WORDSW
ETHI

ADAM POTKAY

Johns Hopkins University Press
Baltimore

© 2012 Johns Hopkins University Press
All rights reserved. Published 2012
Printed in the United States of America on acid-free paper

Johns Hopkins Paperback edition, 2015
2 4 6 8 9 7 5 3 1

Johns Hopkins University Press
2715 North Charles Street
Baltimore, Maryland 21218-4363
www.press.jhu.edu

The Library of Congress has cataloged the hardcover edition of this book as follows:

Potkay, Adam, 1961–
Wordsworth's ethics / Adam Potkay.
p. cm.
Includes bibliographical references and index.
ISBN 978-1-4214-0708-1 (hdbk. : alk. paper) — ISBN 978-1-4214-0758-6
(electronic) — ISBN 1-4214-0708-6 (hdbk. : alk. paper) —
ISBN 1-4214-0758-2 (electronic)
1. Wordsworth, William, 1770–1850—Ethics.   2. Ethics in literature.
3. Music and literature.   4. Music in literature.   I. Title.
PR5892.E8P68 2013
821'.7—dc23   2012008906

A catalog record for this book is available from the British Library.

ISBN-13: 978-1-4214-1702-8
ISBN-10: 1-4214-1702-2

*Special discounts are available for bulk purchases of this book.
For more information, please contact Special Sales at 410-516-6936 or
specialsales@press.jhu.edu.*

Johns Hopkins University Press uses environmentally friendly book
materials, including recycled text paper that is composed of at least
30 percent post-consumer waste, whenever possible.

Contents

Acknowledgments

Behind the writing of this book are debts that extend back to my teachers at Cornell University, where I was an undergraduate some thirty years ago. Although I've since hiked through England's Lake District, the mountains and waterfalls I most associate with Wordsworth remain those of upstate New York's Finger Lakes.

At the College of William and Mary in Virginia, I've enjoyed the company of numerous Wordsworth devotees over the years, among them my colleagues Kim Wheatley and Tim Costelloe. Both of them commented on portions of my manuscript, as did Monica Brzezinski Potkay, keenest of editors (though not yet a Wordsworth fan). Erin Minear shared some of her writing on Shakespeare and music with me at a timely juncture. For many years my students have been delightful and often instructive in numerous courses, theses, and summer projects devoted wholly or partially to Wordsworth's poetry; I am especially grateful to Sean Barry, Lauren Cameron, Lindsay Gibson, and Jonathan Ogden.

Then there are the far-flung Wordsworth aficionados with whom I've corresponded, mainly in cyberspace: these include John Cole, Bruce Graver, Jeffrey Hipolito, David Kaiser, Donald J. Moores, and Steven Scherwatzky. My special thanks go out to Vivasvan Soni, who inspired me to rethink aspects of ethical theory and its relation to literature.

The writing of this book was generously supported by two year-long research leaves, the first provided by the National Endowment for the Humanities—a 2006–7 fellowship to finish my last book, *The Story of Joy: From the Bible to Late Romanticism*. *Wordsworth's Ethics* has its origins in that earlier project. It was completed during a William and Mary Research Leave for 2010–11.

In the five years of composing this book I was assisted, as if providentially, by panel organizers and editors who prompted me to work through my ideas in conference papers and articles. Portions of chapter 1 appeared in *A Companion* to *Romantic Poetry,* ed. Charles Mahoney (Wiley-Blackwell, 2011), 176–94. An early version of chapter 4 was published in *PMLA* 123 (2008): 390–404 (with thanks to the journal's then-editor, Patsy Yeager), and an early version of chapter 5 in *Theory and Practice in the Eighteenth Century: Writing between Philosophy and Literature,* ed. Alexander Dick and Christina Lupton (Pickering and Chatto, 2008), 225–38. Part of chapter 6 appeared in *"Soundings of Things Done,"* a 2008 special issue, edited by Susan Wolfson, of the online journal *Romantic Circles;* the issue was based on a 2007 MLA panel Susan organized. Parts of chapter 7 were originally written for my article on the Romantic sublime forthcoming in *The Sublime: From Antiquity to the Present,* ed. Tim Costelloe, and appear here with permission of Cambridge University Press. Some of my thinking about Wordsworth and Biblical Psalms, which weaves its way through several of my chapters, found earlier expression in a piece I wrote for *The King James Bible after Four Hundred Years: Literary, Linguistic, and Cultural Influences,* ed. Hannibal Hamlin and Norman Jones (Cambridge University Press, 2011), 219–33. To all of these editors and publishers I am immensely grateful. Finally, an earlier version of my reading of Wordsworth's poem *The Old Cumberland Beggar,* included here in chapter 2, was originally published in *The Story of Joy,* 121–28 and is used with permission of Cambridge University Press.

One journal in which I did not publish any portion of this book, but which I nonetheless want to thank, is *The Wordsworth Circle,* edited by the ebullient and ever-sharp Marilyn Gaull, to whom I am deeply indebted: thank you, Marilyn, for drawing me into the circle some twenty years ago. I am beholden to Matt McAdam of the Johns Hopkins University Press for his faith in this project from proposal to final acceptance, and to Michael Baker for his eagle-eyed copy editing.

In working out my ideas for this book with an array of talented editors, I also had the great good fortune during its writing to have been invited to speak at numerous universities, where I tested out ideas, got early and invaluable responses, and enjoyed remarkable hospitality from friends old and new. Proceeding in more or less alphabetic order by university, and including my principal host or hosts at each, I thank David Duff and the University of Aberdeen; Dorota Chabrajska and the John Paul II Institute of the Catholic University of Lublin, Poland; James Engell, Jacob Sider Jost, Matthew Ocheltree, and Harvard University: Sunil Agnani, Adela Pinch, and the University of Michigan; Hannibal Hamlin, Norman Jones, and Ohio State University; Susan Wolfson and Princeton University; William Galperin (a rock of support) and Rutgers University; Emma Sutton and St. Andrews University; and Jane and

Marshall Brown at the University of Washington. Lastly, I would like to thank Christine Dunn Henderson, Senior Fellow at Liberty Fund, for sponsoring my 2008 colloquium on Wordsworth in Hermosa Beach, California, an event that included among its participants Seamus Perry, Thomas Pfau, and Margaret Russett.

This book is dedicated to all those with whom I've studied Wordsworth, both in person and in print: "what we have loved / Others will love, and we may teach them how."

Wordsworth's Ethics

Introduction

We shall acquire
The habit by which sense is made
Subservient still to moral purposes.
—*Wordsworth*, The Ruined Cottage

There is scarcely one of my Poems which does not aim to
direct the attention to some moral sentiment, or to some
general principle, or law of thought, or of our intellectual
constitution.
—*Wordsworth to Lady Beaumont, May 21, 1807*

Why read Wordsworth—indeed, why read poetry at all? Wordsworth hoped his poems might make his readers better or more flourishing persons, attuned to moral purposes through the pleasures of form. According to some of his nineteenth-century readers, it would seem he succeeded. John Stuart Mill records in the fifth chapter of his *Autobiography* (1873) a crucial debt to Wordsworth, whose poems helped to save him from a moral crisis he experienced in his early twenties.[1] As a teenager Mill acquired a desire to reform the world, seeking, according to the familiar utilitarian calculus, "the greatest happiness for the greatest number of people." But what is happiness? Mill experienced a nervous breakdown when he asked himself the pointed question, "'Suppose that all your objects in life were realized; that all the changes in institutions and opinions which you are looking forward to, could be completely effected at this very instant: would this be a great joy and happiness to you?' And an irrepressible self-consciousness distinctly answered, 'No!'" Mill came to realize that the conception of public happiness he had inherited from his father, James Mill, and his father's friend Jeremy Bentham was radically flawed. He came to see that the utilitarian condition for happiness—"every person in the community . . . free and in a state of physical comfort"—is, at best, not a sufficient condition. Why, then, bother to strive for reform? What, if anything, lies beyond a preliminary achievement of distributive justice?

Mill glimpsed an answer to these obstinate questions in Wordsworth's poems: "In them I seemed to draw from a source of inward joy, of sympathetic and imaginative pleasure, which could be shared in by all human beings; which had no connection with struggle or imperfection, but would be made richer by every improvement in the physical or social condition of mankind." Mill attests that Wordsworth's synthesis of "thought, colored by feeling, under the excitement of beauty" made life seem worth living by providing not a means to an end but an end in itself, an "inward joy" that might be universally shared. For Mill, this joy is a perfect thing that nonetheless admits degree; it can build, but is not dependent, upon increases in public happiness. Wordsworth thus offered Mill a vision of the world's value as independent from the standard of utility. This vision may have been of particular relief to a young man groomed as a materialist-utilitarian—and it is worth noting that by the time the mature Mill wrote his autobiography he may well have had in mind the older Wordsworth's denunciation of an age "by gross Utilities enslaved."[2]

For those from whom faith in either God or utility had receded, Wordsworth offered an alternative source of value and of joy. Matthew Arnold wrote in his 1879 preface to Wordsworth's poems:

> Wordsworth's poetry is great because of the extraordinary power with which Wordsworth feels the joy offered to us in the simple primary affections and duties; and because of the extraordinary power with which, in case after case, he shows this joy, and renders it so as to make us share it. The source of joy from which he thus draws is the truest and most accessible to man. It is also accessible universally. Wordsworth brings us word, therefore, according to his own strong and characteristic line, he brings us word "Of joy in widest commonalty spread."[3]

Arnold responded forcefully to what he took to be Wordsworth's ethical program, one redolent of moral egalitarianism ("the simple primary affections and duties"), hopeful of social cohesion, evincing the joys that people have in common with one another and perhaps too with other creatures and things ("in widest commonalty spread").[4]

Mill and Arnold saw in Wordsworth a poet of ethical relations, not of (as Keats deemed him) the "egotistical sublime."[5] Wordsworth's poems examine our obligations to others and invite us to participate imaginatively in the joys proper to all modes of being. The first-person plural of my last sentence runs counter to an influential view of Lake School Romanticism as enacting a "lyric turn" away from the communal personifications of eighteenth-century poetry to "the privatized active self." [6] "I" is certainly a locus of authority for Wordsworth, both in his meditative lyrics and his autobiographical poem, *The Prelude*, published posthumously in 1850; yet pre-1850 readers of Wordsworth must particularly have felt the countervailing weight of Wordsworth's "we" in his lyrics and odes, a usage continuous with the eighteenth-century laud or communal hymn of joy, as in the first climax of *Lines written a few miles above Tintern Abbey*: "While with an eye made quiet by the power / Of harmony, and the deep power of joy, / We see into the life of things." Wordsworth's lyric "I" is often and unexpectedly interchangeable with a communal "we." After 1807, as his poetry takes an increasingly impersonal turn, the first-person plural pronoun often carries emphatic force, as in the final line of his sonnet sequence, *The River Duddon*: "We feel that *we* are greater than *we* know" (my emphases).[7]

The Victorians were apt to find a moral philosophy in Wordsworth's poetry, though they might disagree on whether or not it was a coherent or useful one. Leslie Stephen, in his 1876 essay "Wordsworth's Ethics," sees Wordsworth addressing the foundational question of classical ethics: "What is the nature of man and the world in which he lives, and what, in consequence, should be our conduct?" (250). Stephen, for his part, hears in the complexity of Wordsworth's inconclusive dialogue poem, *The Excursion*, a simple lesson in "the divine harmony which underlies all apparent disorder" (267). Stephen's faith in Wordsworth as a philosopher was challenged by Arnold's counterclaim that Wordsworth's "poetry is the reality . . . his philosophy is the illusion"; with more nuance, however, Arnold maintained that "[n]o one will be much helped by Wordsworth's philosophy of nature, as a scheme in itself and disjoined from his poems."[8] Arnold is of course right: Wordsworth does not expound a systematic philosophy capable of standing without the scaffolding of his poems. Yet all the same Arnold never doubts the ethical orientation of Wordsworth's poems or their power to attach us to "the simple primary affections and duties"—whatever these might be.

I seek to determine what, in Wordsworth's poems, these affections and duties are: that is, to understand the ethics implicated in his poetry. In homage to Stephen, I have titled my book *Wordsworth's Ethics*—I like the simplicity of it. Two caveats, however: first, the ethics I discuss in this book are not, for the most part, peculiar to Wordsworth (as are, say, Kant's metaethics); and second, I am not assessing the moral worth of Wordsworth as a man or biographical subject. On the contrary, my focus is very much on how ethics can get done *in poetry,* and especially through the *music* of poetry. To the extent that I maintain an ongoing conversation with Victorian (as well as Georgian) criticism and moral thought, this book ventures back in order to move ahead, seeking in the past a power that might reinvigorate our contemporary discussion of Romantic and modern poetry—one that, on the far side of poststructuralism and the New Historicism (linger on as these will), can seem stalled, aimless, anomic. I came of age intellectually in the late 1970s and 1980s, when the rigorous exclusion of ethics—or, as one influential critic dismissively put it, "edification"[9]— from the advanced (i.e., theory-dominated) discussion of Romantic texts may have constituted a salutary break from a lingering Victorian mode of moral criticism. By the 1990s, however, moral criticism of a particularly sanctimonious variety had snuck back under the guise of a "political" criticism that judged authors of the past according to their notions of race, class, gender, and empire.[10] According to these criteria, male Romantic poets were judged and often found wanting.

By now the air has been cleared. Being well beyond the Victorians' uncritical elevation of Wordsworth, we can move beyond its antithesis, his arraignment in the courtrooms of late twentieth-century criticism. I hope to recapture some of literary criticism's quondam moral authority, in part, by developing the Victorians' best insights into Wordsworth: the centrality of ethics to his poems, of course, but also the captivating musicality of his verse and the debt of his diction to, in Walter Pater's phrase, "the unconscious mysticism of the old English language."[11] To show the underlying connections between Wordsworth's music, his diction, and his ethics is one of my chief goals.

Unlike the Victorians—or the mid-twentieth-century humanists with whom their work is morally continuous[12]—I do not assume that Wordsworth had a simple or univocal program. I make allowance, rather, for the diversity as well as the subtlety of Wordsworth's ethical intuitions: he has no categorical or consistent answer to Stephen's universalizing question "what should be our conduct?" Nor does he subscribe to any one ethical theory, expressing instead his dismay in his fragmentary "Essay on Morals" (c. 1798–99) that all moral theories are without content: "they *describe* nothing." Lacking imaginative *enactment,* formal ethical systems lack efficacy: "Now, I know no book or system of moral philosophy written with sufficient power to melt into our affections, to incorporate itself with the blood & vital juices of our minds, & thence to have any influence worth our notice in forming those *habits* of which I am speaking" (*Prose Works* 1:103, my emphasis)—namely, the *ethos* or "habit" of action that Aristotle saw as the source of moral virtue, and from which he derives the word "ethics."[13] In another fragment from 1798–99, "There is an active principle alive in all things," Wordsworth likewise indicts "negative morality,"[14] meaning by this phrase either prohibitions backed by sanctions ("Thou shall not") or, more generally, ethical theory types (including most religious ones) that ask, "what am I authorized to do / prohibited from doing?" Judeo-Christian religious commandments, which instance this type of requirement ethic, find no place in the moral universe of Wordsworth's poetry. He rarely if ever admitted them or judgments based upon them, even after turning, in the later 1820s, toward orthodox Christian faith.[15]

Ushering us into a world unmoored from requirement and unreconciled to utilitarianism, Wordsworth reimagines ethics from the ground up, as rooted in encounters with other things or persons that "melt into our affections" and make us feel an interest in them, a part of them, and a responsibility, however undefined, for them. This is morality without moralizing and, beginning with and bequeathed by Wordsworth, it forms the only sort of ethics available to serious poetry.[16] Wordsworth draws us into modernity precisely through encounters with others or other "things" (in the language of *Tintern Abbey*, even we "thinking things" are finally subsumed into "all things"): vagrants, children, a discharged soldier, a leech gatherer, an African woman sailing from Calais, a street corner fiddler and his absorbing music, the churchyard dead, a grinning ass, a numinous doe, a single tree. Each and all command attention and disallow easy judgment, leading poet and reader alike to ask questions about (I adapt a line from "Lines Written in early spring") "what man is *to make of* man," as well as the nonhuman—the phrase linking hermeneutics and ethics in typically Wordsworthian fashion.

Wordsworth's fundamental question would seem to be: "what is my obligation to others—others I cannot fully know or judge—and where does it come from?" In response to this second query, he proposes or implies a wide variety of sources:

1.) the *face* of the other, including abject, nonhuman, and inanimate others;

2.) human nature, which ratifies moral activity through pleasure or joy, including the reflective aesthetic pleasure of beholding beautiful or sublime actions;

3.) the structure of a cosmos which can at least be imagined as governed by law and a world spirit, or as involving one substance, or a life force indexed by the spirit of music;

4.) conscience, rooted in its Latin sense of communal *conscientia*, literally a "knowing together," which may or may not also be the voice of God;

5.) a law or duty one legislates for oneself, thus freeing one from causal determination;

6.) the cultivated impartiality or disinterestedness that allows one to care about the future good of others.

These facets of Wordsworth's ethical poetry have philosophical coordinates—in order: (1) Emmanuel Levinas's ethics of the other/Other; (2) Aristotle's coordination of virtue and joy as developed by the 3rd Earl of Shaftesbury and Francis Hutcheson; (3) the cosmology of the ancient Stoics and the pantheism of Spinoza, plus the music-metaphysics of Pythagoras and Schopenhauer; (4) the conscience of Latin rhetoric and Roman Stoicism, set uneasily alongside the conception of conscience found in Romantic-era evangelical writing; (5) Kant's conception of moral autonomy; and (6) William Hazlitt's metaphysics of future selves and Mill's "religion of humanity." None of these systems will serve, however, as templates for reinscribing Wordsworth in their images. I allow Wordsworth's poetry to read the theory I introduce rather than, as is too often done in contemporary literary criticism, use theory to read poetry. My method is close reading of selected Wordsworth poems from across his career in tandem with ancient, modern, and postmodern ethics, none of which systems he followed systematically, but some of which he drew upon as suited his poetic needs, and some of which (as with Levinas's ethics of the other) he anticipated, giving them a particular content or enactment in advance of their theorization.

In addition to exploring ethical relations and their possible and varied sources, Wordsworth ponders as well the *antinomies* he sees in moral thought or its conditions—that is, in the metaphysics of morals. For example, we feel ourselves to be free (capable of undetermined moral thought or action), but yet we know ourselves, at least insofar as we are material beings, to be causally determined. Wordsworth spins from this basic metaphysical conundrum the specific oppositions of liberty and power (or necessity), duty and desire, independence and interdependence. His poetry variously enacts solutions to and the irresolution of these antinomies or opposed principles, and it is to his art of thinking them through that I devote much, and in particular the later chapters, of this book.[17] In Wordsworth's mature judgment, the "weighing of opposites" enhances the awe and wonder we feel in the world, in and through art. Writing of a portrait hung in his family's parlor, he addresses art more generally, in a coiling sentence of semantic adjustments characteristic of his own poetic art:

To a like salutary sense of awe,
Or sacred wonder, growing with the power

Of meditation that attempts to weigh
In faithful scale, things and their opposites,
Can thy enduring quiet gently raise
A household small and sensitive.[18]

Poetry incites attempts "to weigh things and their opposites," but it may also suggest to us the ways in which these are enmeshed in, to use another Wordsworth phrase, "a finer connection than that of contrast."[19] Wordsworth's verse allows us to think through apparent oppositions including art and nature, person and thing, in- and interdependence, ambition and humility. Doing so, Wordsworth believed, would make us (or so at least he hopes) better persons, alive to "sacred wonder" and "salutary awe" in the working of the cosmos, the moral order, and the art that represents and interweaves them.

In *Wordsworth's Ethics* I hope to contribute to what I see as positive yet still fragile trends within twenty-first-century literary criticism: its so-called ethical turn; a more general interest in thinking about the sort of thought that literature facilitates or makes possible; and a renewed commitment to poetry's meter and rhythm, sounds and forms—that is, what makes it poetry and not prose, at least scientific prose. My focus will very much be on Wordsworth's poetry, although I would also like to suggest a way of thinking about ethics in modern poetry more generally,[20] one that may lead to rereadings of such poets as Wilfred Owen, Robert Frost, Elizabeth Bishop, Derek Walcott, Seamus Heaney, and, moving eastward, Zbigniew Herbert and Czeslaw Miłosz (who in 1945 translated *Tintern Abbey* into Polish, although Soviet-era Poland would not allow its publication).[21] I am particularly intrigued by how poetry, especially lyrical poetry (or the lyrical elements of narrative poetry), can "do ethics" differently and, in certain regards, better than expository or narrative writing, in some measure through musical, lexical, and rhetorical means that exceed or subvert narrative and argument.

Poetry, a border creature moving between constative and performative speech acts, description and prescription, reference and association, semantics and sound, has the power not only to expand our vision (or audition) of ethical concepts and relations but also to *attach* us to them. Attuned to our most primal communicative level of rhythm, pitch, and gesture, poetry can attach us not only to its own sounds, and what they represent, but also to the world itself, as acoustic environment and horizon of poetic reference. In his 1800 Preface to *Lyrical Ballads,* Wordsworth attributes to poetry and "the great and beautiful objects of nature" our "moral attachment" to others

(*Prose Works* 1:126). "You have to love life before you can care about anything," wagers Jane Bennett; "to some small but irreducible extent, one must be enamored with existence and occasionally even enchanted in the face of it in order to be capable of donating some of one's scarce mortal resources to the service of others."[22]

Poetry's connection to ethical *paideia* goes back at least to ancient Greece and remains fixed in the popular imagination: a high school friend of mine used to ask, at least half-seriously, of any literary work a teacher put before him, "will knowing this make me a better person?" In academic circles, however, ethics and literature were severed during what Geoffrey Galt Harpham labels "the Theoretical Era (c. 1969–87)," when the most prominent critical schools (deconstruction, feminism, Marxism, and psychoanalysis) recast ethical claims as hypocritical or deluded assertions of private interest or desire. With the so-called ethical turn that began in the late '80s—its fulcrum based on the French philosopher Emmanuel Levinas (d. 1995) and to a lesser degree a revival of ancient virtue ethics—theoretical ethics returned as a doctrine of "obligation without normativity . . . consistent with postmodernity's emphasis on heterodoxy and dissemination."[23] Yet efforts over the past twenty years to reconnect ethical to literary study, whether undertaken by literary critics or philosophers, have typically been concerned with the study of prose narrative.[24]

What of poetry? Its ethical value has long been shadowed by Theodor Adorno's 1949 claim, still often quoted and contested, that "[t]o write poetry after Auschwitz is barbaric"—a claim that assumes, as Nouri Gana explains, that lyric poets "reenact and continue the foreclosure of veritable otherness in favor of . . . cults of selfhood . . . of which Auschwitz is the product." And if to write poetry after Auschwitz is barbaric, poetry written well before Auschwitz, especially if it has a Romantic or egoistic cast, may seem similarly tainted. Yet a recent wave of critics, taking Adorno's charge seriously, have come to the defense of lyric poets—from Wordsworth and Emily Dickinson to Wallace Stevens and contemporary Arabic poets—arguing the lyric's potential for sociality and ethical address.[25]

The road from Wordsworth to Auschwitz may be a long and tendentious one but not so long as to preclude critical accusations that he, too, has been unethically repressive of the otherness of other people, especially, but not only, of the women in his life and in his poems of encounter ("The Solitary Reaper" has fared especially poorly in postcolonial criticism).[26] Yet such criticism is merely moralizing; it does not grapple with the seriousness and complexity of Wordsworth's engagement with ethics. Nor does it take into account that the ethical imperative of poetry is not to set everything right in the world—poetry is not coextensive with justice. Its fundamental imperative, on the contrary, is to attach us to a world that is always, to a greater or lesser extent, scarred by history and the poet's own complicity with it. This holds true from *Gilgamesh* to the Biblical Book of Psalms to Wordsworth's poetry to the poem by Adam Zagajewski published in the first issue of the *New Yorker* to be published after the attacks of September 11, 2001, titled "Try to Praise the Mutilated World."[27]

Romanticism has not yet given rise to an ethical criticism that matches in depth or complexity the ethical engagements of Romantic poetry. Laurence Lockridge's *The Ethics of Romanticism* (1989) is a useful introductory work, with a fine chapter on Wordsworth's poetry through *The Prelude* (206–48); more recent critics who have sensitively explored aspects of Wordsworth's moral thought include David Bromwich, Nancy Yousef, and Simon Jarvis. But Wordsworth's poetic thinking about morality, as it develops throughout his career, has yet to be engaged with any degree of thoroughness. My chapters thus progress more or less chronologically, selectively treating Wordsworth's writings from the 1780s (*The Vale of Esthwaite* and a translated passage from Virgil's fourth *Georgic* on the power of Orpheus) to the 1830s (Scottish tour poems and *The Cuckoo at Laverna*, his poem on St. Francis of Assisi).

Wordsworth was born in mid-Georgian and died in Victorian England, and so the story of his career is one of three literary eras, as we conventionally understand them—the Enlightenment, Romantic, and Victorian periods—although the Enlightenment and Romanticism are retrospective creations of Victorian-era authors, each crafted to serve as the antithesis of the other.[28] Period divisions in literary and philosophic history can be useful heuristic devices, and convenient ways to organize college courses in the humanities, but we should never let them blind us to the substantial continuities that link any two decades, centuries, or retrospectively imposed periods. It is not as though (to adjust an exam book blooper from a freshman course on European history), "Romanticism bolted in from the blue. Life reeked with joy."[29] Accordingly, in this study I attend closely to the eighteenth-century literary and cultural contexts of Wordsworth's formative years—including the poetic legacy of James Thomson, Mark Akenside, and other "pre-Romantics," which Wordsworth ever honored[30]—as well as to his poetic development, and critical reception, in the first half of the nineteenth century. Like many of his Victorian admirers, at least before Arnold, I am inclined to see his poetic powers—his power to evoke and unsettle, his illuminating strangeness—extending well beyond 1807 (*Poems, in Two Volumes*) or 1814 (*The Excursion*), and into his final decades.[31]

While proceeding chronologically, my chapters are also organized thematically. Chapter 1, "Audition and Attachment," concerns Wordsworth's early loco-descriptive poetry (*An Evening Walk* and *Descriptive Sketches*) and in it the aural power of sound and music to attach us to environments that the eye/I might seek to appropriate. "Close Encounters," divided into chapters 2 and 3, examines the poetry of encounter Wordsworth developed in his narrative or quasi-narrative poetry of the 1790s and early 1800s, from his drama *The Borderers* through *Peter Bell*. Describing face-to-face meetings with people who are not (and by implication cannot be) comprehended, Wordsworth short-circuits the perceptual sharing of sympathy and suggests a less determinate basis for interpersonal ethics. *The Old Cumberland Beggar* concerns the cultivation of moral dispositions and habitual virtue; *The Discharged Soldier*, by contrast, explores the challenge of unexpected and unpredictable encounters, with strangers whose claims on us are imperfect. Moving beyond persons, chapter 4, "The Ethics of Things," explores the ecological ethics Wordsworth grounded on the self's nonassimilative encounters with the otherness of nonhuman things. Engaging the etymological force of the word *things*, Stoic and Spinozan philosophy, and a poetic tradition of assigning a "face" to natural things, Wordsworth arrives, in *Tintern Abbey* and elsewhere, at a lyric apprehension of the "life of things," a life that humans share with other thinking and insentient, substantial and circumstantial things.

Two of my chapters address Wordsworth's poetic attempts in the 1790s and early 1800s to replace the ethical role of *conscience*—typically conceived in Wordsworth's day as a faculty that punishes, and thus deters, transgression—with a nondirective but life-attaching invocation, and enactment, of *music* or verse musicality. Thus, in chapter 5, "Music versus Conscience," I trace the course by which the evangelical's "still, small voice of conscience" becomes Wordsworth's "still, sad music of humanity," the transformation of a punitive force into an ethical, and pleasurable, attunement. Chapter 6, "Captivation and Liberty," explores the antinomy of its title in Wordsworth's 1807 *Poems, in Two Volumes*, particularly in "The Solitary Reaper" and "The Power of Music." In these poems, the Orphic power of music to seduce and distract—to wring the will of its freedom—proves not incompatible with civic liberty, as it brings individuals together, apart from an overly busy commercial world.

My last four chapters follow Wordsworth from *The Prelude* through *The Excursion*, and on to selected later poems including *Laodamia, The River Duddon* sonnet sequence, and the romances (or antiromances) *The White Doe of Rylstone* and *The Egyptian Maid*. In chapter 7, "The Moral Sublime," I argue that Wordsworth's sublime, mischaracterized by Keats and subsequent critics as the "egotistical sublime," is to a large extent the sublime of moral relations, of an impersonal or impartial love that inspires awe through its transcendence of natural inclination and external causation. "From love . . . all grandeur comes," Wordsworth writes in *The Prelude*, "All truth and beauty—from pervading love—/That gone, we are as dust." Wordsworth's commitment to impersonal love, along with the personal traumas of 1807 and his subsequent immersion in Roman Stoicism (with a dash of Kant), lead to his increasing emphasis on the good of independence—from partial attachments, immoderate passions, fortune's wheel, and administered public assistance—coupled with an equally Stoic sense of the interdependence of all things. Both virtues interweave in *Resolution and Independence, Ode to Duty,* and finally *The Excursion,* the central work I address in chapter 8, "Independence and Interdependence." The character of the Solitary, whom modern readers are apt to find the poem's most captivating character, is nonetheless flawed, in that he lacks both independence—he is unreasonably dependent on others, and he is weak—and also a sense of interdependence, the *conscientia* or "knowing together," which the dialogic form of *The Excursion* embodies in the present and the poem's epitaphic mode extends into the past.

My final two chapters treat Wordsworth's exploration, in his late poetry, of the different senses in which an individual can be said to live beyond death—that of others, and of his or her own. Chapter 9, "Surviving Death," begins with a meditation, stemming from *The River Duddon,* on how the truly disinterested or impartial individual, identifying her own good with communal good, ensures a kind of continuing life within the life of the community that survives her, especially as it progresses toward the greater good. This chapter addresses as well Wordsworth's sense of the reciprocal duties that bind the living and the recollected dead. Chapter 10, "The Poetics of Life," centers on readings of *The White Doe of Rylstone* and *The Egyptian Maid,* both of which concern female characters who variously survive death: in the former poem, Emily survives that of her family, living on with and finally through the numinous doe, who is both her comforter and double; in the latter poem, the maiden survives her own death, brought back to life only insofar as it anticipates eternal life in a celestial choir.

In both of Wordsworth's late romances death is meted out for the antipoetic sin of visual idolatry. This narrative detail brings us back, in the end, to Wordsworth's abiding morality of art. Wordsworth variously stressed poetry's service to the past ("memorial tribute"), present (it "sustains the heart in feeling/Life as she is"), and future ("to live, and act, and serve the future hour"),[32] but throughout his career he retains his sense, dating to his early loco-descriptive verse, that *ut musica poesis*. If poetry has a moral effect it is akin to, and partly comprised by, that of music or sound, independent of words.[33] Thus poetry is, or should be, that which, without telling us what to do, opens us up, attunes us to living environments, actual as well as imaginative.

The visual has a place in Wordsworth's poetry, in imagery that is often indefinite, Biblical, and sublime but not "as is a landscape to a blind man's eye" (*Tintern Abbey*). Still, the danger of the eye, to Wordsworth's mind, is that it is given to either illusive dominion or, conversely, abjection before idols. This idea has roots in Luther and Calvin, but the matter doesn't begin and end in theology or the history of the church. Our twenty-first-century lives are to an unprecedented degree indentured to images, the distraction of multiple screens, and an ever-expanding range of image-producing and surveillance technologies. Audition is typically reduced to the audiovisual. Thus resistance to the image now seems the most radical resistance of all. Arguably the most *avant-garde* film of the past twenty years is one that most harkens back to the Protestant Reformation: Derek Jarman's swan song *Blue* (1993), made when the auteur was dying and partly blind from AIDS-related complications, a seventy-six-minute film that is without images except for a blue color projected on the screen, with a soundtrack consisting of narrated text (Jarman's account of and meditation on his illness), music, sounds, and noises. In a film that subverts generic expectation and replaces spectacle with audition, an actor reads these lines as they appear in the published text of *Blue* (1994): "Thou Shall Not Create Unto Thyself Any Graven Image, although you know the task is to fill the empty page. From the bottom of your heart, pray to be released from image."[34]

Chapter 10 ends with Wordsworth's *The Cuckoo at Laverna,* a late poem inspired by the site where St. Francis had a divine vision and, Christ-like, received the stigmata. Wordsworth passes over this spectacle in silence, focusing instead on the springtime cuckoo, whose voice spans and unites the ages, as does the poet's own aural art.

CHAPTER ONE

Audition and Attachment

Ethics begins in listening. Often it begins in listening to a voice from above, as in Exodus 19–20, in which Yahweh, from the sky, speaks the moral law to Moses and Moses, from the mountain, speaks it to the Israelites. In Levinas, it begins in making oneself available, through discourse, to the replies and questions of the Other, who figures as above.[1] Yet listening can be horizontal as well, as when one attends to the sounds that surround one in an environment. In what sense can such listening be called ethical? A certain protoethical stance, or a formal condition for ethics, may be implied in the phenomenology of hearing itself, which involves responsiveness (a step toward responsibility) and vulnerability (a sense of which underscores our obligation to care for others).

In these involvements, the ear contrasts the eye. "Unlike the eyes, the ears have no lids" (John Hamilton, 112). Expatiating on a passage from Heidegger, Gerald Bruns writes:

> [L]istening is not the spectator's mode; listening means involvement and entanglement, participation or belonging for short. . . . The ear is exposed and vulnerable, at risk, whereas the eye tries to keep itself at a distance and frequently from view (the private eye). The eye appropriates what it sees, but the ear is always expropriated, always being taken over by another ("lend me your ears"). The ear gives the other access to us, allows it to enter us, putting us under a claim, driving us mad or something like it. . . . The ear puts us in the mode of being summoned, of being answerable and having to appear. It situates us. It brings us into the open, puts us at risk, whereas the eye allows us to stand or hang back, seeing but unseen. (127–28)[2]

Hearing, unlike seeing, is necessarily a process; it is open-ended, rather than totalizing; it blurs the boundaries of inner and outer, self and other, or indeed transforms how we imagine the self. "To listen is to enter that spatiality by which . . . I am penetrated, for it opens up in me as well as around me, and from me as well as toward me it opens me inside me as well as outside, and it is through such a double, quadruple, or sextuple opening that a 'self' can take place" (Nancy 13–14).

Hearing thus offers a possible solution, or at least a counterforce, to the perceived ethical problem of the possessive "I" and its agent, the visual eye. In literary as well as cultural studies, the appropriative gaze, especially but not only the "male gaze," has been a topic of sustained critical interest. Although the phrase "male gaze" goes back to Laura Mulvey's influential 1975 essay, "Visual Pleasure and Narrative Cinema," moral qualms about the objectifying and possessive gaze antedate that, going back to the work of another British academic, John Barrell, in his 1972 book *The Idea of Landscape and the Sense of Place*. Barrell locates the problem of the gaze within a specific genre—the loco-descriptive poem of the eighteenth century, particularly Thomson's long poem *The Seasons* (1726–44)—and in relation to a particular sociocultural position: the perspective of a detached observer who stands above a landscape, reducing it to a picturesque frame by eliminating its particularities. The superior observer of the prospect poem represents, for Barrell, the deracinated bourgeoisie that will appropriate the countryside without inhabiting it or understanding it as a locality. Barrell finds welcome (if, finally, futile) resistance to this process in the work of the nineteenth-century peasant-poet John Clare. But before Clare there was Wordsworth, who made his poetic debut in the loco-descriptive genre with *An Evening Walk* and *Descriptive Sketches*, both published in 1793. These poems contribute to the genre—and are more interesting than critics typically allow—in developing its animating contradiction, already apparent in Thomson, between (appropriative) eye and (receptive) ear.

Audition and attachment are the unsung and ecologically critical counterparts to the qualities that have come to characterize descriptions of long eighteenth-century loco-descriptive verse: observation and control. The line of critique that extends from Barrell's *The Idea of Landscape and the Sense of Place* is valuable, but it is also partial. What it occludes is the deconstructive energies of a poetic genre in which the I/eye and their basis in empiricism and technology are offset by hearing and the enacted power of music (natural or artificial, instrumental or poetic) to attach us to a world that exceeds linguistic or scientific comprehension or control. In other words, in certain (pre-) Romantic descriptive poems the modernism of abstraction and control is set against the proto-postmodernity of an environmental aesthetic.[3] For music is, in all senses of the term, an "environmentalist" power. It locates us as part of a complex environment: to listen to music or, more broadly, to attend to musicality, is to understand in a discursively indefinite manner that blurs the line between objective property and subjective response, as well as any line between subject and intersubjective (biological, cultural, aesthetic) norms.

Music also reveals our dependency on that which exceeds us: it embodies, as Martha Nussbaum suggests, "our urgent need for and attachment to things outside ourselves we do not control, in a tremendous variety of forms" (272). Building on Nussbaum's analysis, Andrew Bowie argues that music allows us to imagine "a different sense of how metaphysics might be construed" (34), attuning us to a world in which meaning is irreducible to verifiable propositions and thus not incompatible with theology or, in Bowie's alternative, "the needs aroused by the decline of theology" (364). These reflections on a (post-Pythagorean) philosophy *of* music—not just music as philosophy's object but music's suggestion of an alternative metaphysics—may help us construe appeals to natural music in poems from Thomson to Wordsworth (and, as I have analyzed elsewhere, John Clare).[4]

LOCO-DESCRIPTIVE POETRY: THOMSON'S MUSIC

"Loco-descriptive" is a Romantic-era phrase for a poetic genre rooted in the eighteenth century. The Oxford English Dictionary, defining the term as "descriptive of local scenery, etc.," traces it to Wordsworth's Preface to his 1815 *Poems,* although in fact it appears earlier, in the subtitle of a 1780 poem.[5] The *loco*-descriptive cannot be divided too strictly from more generally *descriptive* verse. Wordsworth's Preface categorizes the genre under the heading of "Idyllium,—descriptive chiefly either of the processes and appearances of external nature, as the Seasons of Thomson; or of characters, manners, and sentiments," especially "in conjunction with the appearances of Nature" (*Prose Works* 3:28). As distinct from descriptive verse that renders external nature in a general, abstract, or ideal way, loco-descriptive poetry treats specifically named places or things (estates, buildings, rivers, even a few mines and caves); this distinction, however, pertains more to theory than to practice, as giving a poem a local habitation and name does not ensure any specificity or detail in its delineation. Moreover, Thomson's *Seasons*—a work only intermittently loco-descriptive—is, as I suggest in this chapter, of importance to the Romantic practice of describing places.

M. H. Abrams draws a sharper distinction between eighteenth-century loco-descriptive poems—which he associates with hill prospects—and their "lyricized" offspring, the descriptive-meditative poems or "greater Romantic lyrics," in which the poet's "responses to the local scene are a spontaneous overflow of powerful feeling," preferably expressed unconventionally, "and displace the landscape as the center of poetic interest" ("Structure and Style" 540). The limitation of this thesis lies in the restricted range of Romantic-era poems that qualify, according to Abrams's strictures, as "greater Romantic lyrics." This proposed genre, modeled on "Frost at Midnight" and *Tintern Abbey*, does not accommodate all of Wordsworth's or Coleridge's poems on places, and it clearly excludes loco-descriptive works by such poets as Charlotte Smith, Leigh Hunt, Byron, and Clare. Granted, well-known Romantic-era loco-descriptive (or descriptive-meditative) poems sometimes differ, in degree if not kind, from their eighteenth-century precursors and *arrière-garde* nineteenth-century works, evidencing a greater amount of personal memory and meditation; a more intense metaphysical querying (in lieu of Christian orthodoxy); and less overt political concerns (although New Historicist critics have drawn our attention to covert ones). But the difference should not be overstated. Wordsworth, for one, saw no disruption in the form between John Dyer's *The Ruins of Rome* (1740), William Crowe's "excellent loco-descriptive poem" *Lewesdon Hill* (1788), and his own work (postscript to *The River Duddon*, in *Sonnet Series* 76).

Reflecting on antecedents to his work, Wordsworth paid particular tribute to James Thomson as an inspired poet, whatever his stylistic faults (chiefly poetic diction), who provides with scant exception the only original images of nature between Milton and Wordsworth's own page ("Essay, Supplementary to the 1815 Preface," *Prose Works* 3:72–80). Thomson's "idyllium" *The Seasons* comprises four separate poems, one for each season, from "Spring" to "Winter." In terms of genre, *The Seasons* is a hybrid work, mixing loco-descriptive pieces with generalized descriptions of British (especially Scottish) nature, georgic materials, exotic excursions, and panegyrics on Whig grandees. What Wordsworth and successive Romantic poets gleaned from Thomson, however, were ways of representing the sights—and, I argue, the sounds—of more or less particularized places.

In recent years, one aspect of Thomson's legacy to the Romantics has engrossed critical attention: the picturesque artistry, and ideological agenda, of his loco-descriptive pieces. John Barrell argues that Thomson organized his prospect views (Barrell adduces the view from Hagley Park in "Spring," ll. 950–62) according to painterly principles derived from Claude Lorrain: the eye is drawn hurriedly to the horizon, and then moves back to the foreground, and continues in a back-and-forth movement at a more leisurely pace (*The Idea of Landscape* 14–20). This "eye's journey" requires an elevated and thus detached viewpoint; the composition of poet or painter demands as well the suppression of too much particularity or detail (22–23). For Barrell, this aesthetic does the ideological work required by the enclosure of commons and the extension of metropolitan political and cultural authority: extirpating or glossing over local forms of life, it inculcates the abstract, occlusive, and seemingly disinterested point of view of the gentleman connoisseur.[6] Thus Thomson, as later William Gilpin in his writings on the picturesque, seeks "to control whatever power nature seems . . . to have, by coming to *know* the natural landscape," and this is "part of a wider movement in the eighteenth century, to *explain* the countryside, open it out, and to make each particular place in it more available to those outside it" (84).

Barrell's impress is clear upon subsequent criticism of the loco-descriptive genre. Thomas Pfau traces to Claude Lorrain, Thomson's *Seasons*, and Wordsworth's early loco-descriptive poems an imagined community of the "cultured eye" that reproduces on a symbolic level the productivity and exclusionary violence of a new middle-class formation (44). Blanford Parker adds the exclusion of religion to the cultural work performed by the genre, finding in Poussin, Thomson, and their heirs the very origin of "the literal (and its twin the empirical)" in "the empty space brought on by the erasure of both analogy and fideist theology" (18, 20). Both Pfau (43–49) and Parker (156–73) find in Thomson's representations of the sun a figure for the clinical eye of the poet and the readers he schools in seeing. Ron Broglio censures the picturesque ideal as "optical hegemony" (19), a visual discipline "offering the lure of unity, control, and power to the perceiving subject" (63). Broglio, a sensitive critic, finds in Wordsworth's corpus a tension between, on the one hand, the prospect overview and the mind that would supersede nature, and, on the other, an evasion of subjectivity in poems of walking, interpersonal encounter, and environmental contact with "entities among themselves" (99). Broglio observes that Wordsworth "wants to make the subject more than a spectator of the scene and to represent a sense of space prior to mental abstraction and categorization of sensations" (73), evidencing a keen close reading of the disorientation of the senses represented in the final portion of the Simplon Pass episode of *The Prelude* 6:549–80 (86–101). But although aware of Wordsworth's dissatisfaction with the eye, Broglio does not address the counteractive sense that Wordsworth, like Thomson before him, sets against it: the sense of hearing.

We misunderstand Thomson if we think of him as seeking merely to control nature through striating it into well-defined visual bands (foreground/middle/background) by analogy with visual art. What criticism has neglected is the role of music in his descriptions, the representation of natural music in and through the music of Thomson's own lines. Here, for example, is a passage about the sun's emergence after a shower that Pfau quotes as though it involved no more than a point about the "axis of eye and sun" (43):

> in the western sky, the downward Sun
> Looks out effulgent from amid the flush
> Of broken clouds, gay-shifting to his beam.
> The rapid radiance instantaneous strikes
> The illumined mountain, through the forest streams,
> Shakes on the floods, and in a yellow mist,
> Far smoking o'er the interminable plain,
> In twinkling myriads lights the dewy gems.
> Moist, bright, and green, the landscape laughs around.
> Full swell the woods; their every music wakes,
> Mixed in wild concert, with the warbling brooks
> Increased, the distant bleatings of the hills,
> The hollow lows responsive from the vales,
> Whence, blending all, the sweetened zephyr springs. ("Spring" ll. 189–202)

The passage's first nine lines do indeed describe the painterly, prospect view that Barrell has taught us to see: the eye darts to the sun above the horizon and a background mountain, and then moves forward via a middle ground of forest and streams, to a dew-sparkling plain, which again leads us backward to its own "interminable" blending with the horizon. But offsetting this schematic visual focus, we are surprised by a "laughing" landscape and then given, musically, a scene of music.[7] "Full swell the woods; their every music wakes": this line, with its initial spondee and dramatic caesura, slows recitation and sets us up to accent the "muse" of "music." This music is self-reflexive as well as mimetic: the line establishes a gliding pattern of semivowel "w" alliteration that continues into the next line ("wild/warbling"). This alliteration recurs in a line that arrests us with the appearance of grammatical ambiguity: "The hollow lows responsive from the vales." As a further element of a prepositional list ("with the warbling brooks . . . , the distant bleatings"), the line must refer to the bellowing of cows; yet "low" as a noun is not common (it does not feature in Johnson's *Dictionary*). Thus the line invites us to hear it as a self-contained sentence: "the hollow" as "cavern, den, hole" (Johnson) metonymically "lows," perhaps with more reverberation than usual. Poised uncertainly in space, the line adds indefinitely to the "wild concert" being described, and it adds, moreover, musicality: "hollow lows" is an onomatopoeic as well as echoic phrase that here is about echoing, specifically about how entities in an environment, including entities we cannot with certainty locate or name, "respond" to one another.

Finally, Thomson's last line summons the interdependence of *senses*, both semantically and sensuously: the zephyr that springs from the vales—or is it the woods?—has a force that conjures touch and smell, and a "sweetness" that applies to taste or, figuratively, sound, and perhaps a Hutchesonian "moral sense" as well, although it is clearly not for human sense alone. Wind, like ambient sound, wafts unbidden; it is not, like our visual field, readily subject to framing and control. Insofar, then, as landscape is transmuted into a soundscape or more general realm of the senses, the comprehension and control embodied and figured by the eye ("I see," "that's clear," etc.) is counteracted by absorption in an environment or, poetically, the audition of a corresponding environment.

Thomson's concert here centers on birds of the woods: it is their music that first wakes and finds increase in his depicted environment. Birdsong, in "Spring," everywhere intimates an interconnectedness that may include, but that does not center, in us. At the very outset of the poem, a morning chill makes plovers unsure of the season, and thus of their time "to scatter o'er the heath, / And sing their wild notes to the listening waste" (ll. 24–25). "Listening waste," inasmuch as it at first seems an oxymoron, sparks recognition that places uncultivated by us are not uninhabited. Conversely, what might seem to us a "waste" in the sense of useless expenditure or squandering may be, in a broader environmental context, a gift of love. Having amplified upon a "full concert" of birds (l. 613), with each constituent type (blackbirds, linnets, and so on) designated and characterized, Thomson traces its impetus to erotic attachment: "'Tis love creates their melody, and all / This waste of music is the voice of love" (ll. 614–15).

Here birdsong is no longer simply a salient element of a concerted environment but something more: an index of generative love, the *Venus Genetrix* that Lucretius—an author Thomson sometimes imitates in "Spring"—hymns in the prologue of his philosophic poem *De Rerum Natura* and that Thomson praises, simply, as the all-animating "God" ("Spring" ll. 848–67). Thomson's insistence in categorizing birdsong as "melody," as "music," has the converse effect of making music itself seem a natural sign of the unindividuated libidinal force that manifests itself in all individuated life forms—as indeed Arthur

Schopenhauer will declare it to be in *The World as Will and Representation* (1819). But Thomson, unlike Schopenhauer—and, more to the point, unlike his model Lucretius—does not seek a more or less ascetic liberation from desire but rather offers images of a golden and recoverable age when the music of love attached each creature to every other. In the "first fresh dawn" of the world, writes Thomson, when "Love breathed his infant sighs, from anguish free, / And full replete with bliss" (ll. 242, 252–53),

> music held the whole in perfect peace:
> Soft sighed the flute; the tender voice was heard,
> Warbling the varied heart; the woodlands round
> Applied the choir; and winds and water flowed
> In consonance. (ll. 267–71)

And it is this amorous, musical paradise that Thomson seeks to recover, on the far side of the erotic suffering he limns with Lucretian colors in the penultimate section of his poem (ll. 963–1112), in the poem's ending lines on the "harmony" and "attunement" necessary for virtuous love (ll. 1113–76). That which knits together Thomson's happy family is what attaches them to other creatures as well, both human and, as in his lines against bird-caging, nonhuman:

> Oh then, ye friends of love and love-taught song,
> Spare the soft tribes, this barbarous art forebear!
> If on your bosom innocence can win,
> Music engage, or piety persuade. (ll. 710–13)

Two of Johnson's definitions of "engage" may pertain here: "to enlist; to bring to a party" (verb definition 3); or, my preferred one, "to unite; to attach; to make adherent" (definition 5).

In sum, whereas for many critics since Barrell "Spring" is a poem about cultivated observation and elite control of both nature and falsely naturalized social relations, it is also, and perhaps more centrally, a poem about things one cannot (fully) control—libidinal and other instinctive drives; other beings both like and unlike us. It is a poem about how music at once embodies and responds to these things. Finally, it is about how music might subtend ethical relations. Like the "meaning" of music itself, none of these inferences from Thomson's text is an entirely clear, let alone a verifiable, proposition—this, presumably, is why critics have sidestepped the abundant appeals to music in descriptive poetry—but rather inducements to think beyond "the realm of explanation and legitimation by evidence and argument" (Bowie 280).

This inducement in "Spring" becomes, in "Summer," an injunction: submit, through music, to unreason. From "Spring," we have seen the sun reemerge after a gentle rain; in "Summer," a more astringent poem, the sun emerges after a summer storm whose lightning has turned one of a pair of pastoral lovers into "a blackened corse" (l. 1216).[8] Thomson presents the returning beauty of the day and the sylvan concert it awakes as a reason for not repining at gratuitous suffering and death:

> As from the face of Heaven the shattered clouds
> Tumultuous rove, the interminable sky
> Sublimer swells, and o'er the world expands
> A purer azure. . . .
> 'Tis beauty all, and grateful song around,
> Joined to the low of kine, and numerous bleat
> Of flocks thick-nibbling through the clovered vale.
> And shall the hymn be marred by thankless man,
> Most-favoured, who with voice articulate
> Should lead the chorus of this lower world?
> Shall he, so soon forgetful of the hand
> That hushed the thunder, and serenes the sky,
> Extinguished feel that spark the tempest waked,
> That sense of powers exceeding far his own,
> Ere yet his feeble heart has lost its fears? (ll. 1223–43)

This passage in Thomson from death to natural music is one that Wordsworth will recreate in his own loco-descriptive poems, even as he jettisons Thomson's Christian conviction that human beings stand at the apex of the created world.

WORDSWORTH AND THE "SOCIAL ACCENTS" OF THINGS

Since Geoffrey Hartman's seminal book *Wordsworth's Poetry, 1787–1814* (1964), Wordsworth's visual imagery, at least during his so-called great decade (1797–1807), has been read as being in tension with his imaginative vision. His representation of external nature and other selves is precariously balanced against a desire for transcendence or, following Paul de Man's writings, the self-reflexive and self-confounding energies of literary language itself. Less remarked upon is the tension in Wordsworth between seeing and hearing, or the different kind of knowledge gleaned by the eye and by the ear. At some level this opposition is obvious, as in Wordsworth's well-known lines from "The Tables Turned" (*Lyrical Ballads*):

> Books! 'tis a dull and endless strife,
> Come, hear the woodland linnet,
> How sweet his music; on my life
> There's more of wisdom in it. (ll. 9–12)

But more salient is the opposition, in his loco-descriptive poems of the 1790s, between visualized death and the power of music or euphonious sound to cancel its horror.

The opposition figures in *An Evening Walk*, a series of tableaux drawn from Wordsworth's native Lake District, as well as from his reading and fancy. The logic by which Wordsworth passes from scene to scene is often no more than locomotive progress as dusk proceeds to night, but some collocations are clearly thematic: thus he follows his description of a secure family of swans (ll. 195–240), antithetically, with a lurid tale of a human family that has no security. Wordsworth depicts a vagrant war widow who "haply"—her fanciful origin is strongly implied—has "dragg'd her babes along this weary way" (ll. 242–44) in the summer heat of day, and who will at some point in the future discover them, by lightning's illumination (and perhaps its strike), dead at her breast:

> Soon shall the Light'ning hold before thy head
> His torch, and shew them slumbering in their bed,
> No tears can chill them, and no bosom warms,
> Thy breast their death-bed, coffin'd in thine arms. (ll. 297–300)

Clearly this scene is related to the summer lightning death of Thomson's "Summer," although Wordsworth's version is still more disturbing: what happens unexpectedly to Thomson's happy lovers happens to Wordsworth's miserable vagrants because they are continually exposed to the elements. Pfau assesses the picturesque aspect of this vagrant tale: the mother and her babes, objects of sight, give way to an aesthetic "practice of seeing," undercutting what at first glance might seem a critique of "the systemic indifference of a complex, human economy" (Pfau 101, 103). What Pfau does not engage, however, is the appeal to music that immediately follows this sacrificial tale. Such an appeal was quasi-homiletic in Thomson's "Summer"—a tale of accidental death followed by an exhortation not to murmur but to lead nature's song of praise—but it reappears in Wordsworth as a jarring collocation of corpses and sweet sounds:

Sweet are the sounds that mingle from afar,
Heard by calm lakes, as peeps the folding star [Venus],
Where the duck dabbles mid the rustling sedge,
And feeding pike starts from the water's edge,
Or the swan stirs the reeds, his neck and bill
Wetting, that drip upon the water still;
And heron, as resounds the trodden shore,
Shoots upward, darting his long neck before. (ll. 301–8)

No continuity is articulated between the vagrant mother's abjection and this expansive music (the description of variegated music continues through line 328). In the suggestive power of *un*articulated connection, Wordsworth finds the key to his future tragedies of common life (as well as a cornerstone of modernist aesthetic), tragedies in which natural beauty, and particularly natural music, are offered not as a vindication of the ways of God but nonetheless as a reattachment to life. The sweet sounds of calm lakes are pivotal in *An Evening Walk;* after this passage, soundscape increasingly dominates the poem (ll. 345–78, 433–46), and the practice of hearing ironically counteracts not so much actual suffering in the world as the poet's own visual fancy, which—as in the vagrant mother's tale—distorts tragedy into the "super-tragic."[9] In the shift from eye to ear, there is creative chastening as well as environmental humility.

Another way of getting at the implication of Wordsworth's leap from death to sound is to say: life means inasmuch as, and in the way that, music means. And not only to us: in the lines I quote above "lakes" appear to have the ability to "hear" as we do ("heard *by* calm lakes" is purposefully ambiguous). In his 1794 expansion of the poem Wordsworth elaborated on this intuition, giving us his poetry's first pansensuous passage:

A heart that vibrates evermore, awake
To feeling for all forms that Life can take,
That wider still its sympathy extends,
And sees not any line where being ends;
Sees *sense,* through Nature's rudest forms betrayed,
Tremble obscure in fountain, rock, and shade;
And while a secret power those forms endears
Their social accents never vainly *hears.*[10]

The music of sensate things, in Wordsworth's later loco-descriptive poems, appears in lieu of regret for humans who pass away. In *Descriptive Sketches,* set

among the Alps, an episode concerning a chamois hunter who dies in an ava-
lanche (ll. 366–413) is followed by one in which the speaker/hearer rejoices in
the "Soft music from th' aëreal summit" (l. 421), and in the absence of man:

> —And sure there is a secret Power that reigns
> Here, where no trace of man the spot profanes . . .
> An idle voice the sabbath region fills
> Of Deep that calls to Deep across the hills,
> Broke only by the melancholy sound
> Of drowsy bells for ever tinkling round;
> Faint wail of eagle melting into blue
> Beneath the cliffs, and pine-woods steady sugh;
> The solitary heifer's deepn'd low;
> Or rumbling heard remote of falling snow. (ll. 424–25, 432–39)[11]

These lines decenter not just the world apart from contemplative consciousness
but that consciousness itself in the accumulation of particular sounds conveyed
as though for their own sake. In the "Deep that calls to Deep across the hills," the
basso continuo over which play an array of "melancholy" (but not saddening)
sounds, Wordsworth recalls the first line of Psalm 42:7—"Deep calleth unto deep
at the noise of thy waterspouts [cataracts]"—while signally omitting its second
line, in which the sound of ravines becomes a vehicle for the speaker's spiritual
dejection: "All thy waves and thy billows are gone over me." Wordsworth's lines
reverse the Biblical dynamic; here inner landscape gives way to outer. The deeps
that concern him are those of nature, not of human spirit, and they call, but not
primarily to us, the speaker's witness notwithstanding. Whereas Psalm 42 as a
whole uses natural imagery to describe, analogically, the individual's inner striv-
ing toward God—"As the hart panteth after the water brooks, so panteth my soul
after thee, O God" (verse 1)—Wordsworth, antithetically, describes the elements
of nature in relation to one another, "where no trace of man the spot profanes." In
short, Wordsworth turns the Bible on its head.[12]

Yet even while Wordsworth's ethic opposes that of the Scriptures, what at-
tracts Wordsworth to Biblical locutions, and specifically to those of the King
James Bible (KJB), is their *anti-iconic sublimity*. Wordsworth uses sacred writ-
ings as a storehouse for his antivisual imagination. In Hebrew as in the KJB's
corresponding English, it's hard to say precisely what "deep calleth unto deep"
looks like, and so commentaries vary on what it might mean. Most offer a natu-
ralistic interpretation: in Wordsworth's day, a popular gloss of the verse sug-
gested that "when, at the 'sound' of descending 'water spouts,' or torrents of

rain, the depths are stirred up, and put into horrible commotion," it is as though "the clouds above [were] calling . . . to the waters below, and one wave encouraging and exciting another, to join their forces, and overwhelm the despairing sufferer" (Horne 1:254). Nearer our own day, Abraham Cohen offers another naturalistic interpretation of what it means for a deep to call to a deep: "The melting snows from the peaks of Hermon form thunderous waterfalls; and to these are added the rapids of the Jordan" (132). But Robert Alter gets closer to what attracted Wordsworth to the KJB style when he concedes the ambiguity of Psalm 42's "deeps": "this could be an associative leap from the heights [of v. 7] to the antithetical depths, from the mountains to the seas"; these "deeps" or "abysses" are "geological or cosmic" (150). Indefiniteness shades into an intimation of infiniteness. Alter's gloss is attuned to the indeterminacy, the sublime affront to clear representation, which attracted Wordsworth to the Hebrew Bible and its King James translation. Wordsworth spells out his anti-iconic aesthetic in his 1815 Preface to his *Poetical Works*:

> The grand storehouses of the enthusiastic and meditative Imagination, of poetical . . . Imagination, are the prophetic and lyrical parts of the Holy Scriptures, and the works of Milton. . . . I select these writers in preference to those of ancient Greece and Rome, because the anthropomorphitism [sic] of the Pagan religion subjected the minds of the greatest poets in those countries too much to the bondage of definite form; from which the Hebrews were preserved by their abhorrence of idolatry. This abhorrence was almost as strong in our great epic Poet. . . . However imbued the surface might be with classical literature, he was a Hebrew in soul; and all things tended in him towards the sublime. (*Prose Works* 3:34–35)

Wordsworth's lines on the anti-iconic sublimity of Milton and "the prophetic and lyrical parts of the Holy Scriptures" are in keeping with Edmund Burke's influential assessment that both these sources evince the sublime of the indefinite or obscure.[13]

In *Descriptive Sketches*, Wordsworth's "secret Power that reigns . . . /where no trace of man the spot profanes" is most immediately the power of ambient sound, conveyed in turn by the consoling sonority of Wordsworth's lines and the Biblical echoes they carry. If, additionally, Wordsworth's "secret Power" intimates divinity, it is an indefinite and unenvisioned demiurge that does not set man above the chorus of creation and that in no way commands or assumes verticality—this is not your father's God. It is, rather, as much of power as the ear can admit when the eye is—to anticipate Wordsworth's fine synesthetic phrase in *Tintern Abbey*—"made quiet." Evading the eye and attuning the ear to poetry's sound—here, the sound of poetry imitating a succession of non- or prepoetic sounds—is an ethical imperative for Wordsworth and one that connects the beginning of his poetic career to its end: his last sonnet and poem of any significance, composed in February 1846, censures book and newspaper illustration and a culture that prizes the graphic over the verbal. "A dumb Art," he laments, "best can suit / The taste of this once-intellectual Land." Wordsworth concludes with a tercet that, for all its late-style fustian, is a remarkably direct expression of a concern that animates his entire career:

> Avaunt this vile abuse of pictured page!
> Must eyes be all in all, the tongue and ear
> Nothing? Heaven keep us from a lower stage! (*Last Poems,* 406)[14]

Childhood, for Wordsworth, is the stage of life properly pleased with pictures. Humanity emerges from its nonage, and its narcissism, through the listening cure provided by poets, or at least Hebrew and Protestant ones.

Music, verbal and nonverbal, delights, though Wordsworth never entirely makes clear why this should be so. Beginning in *Tintern Abbey,* with its evocation of the "power of harmony," Wordsworth will increasingly employ *harmony* in the metaphysical manner of an earlier poet he admired, Mark Akenside, to refer allusively to the Pythagorean-Platonic-medieval belief in a cosmic accord that is both analogous to and embodied in musical harmony. Of harmony I will have more to say in chapters 5 and 6. It is not, however, part of the lexicon of Wordsworth's early loco-descriptive poems. Here, rather, if the delight of music is in any way consoling—and Wordsworth, invoking music after depicting loss, seems to think it is—this consolation lies in the very proximity of sound to the motion and force of life, beneath and apart from individual existences. Keats addresses his singing nightingale, "Thou wast not born for death, immortal bird! / . . . / The voice I hear this passing night was heard / In ancient days": neither, in this limited sense, are we hearers mortal. From this insight, later Romantics would elaborate a metaphysics of music, from Schopenhauer, for whom the motions of music are an index to the "will" or sexualized life force that underlies all passing phenomena, to Nietzsche, who claimed, "It is only through the spirit of music that we can understand the joy involved in the annihilation of the individual" (104). Through music we rejoice in the life force that undergirds all phenomenal beings and periodically reclaims them. Although Wordsworth in the 1790s would not have gone so far as this, he is in his loco-descriptive poetry of human suffering and suprahuman song closer to Nietzsche than to Christian or Enlightenment theodicy.

COUNTERACTING SENSES

Tongue and ear are, however, imperiled by the lust of the eye—it is another theme rooted in Exodus, where the Israelites turn from the word to fashion and worship a molten calf. In *The Prelude*, Wordsworth laments that in his day sight has become overvalued on the basis both of science—"telescopes, and crucibles, and maps" (5:330)—and a picturesque aesthetic involving comparative evaluations of landscape, "a comparison of scene with scene, / Bent overmuch on superficial things," a state in which the eye, "the most despotic of the senses," holds "absolute dominion" over heart and mind (11:158–59, 171–75).[15] Wordsworth urges instead a balance or commonwealth of the senses, and their "subservience still to moral purposes" (*Ruined Cottage* 263):

> Gladly here,
> Entering upon abstruser argument,
> Would I endeavour to unfold the means
> Which Nature studiously employs to thwart
> This tyranny [of the eye], summons all the senses each
> To counteract the others and themselves,
> And makes them all, and the objects with which all
> Are conversant, subservient in their turn
> To the great ends of liberty and power. (11:175–83)[16]

Wordsworth defers this argument to "another song" (11:184) that was, in the event, never written.

The senses Wordsworth elicits in his poetry are predominantly hearing and sight, though he may allude here to the sense of one's own body at rest and in motion, and perhaps too the fundamental sentience he sometimes attributes to all entities in nature.[17] The so-called lower senses of touch, taste, and smell play a not insignificant role in Wordsworth's verse. The sense of touch, Nancy Yousef argues (*Isolated Cases* 147), has a "primacy" in the narrative of fleshly attachment that *The Prelude* obliquely tells, from the infant babe "upon his mother's breast" (2:241) to the mature poet liberated from the city at the epic's opening, "cheered by the genial pillow of the earth / Beneath my head, soothed by a sense of touch / From the warm ground" (1:88–90). Touch abides as well in Wordsworth's keywords "feel" and "feeling":[18] the latter, according to Samuel Johnson's 1755 *Dictionary of the English Language*, refers primarily to "the sense of touch," though it extends metaphorically to "sensibility" or "tenderness."

Smell and taste are rendered salient by synesthesia in Wordsworth's pre-cursor Thomson (e.g., "smell the taste of dairy," "Spring" l. 107), and, more often and elaborately, in his admirer Keats ("tasting of Flora and the country green, / Dance, Provençal song, and sunburnt mirth!," "Ode to a Nightingale" ll. 13–14). Wordsworth's own references to taste tend to be figurative rather than papillary, even when evoking infantile nursing: the infant babe "*drinks* in the feelings of his Mother's eye" (*The Prelude*, 1850 version, 2:237, my emphasis); language ought to "uphold, and *feed*, and leave in quiet" (*Essays on Epitaphs* 3, *Prose Works* 2:85, my emphasis). Wordsworth less often evokes scent—indeed, one critic has recently alleged that he could not smell[19]—but smelling is not wholly absent from his work: for example, in *The Prelude*, Wordsworth com-pares the grace-under-adversity of his friend Beaupuy to the enhanced smell of "aromatic flowers on Alpine turf / When foot hath crushed them" (9:304–5). In the late poem "Devotional Incitements," nature teaches us to aspire upward just as odors "rise / In mute aerial harmonies; / From humble violet [,] modest thyme / Exhaled" (ll. 5–8, *Last Poems*, 226). Yet smell and taste are excluded from his most concentrated effort at synesthesia, "Airey-Force Valley" (1835), which incorporates all the other bodily senses, and not exclusively in terms of human bodies. From within a "leafy glen" the speaker observes:

> And yet, even now, a little breeze, perchance
> Escaped from boisterous winds that rage without,
> Has entered, by the sturdy oaks unfelt;
> But to its gentle touch how sensitive
> Is the light ash! that, pendent from the brow
> Of yon dim cave, in seeming silence makes
> A soft eye-music of slow-waving boughs,
> Powerful almost as vocal harmony
> To stay the wanderer's steps and soothe his thoughts. (*Last Poems*, 285)

In these last three lines, a sensuous amalgam oriented toward sight—soft (touch) eye (visual) music (aural)—is rendered analogous to vocal harmony (aural) in its power to halt physical motion (stay steps) and soothe (a term re-lated, by its definition, to touch, as in Johnson's second definition, "to soften").

Here the senses work in concert. For an example of their productive counter-action, I turn to one of Wordsworth's earlier bower poems, the first of the series of "Poems on the Naming of Places," untitled but known as "Emma's Dell."[20] Jacqueline Labbe usefully contrasts the enclosed (and, she argues, feminized) spaces in Wordsworth's poems—glen or dale or dell or covert—to the prospect poems she associates with arrogating masculinity (ix–xix). Yet Labbe's frame of sensuous reference for both modes is resolutely visual: to her, "Emma's Dell" is thus a poem about what one can see in a bower (102–3).[21] What the poem actually represents, however, are three senses presented in counterpoise to one another and arranged in an abcabc pattern—first physical motion (running/ roaming), then sound, and then sight. In the poem running and roaming are what elemental forces do, and what the human body does, aimlessly, indexing the mechanistic drives that propel all things. Sounding or singing, in tandem with desiring and enjoying, is what all things do together, an image of unanimity and the promissory note of a future ethics. Seeing is what the speaker of the poem does alone; it is that which separates him from his environment and characterizes his imaginative individuality. Here is the poem's first abc sequence:

> It was an April Morning: fresh and clear
> The Rivulet, delighting in its *strength*,
> *Ran* with a young man's speed, and yet the *voice*
> Of waters which the winter had supplied
> Was soften'd down into a vernal tone.
> The spirit of enjoyment and desire,
> And hopes and wishes, from all living things
> Went circling, like a multitude of *sounds*.
> The budding groves *appear'd* as if in haste
> To spur the steps of June; as if their shades
> Of *various* green were hindrances that stood
> Between them and their object . . . (ll. 1–12, *Lyrical Ballads* 242)

(The emphases in this quotation are mine except for "*various*," which Wordsworth italicizes in the original.) After these lines, the poem circles back to movement, this time that of the speaker—"Up the brook / I roam'd in the confusion of my heart"—and in his motion he is rendered oblivious, encompassed by a chiasmic *all*: "Alive to all things and forgetting all."

This self-forgetfulness, the shedding of a self that sees and sees ahead (anticipating a uniform summer green in the various greens of early spring), triggers the poem's second and most remarkable fantasia on a sound or voice that unites and endures:

> At length I to a sudden turning came
> In this continuous glen, where down a rock
> The stream, so ardent in his course before,

Sent forth such sallies of glad sound, that all
Which I till then had heard, appear'd the voice
Of common pleasure: beast and bird, the lamb,
The Shepherd's dog, the linnet and the thrush
Vied with this waterfall, and made a song
Which, while I listen'd, seem'd like the wild growth
Or like some natural produce of the air
That could not cease to be. (ll. 20–30)

The motion of these lines pivots on the phrase "common pleasure." At first it appears comparative, the *mere* common pleasure of all things as distinct from the extraordinary sound of the waterfall. But as the verse continues on to celebrate the "song" of circumambient things along with the waterfall, we revise our estimate of *common* to read it as the affirmation of a pleasure shared by all things, even if it took the cut of the waterfall for the speaker to recognize (or posit) this harmonious whole. I know of no eternizing conceit so marvelous as the one Wordsworth then employs, in which the multeity-in-unity of environmental song acquires, if only through simile, the expansion and permanence of air. The poem turns next to the visual field, in which the speaker beholds at a distance the "summit . . . beyond the dell": this is the vantage point of the prospect poem, now seen from below and within participation in a living environment. The speaker concludes by dedicating the dell to Emma but also recognizing that "the name of Emma's dell" is not usurpation but only a "fancy," and one that ultimately depends on the breath of others, the "two or three" shepherds who, having conversed with the speaker, may one day call it by that name after the speaker and Emma are, like the babies of *An Evening Walk* and the chamois hunter of *Descriptive Sketches*, dead. The seeming casualness of this wish scarcely masks a deeper hope that his speech act will, if only for a little while, not cease to be. The poem itself preserves it, of course, but it also suggests to the reader a sense of what we owe the dead, who once participated in a song that seemed, but was not, subjectively permanent. The final ethical act is epitaphic. Having begun in listening, ethics ends in re-calling the transient attachments of interlocutors who have passed away.

I will return to Wordsworth on audition and musicality in chapters 5 and 6. But proceeding more or less chronologically through Wordsworth's poetic career, I turn next to his meditations on the eye, seeing others, and the ethics of the face in the dramatic and narrative poetry he wrote in his Racedown and Alfoxden years, 1795–98.

CHAPTER TWO

Close Encounters I

In his Racedown and Alfoxden period (1795–98), Wordsworth pioneers what has been called "the poetry of encounter," vignettes of meetings with vagrants, itinerants, children, and the laboring poor.[1] In them, a speaker meets face to face with persons (or animals) who are not, and by implication cannot be, fully grasped but for whom, for that very reason, he is made to feel responsible. These encounters revolve around the eye that sees, the faces it sees, and the ethical intuitions involved in this relation. Wordsworth's poetry of encounter begins, as does this chapter, with the blank verse poem *The Old Cumberland Beggar* (1796–99): here the encounter is explicitly theorized, and the poem becomes a lay sermon on the importance both of habit to moral activity and of moral activity to human dignity. Wordsworth eschews such didacticism in his later and greater blank verse poems on the itinerant and the abandoned, *The Discharged Soldier* (1798) and *The Ruined Cottage* (1798–99). These poems involve *close* encounters in a double sense: they are face-to-face encounters, moored in physical proximity but also only approximate or "close" to a full or comprehending encounter with another. Psychic space remains between observer and observed, and in this space we discover the basis of interpersonal morals.

The poetry of encounter derives in part from the character sketches of figures in the landscape (particularly beggars, itinerants, and the unhoused mad) found in loco-descriptive poems from Thomson to Cowper, as well as those met with in sentimental prose tales and the novel.[2] It is through the visual medium of the drama, however—via the sight lines of an imagined stage—that Wordsworth works out the ethical import of face-to-face encounters in *The Borderers* (1796–97). Wordsworth's failure to have his play accepted at Covent Garden does not diminish its importance as a testament to what Wordsworth imagined the theater could do—which is, do ethics better than moral philosophers, and in particular Godwin. Ethics, for Wordsworth, is about concrete relations, not about abstract theories or principles such as justice, which, pursued unconditionally, can sanction cruelty and murder. Wordsworth and his sister Dorothy attributed his play's theatrical rejection in 1797 "to the deprav'd State of the Stage at present" (*Letters* 1:197, note), anticipating Wordsworth's well-known denunciation in the 1800 Preface to *Lyrical Ballads* of "frantic novels, sickly and stupid German Tragedies, and deluges of idle and extravagant stories in verse," all of which exhibit a "degrading thirst after outrageous stimulation" (*Prose Works* 1:128). One such "sickly German tragedy" might have been, for Wordsworth, Schiller's *The Robbers* (1781, English translation 1792)—an important source and subtext for *The Borderers*.

Unlike the genres Wordsworth laments in his satire on present taste, as well as other modes he might have mentioned—particularly the gothic, and the gothic horrors not absent from his own juvenile and loco-descriptive poems (e.g., dead babies revealed by lightning)—Wordsworth in his mature poetry of encounter does not sensationalize. Indeed, he scarcely accedes to the excitements of narrative. For a play, *The Borderers* has very little plot (relative, say, to *The Robbers*, or any Shakespeare tragedy), and Wordsworth's ballads famously can have little or no plot at all: as the narrator says of "Simon Lee" (*Lyrical Ballads*), "It is no tale; but should you think, / Perhaps a tale you'll make it." But even when a Wordsworth poem has a more clearly articulated narrative, as does *Peter Bell*—the last poem I treat in chapter 3—it is one that falls far short of the narrative expectations inherent in the ballad genre. The reader of Thomas Percy's *Reliques of Ancient English Poetry*, Gottfried August Bürger's *Lenora*, or even Robert Burns's seriocomic *Tam o' Shanter*, might reasonably expect ballads to provide scenes of sexual abandonment, betrayal, murder, and the demonic: in the ballad *Peter Bell*, Wordsworth toys with such themes but offers in the main a man's moral education through his encounter with an ass.

In *The Discharged Soldier*, also addressed in chapter 3, Wordsworth's meditative description seems strangely divorced from any narrative purpose. Meeting a stranger on a road, as the narrator of this poem does, brings to mind a good many mythic, parabolic, and romance possibilities, all of which are here ignored, chastening, as it were, the reader's desire for narrative itself. The naked face of the other, and not any tale, becomes the center of the poem's specifically, if indeterminately, ethical attention. In presenting us the other as neither emblem nor prelude to adventure, Wordsworth inaugurates a new type of modern poetry—one that includes, to name a few examples, Edward Thomas's "As the Team's Head-Brass," W. H. Auden's "Easter 1929," Ezra Pound's "In a Station of the Metro," Robert Frost's "The Most of It," and Elizabeth Bishop's "The

Moose."[3] Wordsworth, while illustrating encounters with the other and otherness, also suggests how difficult such encounters can be. Further, Wordsworth suggests the precious fragility not only of goodness but also of models of accounting for it. Through poetry that maps onto divergent ethical frameworks, at moments recalling Shaftesburian moral sense theory and at others anticipating Levinas's (Judeo-Christian) philosophy of the Other, Wordsworth reveals both the inadequacy and the indispensability of theoretical frames, and does so more impressively than could the strictures of philosophical argument.

THE OLD CUMBERLAND BEGGAR:
GODWINIAN JUSTICE, SHAFTESBURIAN BENEVOLENCE,
AND THE SACRED POOR

The first work of moral and political philosophy the young Wordsworth read was most likely Cicero's *De Officiis* ("On Duties"), a work he appears to have encountered at Hawkshead Grammar School, and it, along with other Roman Stoic writings, would play an increasingly important role in his own.[4] But the first work of *contemporary* moral and political philosophy that Wordsworth embraced—and then ostensibly rejected—was William Godwin's *Enquiry concerning Political Justice and its Influence on Morals and Happiness,* published in February 1793 and known by Wordsworth a year later (see Nicholas Roe, 176–77). Godwin's *Enquiry* was, and remains, a radical work, Stoic in its ethics but advancing a utopian anarchism that might be achieved by rational individuals in time, and without violence (of the type that stained Paris in the Revolutionary Terror of 1793). Godwin allows for the utopian possibility of a perfectly just society, in which "prejudices"—including beliefs in rank, entail, primogeniture, and marriage—would be eradicated; "luxury" and gross material inequalities would be eliminated; and individuals, unfettered by all but the most minimal government, would conscientiously strive for the public good or "the greatest sum of pleasure or happiness."[5]

Godwin works out his "system of equality" in book 8, "Of Property" (2:420–554). Here he states as his ultimate goal a perfect equality of condition, modeled on Jonathan Swift's rational-anarchist Houyhnhnm land in book 4 of *Gulliver's Travels.* Godwin imagined that individuals educated to act disinterestedly could cooperate in a "simple form of society without government" (2:420), the welfare of the whole secured by the periodic and voluntary redistribution of goods. Those who benefit from this redistribution will simply be claiming what is properly theirs as members of a coordinated whole. Godwin lamented that under the current order of European society the poor were expected to show gratitude for whatever meager bounty they received, whereas they ought, ideally, to regard their benefactors "with that erect and unembarrassed mien, that manly sense of equality, which is the only unequivocal basis of virtue and happiness" (2:419). The "true object" of societal reform, Godwin concludes, "is to extirpate all ideas of condescension and superiority, to oblige every man to feel that the kindness he performs is what he is bound to perform, and to examine whether the assistance he asks be what he has a right to claim" (2:456). For Godwin, one has a right to claim as many goods and services from one's neighbors as will not depress them below a common level of subsistence. As he writes in "Of Justice" (book 2, section 2 of *Political Justice*), "My neighbor is in want of ten pounds that I can spare . . . unless it can be shown that the money can be more beneficently employed, his right [to it] is as complete . . . as if he had my bond in his possession, or had supplied me with goods to the amount" (1:135).

Political Justice was a work of great importance to Wordsworth. He addresses his deep and tragic love affair with Godwin's social philosophy in *The Prelude*, recalling the "ready welcome" he gave Godwin's philosophy in his early twenties, as well as his eventual disillusionment with it: "Sick, wearied out with contrarieties, / [I] Yielded up moral questions in despair" (10.810, 899–900). He then yielded up Godwin, or at least a perfect allegiance to him, and was from a philosophical point of view quite right to do so. Wordsworth could only be baffled by Godwin's demand that in all determinations of justice we should be able to distinguish, objectively, between the relative moral worth of any two individuals. Indeed, what does it mean, practically, that one ought to give one's spare ten pounds to a needy neighbor "unless it can be shown that the money can be more beneficently employed"? Godwin demands that our moral calculations involve total knowledge (the ability to be "universally capable of discriminating the comparative worth of different men," 1:129–30), and, unlike natural law theory and Kant, he makes no clear distinction between perfect duties (those things one must do, unconditionally—such as tell the truth) and imperfect duties (things that one should do under certain conditions—such as give money to the poor).

Wordsworth did, however, derive certain things from Godwin, including an abiding distrust of interpersonal gratitude (saliently inscribed in the 1798 poem "Simon Lee," a poem about an old man inordinately grateful for a very small service the narrator performs for him).[6] Wordsworth's poem *The Old Cumberland Beggar*—a meditation springing from an encounter with an old beggar who, in turn, encounters many others on his slow, daily rounds—attempts to resolve, in an aesthetic rather than argumentative manner, the central problems

raised by Godwin: the calculus of moral worth, the limits of private benevo-
lence, and the injustice of gratitude. Wordsworth defuses the problem of grati-
tude, as we shall see, by barring it from his imaginative vision. The beggar is not
apparently grateful for the alms given him by the poor; nor are the poor who
give alms sentimentalized. Wordsworth's attention to the alms-deeds of the
poor is not unprecedented in literature: for example, in a magazine tale from
1775 "an honest Negro" gives his last three pence to a wooden-legged, one-
armed sailor.[7] Yet Wordsworth transforms the stuff of sentimental anecdote
into a dry-eyed, philosophical inquiry into routine virtue, and the virtue of
routine.

Wordsworth answers Godwin, in part, by harking back to Anthony Ashley
Cooper, the 3rd Earl of Shaftesbury (1671–1713), and his neo-Stoic ethics of be-
nevolism. Wordsworth appears to have read by 1785 Shaftesbury's collected
opus, *Characteristicks of Men, Manners, Opinions, Times* (1709); Wordsworth's
Rydal Mount library contained a copy of the book; and in 1815 he referred in
print to Shaftesbury as "an author at present unjustly depreciated."[8] Shaftes-
bury maintained that we naturally fulfill our human ends, and in doing so expe-
rience rational joy, in acting benevolently toward our fellow rational creatures.[9]
Wordsworth, however, grounds Shaftesbury's ethics in the practice not, as
Shaftesbury did, of the gentry or middling orders, but of the poor—indeed, "the
abject poor" (*Cumberland Beggar*, line 135). Wordsworth treats the benevolence
of the poor as wholesomely indiscriminate, the antidote to Godwin's inquiry
into another's moral worth.

Wordsworth's poem opens with encounter: "I saw an aged Beggar in my
walk"; "Him from my childhood have I known, and then / He was so old, he
seems not older now." After a finely observed description of the beggar's daily
travels along a mountain tollgate road—moving so slowly that "scarcely do his
feet / Disturb the summer dust"—Wordsworth turns to a public defense of the
beggar's moral usefulness within mountain life, urged against the "Statesmen"
who would put him away.[10]

> While thus he creeps
> From door to door, the villagers in him
> Behold a record which together binds
> Past deeds and offices of charity
> Else unremember'd, and so keeps alive
> The kindly mood in hearts which lapse of years,
> And that half-wisdom half-experience gives

Make slow to feel, and by sure steps resign
To selfishness and cold oblivious cares.
Among the farms and solitary huts,
Hamlets, and thinly-scattered villages,
Where'er the aged Beggar takes his rounds,
The mild necessity of use compels
To acts of love; and habit does the work
Of reason, yet prepares that after-joy
Which reason cherishes. And thus the soul,
By that sweet taste of pleasure unpursu'd,
Doth find itself insensibly dispos'd
To virtue and true goodness. (ll. 79–97)

The villagers' reward for their customary benisons upon a hopelessly poor and old man is "that after-joy / Which reason cherishes," and this reflective delight in turn further ingrains the virtuous habit of alms-giving.

Wordsworth's short passage serves as a précis of ethics itself, the word "ethics" deriving from the *ethos* or "habit" of action that Aristotle and later the Stoics saw as the source of moral virtue. Aristotle states at the opening of book 2 of *Nichomachean Ethics* (1103a): "Moral virtue . . . is formed by habit, *ethos,* and its name, *ethike,* is therefore derived, by a slight variation, from *ethos*" (33). The link between morality and habitual action is translated into Latin terms in a passage of Seneca's that Wordsworth adopted as the epigraph of his *Ode to Duty:* the virtuous person "is trained by habit [*mors*] to such an extent that he not only can act rightly, but cannot help acting rightly" (*Epistulae Morales* 120.10, Loeb edition 3:386–88). Yet Wordsworth evinces his familiarity with "habit" as the root of ethics much earlier in his poetic career: it is evident in the quotation from his *Ruined Cottage* manuscript (1798) I used as the first epigraph to my introduction, and again in the better-known lines of the Preface to *Lyrical Ballads* describing the virtuous (and virtue-inspiring) "habits of mind" the poet must acquire and "blindly and mechanically" obey (*Prose Works* 1:126).[11]

With Shaftesbury and his neo-Stoic followers, Wordsworth concurs in seeing *joy* as the crucial element in the formation of the habitual actions that constitute moral virtue. Wordsworth carefully qualifies this joy as a "sweet taste of pleasure unpursued," anticipating and fending off the charge often leveled against philosophers in the Shaftesburian line that they practice a sort of "moral hedonism," pursuing the good only for the sake of the pleasure it produces.[12] Wordsworth's "pleasure unpursued" neatly encapsulates an argument found in Aristotle's *Ethics,* Seneca's *De Beata Vita,* and Francis Hutcheson's Shaftesbury-influenced work, *On the Nature and Conduct of the Passions* (1728): as Hutcheson puts it, the gratification of any desire, including the desire for the happiness of others, brings "a pleasant sensation of *Joy*" which could not itself have been the object of desire.[13] In other words, pleasure can never be the *direct* object of any desire or activity: one must pursue other objects or activities that with attainment or completion might bring joy. Like Hutcheson, Wordsworth is keen to claim that one cannot pursue joy but that it descends like grace upon certain other pursuits.

Or at least it does so in the country. In *The Old Cumberland Beggar,* ethical joy descends upon encounters with an aged beggar "among the farms and solitary huts, / Hamlets, and thinly-scattered villages" of the Lake District. Wordsworth's poetry through 1805, taken as a whole, casts grave doubt on whether or not such encounters of an ethical kind are available in more densely populated areas, with London posing a particular problem. The old Cumberland beggar is a compelling figure precisely because he is the only beggar in the landscape; add a few hundred or thousand more beggars to the picture and one blunts the sensibilities of those who behold them. Wordsworth concedes as much in *Home at Grasmere* (begun 1800): charity is only possible in remote rural communities where the presence of beggars is not overwhelming, as it is in cities. One of the humane benefits of living in Grasmere, Wordsworth contends, is "That they who want are not too great a weight / For those who can relieve" (lines 447–48, ms. B). Charity, and indeed any sense of community, is killed by metropolitan life: "he truly is alone. . . . / He by the vast Metropolis immured, / Where pity shrinks from unremitting calls, / Where numbers overwhelm humanity" (lines 593–99, ms. D).[14]

Yet even the Lake District is not ideal. Wordsworth did on occasion imagine social arrangements that would preclude the abject poverty that passes without comment in *The Old Cumberland Beggar.* In this poem he brackets rural community from the larger structures of distributive injustice that he elsewhere acknowledges: in *The Prelude* (1805 version), he grants that laborers bear "all the weight / Of that injustice which upon ourselves / By composition of society / Ourselves entail" (book 12, lines 102–5). Some of Wordsworth's later readers grew less patient than Wordsworth with this perceived injustice. Orestes Brownson wrote in the *Boston Quarterly Review* (April 1839): "Wordsworth sings beggars, we admit, and shows very clearly that a man who begs is not to be despised: but does he ever fire our souls with a desire so to perfect our social system, that beggary shall not be one of its fruits?"[15]

Even if moral life in the Lake District is less than ideal, *The Old Cumberland Beggar* still offers an attractive picture of traditional community founded on bonds of benevolence and joy. Here all can exercise bounty, and so all feel a joy that confirms their places in an orderly cosmos. Or, more precisely, all can feel this joy except for the beggar himself. Wordsworth's American editor, Henry Reed, dubbed the beggar "the benefactor of inferior creatures" ("Wordsworth's Poetry" 57)—that is, the birds who enjoy his crumbs—but this act of "charity" is ironic because unwilling. The beggar eats his food in solitude, and his "palsied hand" accidentally scatters crumbs that "the small mountain birds" peck once he moves on. The beggar does not *want* to share anything with the birds: "still attempting to prevent the waste, / [He] was baffled still," the ongoing futility of his efforts underscored by the alpha and omega of "still." The remarkable thing about these lines is that they're the only glimpse we get of the beggar's interior life: all we know about him is his frustrated effort to keep his hand from shaking crumbs to the birds. Beyond this, the beggar's consciousness is a blank.

Wordsworth's poem speculates on the consciousness of the alms-giving poor for the moral benefit of the poem's polite readers. The old beggar, in his stone-like calm, is absolved of self-consciousness altogether, rendering immaterial whether or not he feels pain, for example, or whether or not he feels gratitude for the small kindnesses rendered him. It is upon this denial that Wordsworth builds his poetic solution to the Godwinian challenge: as far as we can tell, the old Cumberland beggar feels no gratitude for what he is given, nor do the villagers with whom he interacts expect him to do so. He claims what is his due, albeit not with an erect mien. Sufficient for the poor who spare him what they can is the joy of acting in accordance with nature, and with habit as a kind of second nature.

Religion has no real bearing on the villagers' interaction with the beggar. Indeed, a point on which the early Wordsworth concurs with both Godwin and Shaftesbury—and with an Enlightenment legacy more generally—is that religion has no essential connection to ethics, properly understood. In *The Old Cumberland Beggar,* and nowhere else in Wordsworth's poetic corpus, we find a reference to "the Decalogue," and the reference is withering. The Biblical passage in which we find the so-called Ten Commandments (Exodus 20:1–17)—the injunctions related by Moses are not actually numbered, and different Christian churches sort them differently—contains nine "thou shalt not's" and one "thou shalt have no," and thus embodies what Wordsworth elsewhere calls "negative morality." In *The Old Cumberland Beggar* this negative morality is the pharisaic comfort of the "many"—including, it would seem, the "statesmen" to whom the poem is addressed as a kind of lay sermon—while true morality, based not on positive law but rather on the "one human heart," belongs to the poor. The many are depicted first:

> Many, I believe, there are
> Who live a life of virtuous decency,
> Men who can hear the Decalogue and feel
> No self-reproach, who of the moral law
> Establish'd in the land where they abide
> Are strict observers, and not negligent,
> Meanwhile, in any tenderness of heart
> Or act of love to those with whom they dwell,
> Their kindred, and the children of their blood.
> Praise be to such, and to their slumbers peace! (ll. 125–34)

The ironies of this passage, subtle but piercing, involve two slippages, the first between "the Decalogue," or the authoritative Word of God, and "the moral law / Establish'd in the land where they abide," which sounds like, and tends to reduce the Decalogue to, a set of rules relative to a certain time and place. A second slippage occurs between the religionist's "tenderness of heart" and, as Wordsworth's unfolding syntax gradually reveals, the blood relations to whom it is limited.

By contrast, the poor, as Wordsworth imagines them, are Good Samaritans, generous by nature rather than precept. They transcend the religious many whose morality is disclosed as wholly negative ("cold abstinence") or constrained ("inevitable charities"):

> —But of the poor man ask, the abject poor,
> Go and demand of him, if there be here,
> In this cold abstinence from evil deeds,
> And these inevitable charities,
> Wherewith to satisfy the human soul.
> No—man is dear to man: the poorest poor
> Long for some moments in a weary life
> When they can know and feel that they have been
> Themselves the fathers and the dealers out
> Of some small blessings, have been kind to such
> As needed kindness, for this single cause,
> That we have all of us one human heart. (ll. 135–46)

The poor are moral because they know from experience the vulnerability that is our shared condition, however far it be from the dreams of the prosperous many who slumber in peace. Although Wordsworth insists on his ethical naturalism, *The Old Cumberland Beggar* is, finally, homiletic: "blessed are the poor in spirit: for theirs is the kingdom of heaven" (Matthew 5:3). Wordsworth's poor trail a certain glory from Christ's Sermon on the Mount; insofar as they do, they may be considered a secularized theological concept.

The process of secularization in which Wordsworth participates is characteristic of "Romanticism," or modernity, more broadly, as theorists from Carl Schmitt to M. H. Abrams have argued; in ethics, however, to truck with secularized theological concepts has, through the Anglo-American reception of Emmanuel Levinas's philosophy, come to be called postmodern. Levinas grounded his ethics on the face-to-face, nonassimilative encounter of one human being with another. Ethics, in his sense—now often known as postmodern ethics—is not a set of moral rules but rather an "orientation" toward or responsiveness to the other that, in his infinite (or divine) otherness, is also known as the Other.[16] In the next section, on *The Borderers*, I hope to show the mutually illuminating connections between Wordsworth's maturing poetry of encounter and Levinas's philosophy or (as Samuel Moyn dubs it) "ethical theology."[17]

THE BORDERERS: ETHICS IN THE FACE OF THE OTHER

The Borderers, Wordsworth's one foray into drama, is indebted to Shakespeare for the stateliness of its blank verse (its altitude unrelieved by Shakespeare's gift for low humor), and to Schiller's *The Robbers* for its basic conceit: as Schiller used a band of outlaws to explore the grounds of morality, so will Wordsworth. For Wordsworth, imagined theatrical space allows for a hyperconscious meditation on *seeing faces*, and how the face of the other solicits a moral response that is prior and preferable to a calculation of justice. *The Borderers* renders the demand for justice problematic vis-à-vis the visage.[18] Godwin demanded that our moral calculations involve total knowledge of the character of others, yet it is a knowledge we do not have; retributive justice can demand blood, but the face of the other disarms. *The Borderers*, using the sight lines of the theater, insists that we visually respond to faces, especially the faces of the unfortunate; the keywords of its dialogue are "see" (thirty-eight occurrences), "saw" (nineteen), "look" (twenty-seven, sixteen as a verb and eleven as a noun), "aspect" (two), "countenance" (four), and "face" (twenty, including two "faces").[19] What we are supposed to see above all in the beheld, recollected, or imagined face of the other is an element of the Decalogue inscribed in nature: "thou shalt not kill."

The play, set on the borders of England and Scotland during the reign of Henry III, has as its backdrop the so-called Barons' War of the 1260s, a civil conflict against which Mortimer's band of "borderers" acts either for the public good, protecting the weak from predation, or for more selfish reasons— Mortimer is called at one point "a base freebooter" who "doth prey alike on two distracted countries" (I.i.175–77).[20] This is the judgment (never contravened) of the elderly, blind, and dispossessed Herbert, whose baronial lands have been usurped whilst he was on Crusade. He has, as the play begins, returned to the borders seeking to repossess his lands, led by his loyal daughter Matilda, whom he had rescued from a fire in Antioch at the cost of his eyes. Matilda loves Mortimer, but she loves Herbert still more as he faces her: "When I behold the ruins of that face, / Those eye-balls dark—dark beyond hope of light, / And think that they were blasted for my sake, / The name of Mortimer is blown away" (I.i.106–9). Yet she recurs to Mortimer in speech, believing that her father would be reconciled to him could he hear him and, crucially, could he see: "O could you hear his voice— / Alas! you do not know him. He is one / (I guess not what bad tongue has wronged him with you), / All gentleness and love. His face bespeaks / A deep and simple meekness . . ." (133–36).[21]

Meanwhile, amidst the band of borderers, the Iago-like villain Rivers has "wronged Herbert with his bad tongue," deceiving Mortimer into thinking him an evil man who earlier purchased the infant Matilda from a poor woman and now seeks to sell her to a wastrel lord. The justice Rivers urges—Herbert must be killed—is *blind* in two senses: impartial in theory, and in practice capable of blinding Mortimer to what lies right before his eyes. Mortimer is moved by the sight of Herbert, whom the two men befriend in order to betray: "I would fain hope that we deceive ourselves: / When I beheld him sitting there, alone, / It struck upon my heart—I know not how" (I.iii.1–3). Mortimer's intuitive response to Herbert's face is what Rivers must block for his plot to succeed. Rivers appeals to justice in its two aspects, distributive and retributive, the latter directly and the first through the beggar woman he suborns to pose as Matilda's true and wronged mother. This beggar woman eloquently addresses the unfair distribution of goods, an inequity that troubled Godwin and the young Wordsworth alike. Chided by Rivers for sleeping outside, the beggar responds, as if on cue:

Oh Sir! You would not talk thus if you knew
What life is this of ours, how sleep will master

> The weary-worn.—You gentlefolks have got
> Warm chambers to your wish—I'd rather be
> A Stone than what I am—but two nights gone
> The darkness overtook me, wind and rain
> Beat hard upon my head—and yet I saw
> A glow-worm through the covert of the furze
> Shine [ ] as if nothing ailed the sky
> At which I half-accused the God in heaven—
> You must forgive me, Sirs— (I.iii.45–55)[22]

Although inequity is, the beggar woman implies, built into nature by heavenly ordinance, it also reflects the unjust distributions in medieval (and Georgian) society, the distance between her own poverty and the warm sleep of gentlefolk (though in this play we hear of no one who sleeps warmly), and the gaping distance between the (alleged) luxury of the lord who would buy her daughter from the (falsely alleged) false father who purchased her as a child. And yet my parenthetical qualifications in the above sentence reflect as well Wordsworth's sense of how difficult judgments of justice can be.

Mischaracterizing such judgments as simple ones, Rivers attempts to stir Mortimer to an act that will, in fact, be murderous but that Rivers designates "an act of justice" (II.i.57), one that ought to prevail over unregulated sentiment: "Benevolence that has not heart to use / The wholesome ministry of pain and evil / Is powerless and contemptible" (73–74).[23] After Mortimer proves unable to slit Herbert's throat in his sleep—a deed Rivers had encouraged—Rivers again invokes justice as though the very word had or should have efficacy: "Justice! Is there not thunder in the word?" (II.iii.199). Mortimer later pleads, "But his aspect: / It is so meek, his countenance is so venerable" (376–77) and conjures as well his pitiable sickness, oldness, and blindness. Rivers responds that justice does not distinguish young from old, strong from weak: "Wisdom, if justice speak the word, beats down / The Giant's strength, and at the voice of Justice / Spares not the worm—The Giant and the worm, / She weighs them in one scale" (385–88); "Justice, / Admitting no resistance, binds alike / The feeble and the strong" (396–98). Mortimer, distraught and yet finally unable to kill Herbert with his own hand, subjects him to trial by ordeal, abandoning him, blind and alone on the heath (III.iii). Herbert dies there, after Mortimer is disabused: the old man had been innocent. Rivers equivocates about what he has sought in duping Mortimer into murder: it is that Mortimer might share either his own freedom from conventional morality, or his burden of guilt for crimes in his past (III.v–IV.ii).[24]

Rivers's disingenuous verbal appeals to justice thus succeed, tragically, to distract Mortimer from that to which the play's reader or viewer has never been blinded: the revelation of ethics in the face of the other. Mortimer, while thinking that Herbert ought to die, *looks* on him as on a father or god: "yet in plumbing the abyss of vengeance. . . . / I look at him and tremble like a child—" (II.iii.65). He later recounts to Rivers his failed effort to kill the old man:

> 'Twas dark, dark as hell—yet I saw him—I tell thee I saw him, his face towards me—the very looks of Matilda sent there by some fiend to baffle me—It put me to my prayers—I cast my eyes upwards, and through a crevice in the roof I beheld a star twinkling over my head, and by the living God, I could not do it— (II.iii.286-91)

Herbert's face, with Matilda's superimposed on it, inspires a religious awe consonant with that felt (by Mortimer as by Kant) beneath the starry heavens above.[25] Mortimer sees, as it were, the "living God" in the face of the man he wants to kill, without wanting to kill God in the face. The overflowing quality of Herbert's face—its edges blurring into Matilda, a star, God—comes to an end in death, when the frozen mien no longer expresses. After Mortimer has seen the dead Herbert—offstage, within the cottage of the peasant, Robert, who has brought him in from the freezing heath—his sole comment is: "The dead have but one face" (V.iii.46). A dead person, that is, has a face that no longer changes or expresses, yet the phrasing suggests as well that all the dead look and are the same, an undifferentiated totality, having lost the sheer *otherness* of each living face we encounter.

By now, the reader acquainted with Levinas's philosophy will be aware of its uncanny resemblance to Wordsworth's concerns in *The Borderers*. Wordsworth gives descriptive content to Levinas's moral theory, while this theory, in turn, gives salience to aspects of Wordsworth's play. Both authors ground ethics in the face-to-face encounter with an other that cannot be fully comprehended. Levinas's idiosyncratic definition of *face* as something that transcends even as it remains rooted in its physical appearance captures some of the strange fluidity in Wordsworth's use of the term: "The way in which the other presents himself, exceeding *the idea of the other in me*, we here name face. This *mode* does not consist in figuring as a theme under my gaze, as spreading itself forth as a set of qualities forming an image. The face of the Other at each moment destroys and overflows the plastic image it leaves in me, the idea existing to my own measure and to the measure of its *ideatum*—the adequate idea" (50–51). The face of the other, so defined, is *infinite* in the sense of being "non-adequate" to one's finite idea or representation of it (27, 34). Thus the face, if it is to remain a face, is what one cannot assimilate to one's own measure or (self-) understanding, and still less what one can appropriate for one's own enjoyment or projects. Rather, the face calls into question one's spontaneity and power—one's very oneness—and demands a response *to* the other that is, in Levinas's telling, tantamount to responsibility *for* the other. (It is when the other—in French, *autre*—is attended to *as* an other that Levinas calls him *autrui,* the "you" or "personal other" that is translated into English as the capitalized *Other.*)[26] Response and responsibility are, for Levinas, the basis of ethics: "We name this calling into question of my spontaneity by the presence of the Other ethics" (43). Ethics so understood is anticipated in *The Borderers* each time Mortimer freely undertakes to kill Herbert, and, seeing his face, finds that he cannot.

The vulnerability of Herbert's face, as well as its antithetical power to command, also finds theorization in Levinas. In Levinas as in Wordsworth, the absolute Other is at once the defenseless one, who by eluding our power tempts us to kill him, and also the transcendent God, who voices a prohibition against murder. The infinity of the Other, writes Levinas, "stronger than murder, already resists us in his face, is his face, is the primordial *expression,* is the first word: 'you shall not commit murder.'" (Wordsworth, with his distrust of negative morality, might have preferred as a Biblical touchstone David's explanation to King Saul of why he spared his life: "some bade me kill thee: but *mine eye spared thee;* and I said, I will not put forth my hand against my lord" [1 Samuel 24:10, my emphasis].)[27] Murder is, Levinas continues, an "ethical impossibility" because as an attempt to negate otherness it abrogates the very possibility of ethics (199). It is also impossible because one cannot kill the living God, and Levinas's Other is modeled in part on the incomprehensible and radically transcendent God of Judaic and, as Samuel Moyn has persuasively argued, Protestant-existentialist tradition.[28] "Ethics is the spiritual optics," Levinas maintains; conversely, it is the only way to behold "the Stranger, the widow, and the orphan," figures of precarious life (78).[29] For Levinas, the abject becomes God, God the abject, a chiasmus related to the gospels'—and Wordsworth's—sacralization of the poor.

All this assumes, of course, that the needy will always be with us, in their concretion as well as their abstract significance as figures for the vulnerability shared by all. This assumption appears retrograde to those who believe that social systems can be perfected and distresses eradicated. That hunger and want can be ameliorated, and in their extremity—at least for the industrious poor—abolished, was the point that Orestes Brownson made against *The Old Cumberland Beggar;* it is also the point of the French Revolution as Wordsworth, in *The Prelude*, claims to have once understood it. Recalling his political education by Michel Beaupuy in an early stage of the Revolution (1792), in the Loire River town of Blois, Wordsworth focuses on an encounter with one of the poorest of the poor:

> And when we chanced
> One day to meet a hunger-bitten girl
> Who crept along fitting her languid self
> Unto a heifer's motion—by a cord
> Tied to her arm, and picking thus from the lane
> Its sustenance, while the girl with her two hands
> Was busy knitting in a heartless mood
> Of solitude—and at the sight my friend [Beaupuy]
> In agitation said, ''Tis against that
> Which we are fighting,' I with him believed
> Devoutly that a spirit was abroad
> Which could not be withstood, that poverty,
> At least like this, would in a little time
> Be found no more, that we should see the earth
> Unthwarted in her wish to recompense
> The industrious, and the lowly child of toil . . . (1805, book 9, ll. 511–26)[30]

Written in 1805, thirteen years after the event described here, the phrase "would in a little time" is ironic, a testament to a (secularized) millenarianism to which Wordsworth no longer subscribed.

By the time he wrote these lines, his belief in political solutions had been chastened by the violent turn taken by the French Revolution under Robespierre and Saint-Just—men who maintained, like Rivers in *The Borderers*, that justice must not be corrupted by clemency, that good motives alone count in what constitutes a virtuous action, and that even in the slaughter of the innocent there is something that does not displease us.[31] Indeed, Wordsworth's experience of the French Revolution left him suspicious of *action* more broadly, a suspicion that extends from the narrative of *The Borderers*—where Mortimer's reluctant moral action, based on an erroneous assessment of his (and Rivers's, and Herbert's) situation, issues in disaster—to Wordsworth's last great narrative poem, *The White Doe of Rylstone*, in which the heroine, Emily, having renounced action in the world, is exalted by her moral suffering and face-to-face contact with a numinous doe, her animal familiar or semi-secularized Paraclete. Wordsworth's dilemma with regard to action, as one critic perceptively writes, is that "one can act with relation to something only if one is *not* distant from it, but to Wordsworth only if one *is* distant can one have the proper perspective and thus act properly with relation to it." Thus in *The Prelude* Wordsworth claims to have made errors during the Robespierre and post-Robespierre years, 1793–95, "into which I was betrayed / By *present* objects" (10:882–83, my emphasis); the "sounder judgement" of his earlier engagement with the Revolution, during his friendship with Beaupuy, was possible only when he was "by objects *over near* / Not pressed upon, nor dazzled or misled / By struggling with the crowd for present ends" (9:345–47, my emphasis).[32]

What finally connects Wordsworth and Levinas is their shared turn from political utopianism to an ethics based on interpersonal encounter.[33] In Wordsworth, this turn is already prefigured in his retrospective grounding of his own Revolutionary zeal not on abstract principles but on an encounter with a specific girl. Alienated by Robespierre and the Terror from the French Revolution and the eschatological promise it held for English radicals,[34] Wordsworth alighted on the nonviolent and systematic utopianism of Godwin's *Political Justice*, a work from which he gradually disassociates himself in *The Old Cumberland Beggar* and *The Borderers*. Wordsworth participates in the first "ethical turn" from progressive history: in such turns, the riposte to utopian thinking is, as Moyn characterizes it, "that existence remained unsurpassably individual rather than collective and has to be lived morally in the present rather than gambled recklessly on the future" (221).

In Wordsworth, this living-in-futurity is embodied by Rivers, who professes that having left behind "the opinions and the uses of the world, / I seemed a being who had passed alone / Beyond the visible barriers of the world / And travelled into things to come" (IV.ii.142–45). Mortimer's final rejoinder to Rivers brings us back to the face he had been taught not to trust: drawing Rivers toward the cottage where Herbert's corpse lies, Mortimer says, "here is another face hard by. / Let's in and take a peep . . . / 'Twill be a comment on your morality" (V.iii.244–46). That "comment," had Rivers made it inside (in the event, he is forgiven by Mortimer and murdered by the other Borderers), would have been that ethics, rather than liberating us from the face of the other (via appeals to justice or, as in Schiller's *The Robbers*, the autonomy of morals),[35] instead binds us in responsibility to it. Levinas makes this comment most eloquently in an essay of 1950, "Place and Utopia," his rejection of the Marxist ideology prevalent among intellectuals, most notably Jean-Paul Sartre, in postwar France (and that still lingers on):

Utopia seems not just vain in itself but also dangerous in its consequences. The man of utopia wishes unjustly. Instead of the difficult task of living an equitable life . . . he pursues a dream as though he were still sleeping, as though another day should dawn within his day, and with it another waking that would rid him of his suffocating nightmares. . . . To move toward justice while denying, with a global act, the very conditions within which the ethical drama is played out is to embrace nothingness and, under pretext of saving everything, to save nothing.[36]

Wordsworth insists as well that the moral value of the individual in the present should not be compromised by political calculations about collective good in the future: this is the moral of *The Borderers,* and it also inflects his 1800 *Lyrical Ballad* poem "A Poet's Epitaph," which begins (as though where *The Old Cumberland Beggar* leaves off):

Art thou a Statesman, in the van
Of public business train'd and bred;
—First learn to love one living man;
Then may'st thou think upon the dead.

Wordsworth places a typographical emphasis on "then," but an equal emphasis is implied in the "*one* living man"—the nonstatistical individual—that the statesman must be able to love before validly projecting a future—the *van,* or front line, of politics that marches onward—or understanding a past that recedes backward. The poet who calls from that past, in Wordsworth's epitaphic mode, then calls into being an exemplary individual—another poet, one who roams the countryside "murmur[ing] near the running brooks / A music sweeter than their own"—as a case of one living man who must be loved because he cannot be (otherwise) understood:

He is retired as noontide dew,
Or fountain in a noonday grove;
And you must love him, ere to you
He will seem worthy of your love.

Leslie Stephen, in "Wordsworth's Ethics," thought that these lines expressed a "doctrine [that] corresponds to the *crede ut intelligas* [believe so that you may understand] of the divine" (2:282), but this seems not quite right: the other that Wordsworth evokes is not necessarily to be understood but rather esteemed ("he will seem worthy"), and this esteem proceeds not precisely from believing but from the related imperative of loving. Turned on its head here is Godwin's conception of justice as dependent on the respective moral worth of individuals. For Wordsworth, there is no worth, or understanding, prior to love, emphatically the love of an individual.

But for all of Wordsworth's seeming opposition to a future-oriented utopianism, some nineteenth-century readers nonetheless detected utopian possibilities in his descriptions of place. Although Wordsworth sometimes grounded his normative values in the folkways of England's past, or England's passing folkways—as in *The Old Cumberland Beggar,* or the Preface to *Lyrical Ballads,* or book 12 of the 1805 *Prelude*—this past could be understood, *mutatis mutandis,* as a regenerative vision for the future. As the American critic Edwin Percy Whipple wrote in 1844, Wordsworth's heart lies in "a period when universal benevolence will prevail upon the earth" (383). "Wordsworth may be a politician of the past, but he is emphatically a poet of the future"; "His England of a thousand years past is the Utopia of a thousand years to come" (381–82). Whipple's claims are provocative, but he does not ground them in readings of specific poems: one wonders which ones he might have in mind. To glean a prophecy of universal benevolence from Wordsworth's verse requires overlooking there all that is at enmity with joy, including abject poverty, social inequity, misplaced gratitude, war, disease, madness, and the malice and intellectual tergiversation of a Rivers. And yet this overlooking of impediments admits us to the side of Wordsworth that is optimistic, even utopian, and certainly underappreciated in our present moment. Even in *The Borderers,* a utopian future lies in the restoration of the ethical possibilities that are contingently, rather than necessarily, lost when Mortimer turns from the face and toward abstract calculations of abstract justice. The ethical remains in the play a missed, but not a foreclosed, opportunity: the ethical is what stares us in the face when we envision (or see) the play's staging.[37]

Similarly, if we subtract the impediment of abject and involuntary poverty from *The Old Cumberland Beggar,* we are left with an ethics of cascading benevolence among multiple agents, without reference to sympathy, pity, or any other egocentric standard, but rather where all are joined by habit and the attendant joy that reason cherishes. This utopian side of Wordsworth, ethical and apparently anarchistic, is the abiding legacy of Godwin, whose influence he never wholly surrendered; of the ancient Stoics and Shaftesbury, whose influence he increasingly acknowledged; and of Biblical religion, an influence he shares with Emmanuel Levinas.

CHAPTER THREE

Close Encounters II

Much of Wordsworth's poetry of the 1790s bears witness to what Wordsworth would later call "the dignity of individual man" (*Prelude* 12:183)—not "man" in the abstract ("the rights of man") but individual men, women, and children, with their quirks, limitations, delusions, and joys, and, above all, their mystery. The dignity of certain ranks or classes of men—royalty, aristocracy, clergy, and gentry—had long been assumed, even, as a normative value, in satires on members of these classes for their shortcomings or hypocrisy. What Wordsworth did was dignify characters drawn from the lower and lowest orders of society: laborers, peddlers, potters, waggoners, vagrants, beggars, criminals, elderly cottagers, madwomen, idiots, and even working animals (horses, asses). Wordsworth is remarkable not so much for welcoming such characters to literary culture but for suggesting that there are more to them than meets the eye. Traditional comedy invites us to laugh at "low" characters, and sentimental literature to weep for them or, assuming their place, to weep in their stead. Wordsworth, by contrast, makes us confront, and care for, their otherness.

Wordsworth's poetry of the 1790s is peopled with socially marginal, "border" creatures, including figures of death-in-life (like the Old Cumberland Beggar) and life-in-death (Lucy), ghostly figures (the Discharged Soldier) and figures who seem as solid as stone (the leech gatherer).[1] They are figures that trouble narrative, neither assimilated into any conclusive story nor absorbed into a sympathetic response. These characters remain strangers. In established narrative forms (tragedy, comedy, epic, romance, the emerging novel, the ballad), strangers appear in order that their identities may eventually be revealed; typically, an apparent outsider is unmasked as an insider. But, as David Simpson writes,

> Wordsworth abandons the world of the eighteenth-century picaresque (which
> would live on in the novels of Dickens) where there are no strangers, where every

chance meeting embodies the providence of a narrative as well as moral closure, where an unknown person met at a country inn in chapter 2 must reappear fully identified in chapter 40 as a long-lost family member or friend or at least a figure crucial to the proper development of the story. Wordsworth's strangers remain strangers, often ghostly strangers open only to minimal intimacies that dramatize alienation rather than community.[2]

For Simpson, the strangers of Wordsworth's poetry signify the dislocations caused by the forces of modernity: capitalism, industrialism, empire, and the elusive process of "commodification," whereby objects and social relations alike are reduced to cash value. Simpson, drawing on the work of Alan Bewell, finds the historical referent of *The Discharged Soldier*—a manuscript poem of 1798 later revised and incorporated into the 1805 *Prelude*, book 4, ll. 363–502—to be the plight of soldiers in and returned from the West Indies, a locale readily associated in Wordsworth's day with malnutrition, disease, and contagion.[3] This knowledge is undoubtedly useful with respect to a poem in which a narrator (the "I" whom we are apt to identify as Wordsworth) meets a soldier who, apparently ill, has been discharged from service in "the tropic isles" (l. 99) and is attempting to make his way back home.[4]

Yet this historical knowledge applies to the *background* (to use a very unfashionable term since *context* became king) from which the soldier emerges. The foreground of Wordsworth's poem—the narrator's solitary ramble followed by his encounter with a discharged soldier—is not an encrypted version of what we are not told about its background or, to use another metaphor, of the roads that have brought its protagonists together. The British colonial context of the itinerant soldier is useful but tangential knowledge, and we should avoid the temptation of reading a poem as an allegory for its historical context.[5] If we do not read the poem in this manner, the *alien*ness of the soldier—which troubles Simpson and other New Historicist readers of the poem—is not necessarily a problem, either for political society (in which it is a problem only insofar as it derives from alienation in a Marxist sense) or for ethics (in which it is a problem only if we assume that ethics depends upon sympathetic identification).

THE DISCHARGED SOLDIER: A "LESS IMPERIOUS SYMPATHY" AND THE ETHICAL ORDINARY

As I read it, *The Discharged Soldier* gives descriptive content to a question of ethics: are we obligated, and if so how far are we obligated, to help a stranger who is or appears to be in need? What makes the question pressing in *The Discharged Soldier* is the shocking suddenness with which the unknown becomes proximate. *The Old Cumberland Beggar,* by contrast, centers on a recurrent figure that has long ago been incorporated into habits of goodness. In social terms, the beggar has contributed in his monstrous abjection or bare humanity to consolidate a community in response to him. What happens, however, when one meets an unexpected stranger, one with whom one has no habitual relation? The question is one of undefined positive duties as distinct from the negative duties laid out in the Decalogue or in Kant (do not lie, kill, and so forth). The Bible enjoins the believer to "love your neighbor as yourself" but offers neither parameters for that love nor a clear definition of "neighbor."[6]

Levinas, working within Judaic tradition, proposes that one infinitely owes the neighboring other because of his otherness: "this gaze that supplicates and demands" is "entitled to everything"; "to recognize the Other is to give" (75). To give—everything? Does Levinas think that one's giving should correspond to the extent of the Other's (theophanic) entitlement? It seems more reasonable to maintain, with Paul Ricoeur (337), that Levinas uses hyperbole to produce a jarring sense of both the other's otherness and the ego's preethical separation from the other. As Terry Eagleton writes, "Responsibility to others, *pace* Levinas . . . is not absolute and infinite, but must be tempered by justice, prudence, and realism" (324). In practical terms, then, what should we, what can we, give? *The Discharged Soldier* answers this question, provisionally, by depicting a specific act of charity; but by not presenting this act as conclusive or satisfactory suggests at the same time the difficulty of setting limits to one's responsibility to the other. If *The Discharged Soldier* were to have an envoy, it could be: what can be done is done for now.

The poem begins not with an encounter but rather with a thirty-four-line verse paragraph on a nocturnal ramble undertaken in solitude, the speaker's inner trouble or fatigue eased by his environment and the process of walking. Critics tend to pass quickly over this opening movement or neglect it entirely, despite its comprising a fifth of the poem's overall lines. Why are these lines here? They set the scene of the eventual encounter, surely, but they soon do something more than that:

> I love to walk
> Along the public way, when, for the night
> Deserted, in its silence it assumes
> A character of deeper quietness

> Than pathless solitudes. At such a time
> I slowly mounted up a steep ascent
> Where the road's watry surface, to the ridge
> Of that sharp rising, glittered in the moon,
> And seemed before my eyes another stream
> Stealing with silent lapse to join the brook
> That murmured in the valley. (ll. 1–11)

The unfolding irony of these lines is that the *public* way is loved precisely for the absence of the people for whom, or for whose benefit, it is so called. The poem begins in a retreat from publicity and a scene that acquires depth ("deeper quietness") antithetically, in relation to the negated possibility of other people. The speaker then moves inward, from the "I" that walks alone to the imaginative eye that transforms a wet road into a stream; he conveys this visual metamorphosis in sound that echoes sense, effluent lines built on sibilance, the animating trochee of "stealing," and the onomatopoeic "murmur."

As aurally seductive as these lines are, the metaphoric equation they represent may not be innocent in *The Discharged Soldier*—a poem, we shall see, that dramatizes the ethical movement *away* from imaginative interiority. The structure of metaphor, identifying this with that, troubled the later Wordsworth. In an 1822 poem set in the Alps, Wordsworth sees in a Catholic procession ("the living Stream / Of white-robed Shapes") a reflection of "the glacier Pillars" above, and this "metamorphosis," as he calls it, fissures into still other forms: "virgin-lilies marshaled in bright row, / . . . swans descending with the stealthy tide." Reflecting on this metaphoric proliferation, Wordsworth chides "that licentious craving in the mind / To act the God among external things, / To bind, on apt suggestion, and unbind."[7] The poet as God of external things, imaginatively *creating* (with the full Biblical force of that term) in a manner analogous to divine creation, is, of course, a commonplace of critical understanding of Romanticism in general and of Wordsworth in particular.[8] Yet Wordsworth not only praised the creative imagination but also chafed against it, particularly the imaginative principle of binding or identifying things that are and ought to remain distinct. Thus a passage incorporated into *The Prelude*— "I had a world about me; 'twas my own, / I made it" (3:142–43)[9]—should be read in counterpoint to poems that eschew imaginative distortion, including *Resolution and Independence, Elegiac Stanzas, Suggested by a Picture of Peele Castle*, and, I would argue, *The Discharged Soldier*.

As this poem proceeds, the speaker distances himself from the imaginative "amusement" of seeing "near objects" either as some other thing (a watery road as another stream) or as connected to his self, idly "disposed to sympathy" (ll. 13–16). Such fanciful amusements are esteemed below "the deeper joy," which for fatigue he then felt himself "all unworthy of," "which waits on distant prospect, cliff, or sea, / The dark blue vault, or universe of stars" (18–20)—that is, in the sublime intuition of a correspondent inner depth or grandeur. This joy, arising from a perception of depth and itself perceived as deep, is one that Wordsworth took over from earlier eighteenth-century poetry (Mark Akenside, Thomas Warton, Anna Laetitia Barbauld), elaborating upon it in other poems of 1798, from the manuscript "A Fragment [A Night Piece]" to the great ode *Tintern Abbey*.[10] In *The Discharged Soldier* this joy is introduced negatively, in contradistinction to his sensual and imaginative enjoyment.

In the lines that follow, his enjoyment is further delineated:

Thus did I steal along that silent road,
My body from the stillness drinking in
A restoration like the calm of sleep
But sweeter far. Above, before, behind,
Around me, all was peace and solitude,
I looked not round, nor did the solitude
Speak to my eye; but it was heard and felt.

And in this sated state, "beauteous pictures" arise on the inner eye, which mingle with "a consciousness of animal delight" felt in "every pause / And every gentle movement of my frame" (ll. 21–35). The poem's speaker here occupies, in Levinas's terms, the preethical state of man, his primordial and egocentric state of "enjoyment" (*jouissance*), in which the things one lives on—food, air, light, bodily movement and work, tools, ideas, sleep—are objects of pleasure.[11] (In stressing our enjoyment of what sustains us, Levinas opposes his teacher Heidegger, in whose phenomenology things serve an instrumental function: objects as mere implements.) While richly appreciating this state, Levinas thought it antecedent and inferior to the ethical, which alone satisfies our "metaphysical desire" (in Levinas's particular sense) for "the *absolutely other*" (33). The "essence of enjoyment," he writes, is "nourishment, as a means of invigoration," which necessarily transmutes the other into the same, absorbs the exterior into oneself (111). Enjoyment as alimentation figures complexly in

Wordsworth's poem: "My body from the stillness *drinking* in / A restoration like the calm of sleep / But *sweeter* far" (my emphases). Here Wordsworth's speaker enjoys objects and features of his environment, but elsewhere in his poetry the human other comes perilously close to being consumed as well. Thus in "The Solitary Reaper," as Wordsworth originally wrote it, the speaker comments of the Highland reaper's song, "I listen'd till I *had my fill*"; only later did Wordsworth exchange this alimentary metaphor for the nonmetaphoric (and logically redundant) adjectives, "motionless and still," salvaging both song and, by extension, singing woman from consumption.[12]

In *The Discharged Soldier* the speaker's independent enjoyment is interrupted by a turn in the road that reveals ahead a tall, "uncouth shape" (l. 38) in soldier's dress. The speaker thus passes from enjoyment to the border of ethics. He initially does not greet the man but rather, from fear or alarm, examines him from a hiding place behind a thick hawthorn:

> His visage, wasted though it seem'd, was large
> In feature, his cheeks sunken, and his mouth
> Shewed ghastly in the moonlight . . . (ll. 49–51)

In *The Prelude*, these lines are condensed to "his mouth / shewed ghastly in the moonlight," a mouth without a face, an index of hunger or need. "Before the hunger of men," writes Levinas, "responsibility is measured only 'objectively' . . . the face opens the primordial discourse whose first word is obligation, which no 'interiority' permits avoiding" (201). The ghastly mouth announces need, but it is also the site of (at this point) potential speech, should the speaker engage him in discourse—that is, to welcome the stranger and surrender his egotism to the diversity of dialogue.

At first, however, the proprietary gaze threatens to turn the other into the self. The man "appeared" to the speaker "cut off / From all his kind" (ll. 57–59); "in his very dress appear'd / A desolation, a simplicity / That appertain'd to solitude" (62–64). Is the speaker here looking outward or inward? In his own moment of enjoyment he had been encased in an epistrophe of "solitude": "Around me, all was peace and *solitude*, / I looked not round, nor did the *solitude* / Speak" (24–26). But now, in or through the soldier, solitude is haunted by the strange reflection that it entails "desolation" as well as "simplicity." Wordsworth's representation of the soldier's dress slights iambic regularity for a stark, balanced rhythm of two strong stresses a line—"A *de*solation, a sim*pli*city / That apper*tain'd* to *so*litude"—and this complication of the metrical contract arrests the reader. All is no longer a flowing ("Stealing with silent lapse . . ."); choices

have to be made, between meter and rhythm as between the simplicity of soli-
tude and its desolation.

"From his lips, meanwhile, / There issued murmuring sounds, as if of pain / Or
of uneasy thought" (68–70). This murmuring may provide another link be-
tween speaker and soldier. Taking the speaker to be Wordsworth (as he appears
to be in the *Prelude* version of this poem), Celeste Langan notes the tendency of
both men to "murmur," in the sense of making low steady sounds, although
Wordsworth's murmurings, consonant with the stream's murmurings (l. 11),
are poetic mumblings ("I sauntered, like a river murmuring / And talking to it-
self," *Prelude* 4:110–11), and the soldier's are "as if" of pain.[13] From my point of
view, this "as if" has protoethical heft: it is the means by which the speaker dis-
entangles the soldier from himself (and from the reader), conceding that he has
no real idea of what the other is thinking or feeling.[14]

This dawning recognition of the otherness of the other is accompanied by a
sublimated desire to kill the other who resists absorption and enjoyment. This
desire registers in the locution "an arrow's flight," never before (and only once
later) employed by Wordsworth:

> In a glen
> Hard by, a village stood, whose silent doors
> Were visible among the scattered trees,
> Scarce distant from the spot an arrow's flight.
> I wished to see him move; but he remained
> Fixed to his place, and still from time to time
> Sent forth a murmuring voice of dead complaint,
> A groan scarce audible. (72–79)[15]

The other who resists our wishes, who is defenseless but incompliant, is the one
whom we wish to kill, according to Levinas (see my reading of *The Borderers*, in
chapter 2). That the man stands "an arrow's flight" from the village implies that
he could either be shot by the villagers or could shoot them, and since he is
clearly unarmed, the former possibility prevails. The soldier vexes with his
strange and extreme stillness, and the speaker fantasizes, fleetingly, that he
might die. Adding to the (projected) hostility of the village, this passage is im-
mediately followed in *The Discharged Soldier* by a mastiff, who appears hostile to
the stranger: "Yet all the while / The chained mastiff in his wooden house / Was
vexed, and from among the village trees / Howled never ceasing." Wordsworth
deleted these lines from his *Prelude* version of this tale, presumably aware of the
blood lust they obliquely admit.

Although aggression never sleeps, *The Discharged Soldier* dramatizes the choice of the ethical life:

> I left the shady nook where I had stood,
> And hailed the Stranger. From his resting-place
> He rose; and, with his lean and wasted arm
> In measured gesture lifted to his head,
> Returned my salutation. A short while
> I held discourse on things indifferent
> And casual matter. (85–91)

"I . . . hailed the stranger": the slightest of gestures, it arrives in the context of Wordsworth's poem with momentous force. It signals emergence from a solitude that had come to feel like desolation, a going out of one's way to speak and give to a stranger whose strangeness is recognized and respected. The ethical choice, for Wordsworth as for Levinas, is to welcome the stranger without assimilating or trying to make use of him—and, of course, without killing him. The irrepressible possibility of inexplicable violence enters Wordsworth's poem intertextually, in relation to a poem he himself had earlier worked on in the fall of 1797: Coleridge's *The Rime of the Ancyent Marinere* (1798).[16] There the act of welcoming—the mariner recounts of the albatross, "We hail'd it in God's name" (l. 66)—is reversed by the arrow: "With my cross bow / I shot the Albatross" (81–82). In *The Discharged Soldier,* by contrast, hailing issues in dialogue, question and answer, some sense of the soldier's tribulations, and finally the speaker procuring a night's food and lodging for him in the nearby home of a laborer, "an honest man and kind" (111). Language writes Levinas, "abolishes the inalienable property of enjoyment. The world in discourse is no longer what it is in separation, in the being at home with oneself" (76). The discursive world is divisible and ongoing, and in this it opposes as well the potential totalitarianism of panoramic vision. Wordsworth's own dialogic mode, turning on the otherness of others, continues through *Lyrical Ballads* (more than half the poems in the volume include dialogue or reported speech) and the narrative poems *Peter Bell, Benjamin the Waggoner,* and *The White Doe of Rylstone,* culminating in the extended philosophical dialogue of *The Excursion.*[17]

The defining characteristic of genuine dialogue (as opposed to Socratic dialectic, religious catechism, and absurdist echolalia) is that one does not know what the other is going to say next. This is particularly evident in *The Discharged Soldier,* where speaker and soldier remain strangers to one another despite their communication, and expectations of sympathetic connection (such as Wordsworth's original readers, steeped in the sentimental novel, would have had) are roundly frustrated. Such frustration is registered as well by Nancy Yousef, in a recent essay that first got me thinking seriously about the poem:

> Thus far [at the hailing of the stranger], the episode would seem to be a straight-forward moral tale in which a minor act of ethical bad faith (cowardly withdrawal from the other) is overcome, the need of a stranger met, and the indulgence in self-absorption rectified by irresistible recognition of kinship. But this greeting is just the beginning of what proves to be a curiously disappointing encounter in which sympathetic expectations are roundly frustrated. The youth has been moved from his solitude, but does not . . . come to know the stranger. ("Words-worth, Sentimentalism, and the Defiance of Sympathy" 211)

The stranger, when asked by the speaker, tells his tale: he had been a soldier in the Indies, dismissed from service upon return to England, and is now trying to make his way back to his home on foot but has tarried because (in lines Words-worth cut from his *Prelude* version) "my weakness made me loath to move" and "the village mastiff fretted me" (ll. 128, 130). As Yousef points out, however, the soldier's tale is not the one the speaker had expected to hear, at least not as it is presented: "in all he said / There was a strange half-absence, and a tone / Of weakness and indifference" (ll. 140–42). Yousef concludes, "For the youth who wishes to himself be moved . . . their conversation is clearly an anti-climax" (211). The poem as a whole thus leaves "ethical urgings" at odds with "epistemo-logical uncertainties," or the inability to know the other (210).

As I see it, however, the ethical relation presented in Wordsworth's poem is not countered but rather underscored by uncertainty and an inability, on the part of both main characters, fully to sympathize with the other. What Words-worth depicts, well in advance of Levinas, is the ethical centrality of the abso-lutely other, who remains in his inequation to our idea of him "infinite" or over-flowing. Wordsworth thus belies an eighteenth-century model of sympathy as a mechanism for perceptual sharing and the transmission of emotion—that is, for a more or less total identification with the condition and feelings of the other.[18] This identification, however, typically converts the other into a version of one's self, so that feeling with another becomes feeling what one imagines one would feel were one in the other's position. This allows for the paradoxical possibility of feeling what the other feels more than the other feels it, especially when the sympathizer is of the upper and the sympathized-with of the lower orders. Thus Thomas Gordon assures his polite readers in a *Cato's Letters* essay of 1722 that on seeing a "beggar, shivering and naked on a cold wet day, with humble, pale, and hungry looks . . . the human sympathy in our souls raises a party for him within us, and our fancy immediately represents us to ourselves in the same doleful circumstances; and, for that time, we feel all that the beggar feels, probably much more; for he is used to it, and can bear it better."[19] The beggar, stripped of his otherness, becomes a placeholder for what the reader can imagine feeling in a (novel and temporary) condition of want. This type of sympathetic usurpation is what *The Discharged Soldier* disallows.

Wordsworth's chastisement of sympathy in his poems of the 1790s—and thereafter—is to some degree a self-chastisement, as he himself had, at the outset of his poetic career, traded in sentimental extravagance. His first (anonymously) published poem, "Sonnet, on seeing Miss Helen Maria Williams weep at a Tale of Distress" (1787), concerns the communication of the authoress's tears to the speaker's own eyes ("She wept . . . Dim were my swimming eyes"), and ends with a wild claim about sympathy's ethical centrality: "That tear proclaims—in thee each virtue dwells." *Each* virtue? Even the list sketched by the fourteen-year-old Wordsworth in his Hawkshead School bicentenary exercise admits Roman (Stoic) self-control and justice alongside "the gentler manners of the private dome" and sympathy with virtue in distress.[20]

The moral clarity of Wordsworth's Hawkshead exercise owes both to its genre (eulogy to one's grammar school and its moral office) and, presumably, to its composition before the full swing of puberty. In the sentimental and gothic modes young Wordsworth subsequently adopted, sympathy with pain and terror—for example, in the scene of the vagrant mother's dead babies in *An Evening Walk*—functions in lieu, not in the service, of ethics. In *The Discharged Soldier* (as well as *The Ruined Cottage*), Wordsworth steps back from the enjoyment of sympathy. He consigns sympathy to the preethical sphere in the poem's opening movement: "disposed to sympathy / With an exhausted mind," he receives "amusement" from the near objects he passes (ll. 12–17). (Wordsworth does not here characterize these nocturnal objects but later provides a daylight catalogue of sympathetic amusements—with daisies, daffodils, small celandines, robins, butterflies, and so forth—in the 1807 *Poems, in Two Volumes*.)[21] Other humans, by contrast, cannot be so readily incorporated into sympathetic identification. In a poem of Wordsworth's maturity, "Composed by the Sea-Shore" (1833), the poet encourages "a less imperious sympathy" with sailors—a brilliant phrase that concedes that sympathy can indeed be imperious (which Johnson defines, with brio, as "commanding, tyrannical, authoritative, haughty, arrogant, assuming command"). In Wordsworth's poem, *imperious* shades into *imperial*: what Wordsworth seems here to recommend is a sympathy with sailors less as agents of empire (who "welcome glory won in battles fought") than as domestic beings, actual men, and as such not fully knowable.[22]

The Discharged Soldier ends without mutual understanding but rather with its two main characters arriving at a reciprocal blessing that, given the poem's gradual scaling down of narrative expectation, seems nearly momentous. The speaker assures the cottager who houses the soldier "The service if need be I will requite" (l. 152)—allowing (or forcing) him to reckon the need—and then admonishes the soldier:

> I entreated that henceforth
> He would not linger in the public ways
> But at the door of cottage or of inn
> Demand the succour which his state required,
> And told him feeble as he was, 'twere fit
> He asked relief or alms. At this reproof,
> With the same ghastly mildness in his look,
> He said, "My trust is in the God of Heaven
> And in the eye of him that passes me."
> By this the labourer had unlocked the door,
> And now my comrade touched his hat again
> With his lean hand, and, in a voice that seem'd
> To speak with a reviving interest,
> Till then unfelt, he thanked me; I returned
> The blessing of the poor unhappy man,
> And so we parted— (ll. 154–70)

Wordsworth's art of the ethical ordinary demands a slowing of the pulse such that upon reading this passage, or at least rereading it, slight details acquire resonance. The speaker now calls the stranger his "comrade," which means, according to Johnson's second definition, "a companion," but more specifically "a partner in any labor or danger"—the implication is that the two men have undergone an experience together, one that has brought them together even as it has left them separate beings, a close encounter. The soldier, now "comrade," "touched his hat again": it appears a valedictory gesture, but in advance of the thanks he offers it seems as well to acknowledge, without the servility of tipping his hat, the favor—or is it the justice?—done him. His interest in discourse (and the ethics on which it is based) revives, and the thanks he offers seems to be in the form of a blessing (presumably "God bless you"), since it is a blessing that the speaker returns. Blessing here carries something of its Old Testament weight as an authoritative pronouncement of God's favor, as well as a passing on of vitality—it is, as Wordsworth as well as Coleridge seem to have understood it in this period, the final resting place of the ethical struggle.[23] With it, the poem should end in peace—and yet, curiously, it does not.

Unsettled questions ruffle our experience of the poem's ending. Ought the soldier to claim "relief or alms" (and what is the difference?) as his due—or ought he, as he is inclined to do, claim nothing (at least verbally), trusting in God and "the eye of him that passes me"? The poem inclines toward, without settling on, the latter option, as in the next question it prompts: ought the speaker have simply recompensed the laborer for his pains, or is giving him the option to exercise charity on the poorest of the poor (as in *The Old Cumberland Beggar*) the right thing to do? In a related matter, and finally: why doesn't the speaker take the soldier home, to his own house? In the 1805 *Prelude*, Wordsworth supplies a simple answer to a question left open-ended in *The Discharged Soldier*: there, the speaker's home is far away (book 4 ends with the line, "Then sought with quiet heart my distant home" [l. 504]). But in the earlier poem, the speaker's implied inability to take the soldier home may be interpreted, charitably, as an unwillingness to incorporate the stranger, especially into the totality that Wordsworth desperately imagines home to be in his own homecoming poem, *Home at Grasmere* ("A Whole without dependence or defect, / Made for itself and happy in itself, / Perfect contentment, Unity entire").[24] The soldier is, instead, allowed his distance, which is the distance that makes ethics possible. As Levinas writes, ethics is a movement "from an 'at home' [*chez soi*] which we inhabit, toward an alien outside-of-oneself [*hors-de-soi*], towards a yonder" (33).

The last line of *The Discharged Soldier*—"And so we parted"—is inconclusive and anticlimactic, chastening our narrative expectations and leaving unanswered questions about home, the speaker's and the soldier's own (will he make it there?), and predominantly about justice, a political concept that Wordsworth never quite relinquished in the wake of the French Revolution and Godwin. What, if anything, does society owe the soldier? Oughtn't the army at least get him home? Is a just and rational scheme of publicly administered military relief preferable to the ethical demands made by the face of the other on the eye that passes him by? Such questions hover uneasily about the borders of the poem, as of Wordsworth's poetry of encounter more generally. They trouble Laurence Lockridge in his effort to think through what he sees as one of Wordsworth's chief ethical imperatives, namely, "the virtue of receptivity, an ability to monitor another without egoistic distortion." Lockridge continues: "The [consequent] imperative it [receptivity] ordinarily leads to is distributive justice: pain should be eradicated and the fruits of the earth spread about equally. Wordsworth's poems of dialogic encounter stop short of any such imperative, however" (219). That this is so, Lockridge suggests, is because Wordsworth is a poet, not a propagandist. Still, the contortions of Lockridge's prose (the imperative of receptivity ordinarily leads to that of distributive justice, but not here) register the unspoken question of justice as an unspoken presence in the poems of encounters as a proverbial elephant in the room.

Complicating the matter further, in his poetry of encounter Wordsworth blurs the distinction between monitoring things, a descriptive project, and endorsing them as how they ought to be, an evaluative one. In *The Discharged Soldier* as in *The Ruined Cottage,* political injustice remains eccentric to a central Stoic sense that "whatever is, is right," according to which causal necessity (things must be as they are because of intricate webs of material cause and effect) passes into a confirmation of the given as the good.[25] The Stoics held, as Nicholas White summarizes, "that all events, at least in the external world, are completely determined by prior states of the universe as a whole. . . . In addition, the Stoics seem to have viewed the world as organized by a perhaps even stronger sort of coherence than mere determination of future events by past events. For they held that the universe is an organic and perfect whole, exhibiting an orderliness that somehow links all of its parts together." The Stoics sought to bring human desires "into line completely with the way the world actually is. . . . The inconceivability of alternatives would . . . rule out dissatisfaction with things as they actually are."[26]

Thus in *The Discharged Soldier* Wordsworth suggests a further ethical charge—in addition to responding to alterity, and monitoring pain without distortion—namely, a prohibition against *murmuring.* The soldier's initial "murmurings" are typically understood by critics as a low, pained noise he emits, but we cannot discount Johnson's second definition of the verb *murmur:* "grumble; to utter secret and sullen discontent." This sense seems pertinent in Wordsworth's poem, given that its speaker passes from describing the soldier's *murmuring* (ll. 69, 78) to his *complaint* (ll. 78, 91), describing its eventual cessation: "he meanwhile [during their discourse] had ceased / From all complaint" (ll. 90–91). The speaker then assures the soldier of the laborer who is to help him in the middle of the night: "He will not murmur should we break his rest" (l. 112). "Murmuring" in this sense is always a bad thing to do, in large part because it's what St. Paul in his Epistle to the Philippians says we shouldn't do: "do all things without murmurings and disputings" (2:14), that is, without protests against divine order.[27]

Murmuring in this pejorative sense is what Wordsworth clearly has in mind at the close of one of his last poems of encounter, one of the *Sonnets Dedicated to Liberty,* titled with the date "September 1st, 1802," which I offer as a pendant to my discussion of *The Discharged Soldier:*

> We had a fellow-Passenger who came
> From Calais with us, gaudy in array,
> A Negro Woman like a Lady gay,
> Yet silent as a woman fearing blame;
> Dejected, meek, yea pitiably tame,
> She sate, from notice turning not away,
> But on our proffer'd kindness still did lay
> A weight of languid speech, or at the same
> Was silent, motionless in eyes and face.
> She was a Negro Woman driv'n from France,
> Rejected like all others of that race,
> Not one of whom may now find footing there;
> This the poor Out-cast did to us declare,
> Nor murmur'd at the unfeeling Ordinance.[28]

Like the soldier of the public road, or the sailors of "Composed by the Sea-Shore," the African woman—the colonized not the colonizer, though Wordsworth blurs the line between them—is spared imperious (or imperial) sympathy. She is allowed her otherness; as Judith Page observes, "Her silence seems to be a sign of strength rather than weakness: she refuses to enter into a discourse that does not fully recognize her humanity. . . . Nor does the black woman become a vehicle for the poet's or the reader's consolation" (72–73). The ordinance to which the poem's last line refers, enacted on July 2, 1802—which, as Page notes (69), forbade people of color from entering continental France but did not expel all people of color currently resident—is deemed "unfeeling," yet the woman does not murmur against it; in this she is unlike the female vagrant of an early *Salisbury Plain* fragment who owned "such reproach of heavenly ordonnance / As shall not need forgiveness" (see chapter 2). A complaint against divine injustice (why has the glow-worm shelter and I no shelter at all?) has given way, in this later poem, to a Stoic acceptance of, and indemnification against, whatever is.

Yet this Stoic sense that what is cannot be otherwise is not uncontested in Wordsworth's work. It is balanced against dissatisfaction with what is and, to anticipate *The Prelude*, hope in "something evermore about to be" (6:542). Thus the black woman's magnanimity—she does not *deign* to murmur—is designed to make the English reader all the more antipathetic to, and able to see beyond, both the French statute that persecutes her and, by extension, Napoleonic France itself. Wordsworth's sonnet is, after all, a poem of wartime. We do not entirely lose sight of unsettled and unsettling questions of political justice that frame Wordsworth's poetry of ethics.

PETER BELL:
THE ANIMAL OTHER AND THE NATURE OF JOY

There is a kind of "ballad justice" in *Peter Bell*: the unjust man gets his just desert of terror and remorse. Yet, as Steve Newman argues (159–64), Wordsworth's poem is also faintly parodic of ballads and their late eighteenth-century revival, as it distances its readers, through doggerel and humble subject matter, from their absorptive power. Violence and abandoned women feature in *Peter Bell* as in other ballads (including those by the then-popular Gottfried August Bürger), but they do so differently, within a space for critical reflection on the genre. Wordsworth's poem also distances us from justice as it is served in traditional and revival ballads. Peter Bell finds, in the end, not death and damnation—the typical deserts of the errant in ballad literature—but, rather, moral reformation.

Peter Bell, drafted in 1798 but not published until 1819, is one of the "lyrical ballads" Wordsworth experimented with in the year before and after the appearance of the first volume of *Lyrical Ballads*. Like *The Thorn* in that volume, it has a fallible narrator clearly distinct from Wordsworth himself, here one who describes himself as "a happy and a thoughtless man" (1799 version, l. 982).[29] Incongruously, he tells the tale of a vicious and cruel man, Peter, a middle-aged "potter" (itinerant seller of earthenware) who "had a dozen wedded wives" (l. 250)—presumably he had (or has) some of them simultaneously, unless his wickedness managed to send each of them consecutively to an early grave (in the course of the poem we hear of just one wife, a Highland girl, who dies young and pregnant of a broken heart [ll. 1136–65]). This is the stuff of melodrama not comedy, although the poem, especially at the outset, has its comic effects. The ballad's verse form—a five-line, roughly tetrameter stanza rhyming abccb— allows for the surprise of coming up short in the last line, often in trimeter, a surprise sometimes accentuated by the polysyllabic rhymes we tend to associate with the first canto of Byron's *Don Juan* (published just three months after *Peter Bell*). In the poem's first of three parts, "river/quiver" features twice (cf. "river/Guadalquiver" of *Don Juan* canto 1, stanza 8), along with "river/shiver," "ether/beneath her," and "river Dnieper / from all evil keep her!"

But the tone shifts toward greater seriousness as the poem progresses. As Hazlitt later recalled, Wordsworth, reciting the poem, rose to "prophetic tones" as "the fate of the hero" unfolded.[30] At the heart of the tale lies Peter's entry into the ethical ordinary through a face-to-face encounter with "a solitary ass" (l. 380). He spies the ass at night, hanging its head over a silent stream, and thinks to take it for his own—but the ass remains stubbornly immobile.

> Quoth Peter, "you're a beast of mettle;
> I see you'll suit me to an ace."
> And now the ass through his left eye
> On Peter turned most quietly
> Looked quietly in his face. (ll. 416–20)

That look enrages Peter, who prepares to beat the ass with a sapling—and when he does so, feels joy in the animal's pain. What the ass teaches Peter, finally, is to take joy in the right not the wrong things—to take joy in what is good or, to use a Stoic term that is now much contested, *natural*.[31] We have seen this Stoic notion in Shaftesbury's ethics of benevolence: we fulfill our *nature*, and in doing so experience rational joy, in acting benevolently toward our fellow rational creatures. Yet leaving aside Shaftesbury's rationalism, *Peter Bell* concerns the moral joy and sorrow that it is natural for us to feel in common with certain animals. Domestic animals share in the joy of being, and particularly the primal joy of being (re-) united with those or that which they love: this is what the poem teaches. In this sense, and this sense only, it is a didactic poem—though hardly the "didactic little horror" that Leigh Hunt called it (*Examiner* May 2, 1819). Rather, it fulfills education's crucial function, as Aristotle understood it: to teach people to feel joy and grief at the right things (*Politics* 1339a-1340a, *Nichomachean Ethics* 1157b-58a). In the course of the one moonlit night, Peter learns what it means to live according to nature, or at least human nature as moral philosophy has defined it (versus, say, the appetitive nature that Peter freely though destructively indulges through double-digit polygamy).

Critics have made much of Peter's overhearing the field preaching of "a fervent Methodist" toward the end of the poem (pt. 3, ll. 1186–1220), yet his being stirred to a sense of salvation by the Holy Spirit is only a fleeting implication of the poem. Peter is more fundamentally stirred to a sense of his humanity and place in the natural order through the ministrations of an ass. *Peter Bell* is not the "Methodistical nightmare" Hunt accused it of being; closer to the mark was the reviewer who noted (alas, with disapproval), "Wordsworth . . . is too fond of the ass."[32]

The sign and perhaps the source of Peter's viciousness is his obliviousness to the beauty of things. Whereas it is nature's privilege to lead us from joy to joy, "In vain through every changeful year / Did Nature lead him as before; / A primrose by a river's brim / A yellow primrose was to him, / And it was nothing more." He is, in short, alienated from external nature, and by implication his own nature: "Nature ne'er could find the way / Into the heart of Peter Bell" (ll. 214–20). The things of nature—after primroses, the narrator lists asses enjoying vernal grass; the sounds of water, earth, and air; the "soft blue sky"—remain to him mere concepts without sense, emotional association, or aesthetic appeal.

We see Peter's emotional nature flare out only in response to the thwarting of his will—the ass he would take for himself will not move. The ass reveals itself as strangely other, especially when it challenges Peter's observational control by observing him in turn, with a calm "quietness"—"looked quietly in his face"—that Peter perceives as an assault to what he thinks he knows about, and to his assumed authority over, animals.[33] Inasmuch as this look levels the field, so to speak, or suggests the ass's superiority to the man who would appropriate him, Peter responds with violence. He is a man, we are later told, who earlier killed his dog, though his motive in this is not given: "close by such a gate as that / Did I by a most heinous murther / Destroy my good dog" (1126–28, omitted from 1819 text).

Short of killing the ass, he beats it mercilessly—this is his "merriment"—and when it falls on its side rather than move, he threatens it with death:

For Peter's merriment is flown,
His lips with rage and fury quiver—
Quoth he, "you little mulish dog!"
Quoth he, "I'll fling you like a log
Headforemost down the river,

By God I will!" When this was said
As stretched upon his side he lay,
To all the echoes south and north
And east and west the ass sent forth
A loud and horrible bray.

This outcry on the heart of Peter
Seems like a note of joy to strike;
Joy on the heart of Peter knocks,
But in the echo of the rocks
Was something Peter did not like. (491–505)

The ass's bray—is it in pain, or is it in protest?—occasions Peter's sadistic joy. Yet Peter's joy in mastering the ass is not complete, because he is troubled by the bray's echo. Peter seems to feel a glimmer of guilty self-consciousness, a mental reflection *on* the aural reflection *of* the cry. His moral sense is elicited when the sound of horror comes back to him as a kind of music or commentary on his action: a type of musical commentary not unlike the office that poetry performs. Still, Peter would continue to roughhandle the ass—"in a fit of dastard rage / He stoops the ass's neck to seize" (526–27)—but that in stooping he sees a face beneath the water of the stream. Thinking it "a fiend with visage wan" (578), he swoons.

Upon reviving, he sees it is "a dead man's face" (611) and, feeling some inexpressible obligation to it, begins sounding the stream with his staff: at which point the ass stands up, revived. Just as Peter stands on the brink of the ethical life, the animal models natural joy for him, the joy of reunion, even if here it is with a corpse, one that might be retrieved from the water by the potter. Peter sees the ass

in his uncouth way
Expressing all the joy he may
In every limb and every feature.—

His meagre bones all shake with joy,
And close by Peter's side he stands;
While Peter o'er the river bends,
The little Ass his neck extends
And fondly licks his hands. (628–35)

In 1819 Wordsworth changed the ass's "meagre bones" to "staring bones," accentuating the ass's gauntness—its bones "stare" or stick out from its skin—while suggesting that the ass focuses with not only its eyes but its very bones on the submerged and now salvageable master. The ass's licking of Peter's hands represents on one level the sheer ebullience of its joy, on another its gratitude for Peter's intervention. But it is not a servile gratitude. The ass licks purposefully, prompting Peter to continue to work with his hands. Retrieving the corpse, along with recounting the master's fate to his family, are the two things the ass cannot itself do.

This scene between ass and master expresses the essence of *joy*—which is, as I've elsewhere defined it, the mind's delight in a good thing that comes to pass or seems sure to happen soon. It is often, as here, the experience of union or reunion, of desire at least temporarily laid to rest.[34] The ass rejoices in its master's being found by Peter just as the father rejoices at the return of his wayward son in Luke's parable, explaining to his dutiful son, "this thy brother was dead, and is alive again; and was lost, and is found" (Luke 15:32). Like the so-called Prodigal Son, the ass's master was lost (or at least out of reach) but now is found (or retrieved). The ass's bone-shaking joy in re-union with his master is surpassed in Wordsworth's canon only by that of the doting mother reunited with her son, a parodic prodigal, in the lyrical ballad *The Idiot Boy*.[35] Yet it would have been for Wordsworth's early readers, and to some degree still is, more surprising to see joy in an animal than in a hu-man. To argue that animals know *pleasure* was uncontroversial: John Donne, for example, conceded in his sermons that animals have *delectatio* or "sensual delight." Wordsworth is original in his detailed attribution to animals of joy, the *gaudium* that Donne, as before him the Stoics, thought proper only to hu-mans, a joy grounded in reason.[36] For Wordsworth, as for many an eighteenth-century *philosophe* before him, animals share with humans basic capacities for empirical reasoning, for affection and bonding—but Wordsworth adds his fine poetic eye for the joy and sorrow animals share with and model for us.[37]

As *Peter Bell* progresses, its protagonist's dawning moral consciousness is expressed through a variety of superstitions that the poem's simpleminded narrator may or may not share with him: a fear of demons, of wraiths, and—in no way distinguished from these—of damnation.[38] But what punctuates the course of Peter's moral enlightenment are his encounters with faces and ago-nized vocalizations, first those of the ass and then, as he finds them, of the dead man's now-fatherless children and widowed wife, whom he responds to fully as widow and orphans, strangers who hunger.[39] It is the ass above all who ori-ents Peter to the ethical life by diverting his joys away from an exclusive focus on his own good. Thus as Peter rides the ass, in quest of the dead man's home, he is perturbed to see drops of blood mysteriously falling upon the ground and, finding that their appearance is not supernatural but, rather, perfectly natural—they fall from the beaten ass's head—at first rejoices, and only then feels his first pangs of pity:

At length he spies a bleeding wound
Where he had struck the ass's head;
He sees the blood, sees what it is—
A glimpse of sudden joy was his,
But then it quickly fled.

He thought—he could not help but think—
Of that poor beast, that faithful ass,
And once again those ugly pains
Across his liver, heart and reins
Just like a weaver's shuttle pass. (916–25)

Again, when Peter begins to console himself with supernatural excuses for his behavior—it must have been the devil that set him on to steal the ass (1006–10)—he is disabused by another knowing look from the ass: "The quiet creature made a pause, / Turn'd round his head and grinn'd" (1024–25). By this point in the tale, Peter does not rebuke the ass for his mockery of him but attempts only to smile back—an attempt curtailed by an underground mining blast he hears, which again makes him think of being dragged to hell.

Wordsworth's seriocomic description of the ass who is superior to its rider harkens back to the similarly seriocomic Bible story of Balaam and the ass (Numbers 22): there the magician Balaam is saved by the ass he rides from being slain by an angel of the Lord, an angel that the ass three times sees and three times avoids running into but that Balaam does not see. Balaam's rage at the ass who won't take his direction lies behind Peter's: "Because thou hast mocked me: I would there were a sword to my hand, for now would I kill thee" (22:29). The angel then appears to Balaam and assures him the ass has been his savior: "the ass saw me, and turned from me these three times: unless she had turned from me, surely now also I had slain thee, and saved her alive"; Balaam replies, "I have sinned" (22:33–34).

In *Peter Bell*, it is the ass that similarly saves Peter, although here it is from the blindness of his enjoyment. No supernatural force actually threatens to slay him or, alternatively, conspires to save him. Granted, Peter in shedding his old life feels a joy akin to that inspired by the Holy Spirit in a traditional scene of Christian conversion: the Methodist's call to "repent, repent!" brings him "joy [that] was more than he could bear; / He melted into tears" (1196–1210). But effected here, tying Peter back to the ass that redeems him, is a transformation of "the animal within":

Each nerve, each fibre of the frame
And all the animal within
Was weak, perhaps, but it was mild
And gentle as an infant child,
An infant that has known no sin. (1216-20)

As the tale ends, Peter directs his final prayer not to God but to the ass: "Oh would, poor beast, that I had now / A heart but half as good as thine!" (1339-40). Through the ass's intercession, nature makes his heart tender to the joys and sorrows of the world, at least the little corner of it to which the ass carries Peter. Hearing the dead man's widow cry for her now-fatherless children, Peter experiences a new birth that is moral rather than spiritual: "And Nature, through a world of death, / Breathes into him a second breath, / Just like the breath of spring" (1313-15). (Wordsworth improved this last line in 1819: "More searching than the breath of spring.") Reanimated, and confronted with the hunger of the other, Peter would give, though he feels—more acutely than the speaker of *The Discharged Soldier*—that what is most needed cannot be given:

Upon a stone the woman [widow] sits
In agony of silent grief.
From his own thoughts does Peter start;
He longs to press her to his heart
From love that cannot give relief. (1316-20)

In 1819 Wordsworth changed the last line to "love that cannot *find* relief" (my emphasis)—a significant distinction, it would at first seem, but one that finally does not, in the circuit of love, make a difference.

In a final turn away from the Christian conversion mold, the narrator's brief, deliberately anticlimactic coda to *Peter Bell* informs us that "after ten months' melancholy, / [Peter] Became a good and honest man" (1184-85)—not, necessarily, a Christian or a pious man. And there the poem ends. Were the tale a Christian conversion narrative, it would extend beyond the crisis of conversion into the activity of the Christian life: proselytizing, for example, and/or the drama of maintaining faith against the threat of backsliding into doubt and fear (as in Bunyan's *The Pilgrim's Progress* and Defoe's *Robinson Crusoe*). If it were a nondoctrinal conversion narrative of the type sketched by Coleridge (*The Ancyent Marinere*) and later popularized by Dickens (*A Christmas Carol*), it would at least show some of the practical consequences of becoming a good and honest man (doing something for the dead man's family, say, or advocating against cruelty to animals). But here Peter becomes to us, after his moral education, a stranger, someone the reader no longer knows, a lost connection—as Peter presumably never again connects to the ass and its dead master's family; as the speaker of *The Discharged Soldier* presumably never again encounters the soldier whose one-night lodging he helped to secure. In Wordsworth's poems there is only the mystery of other lives as they were before, and as they persist after, the limited time of encounter and epiphany—and this is part of his modernity.

We have seen in these last two chapters visible encounters with human and animal faces. Turning next to Wordsworth's lyric poetry of the *Lyrical Ballads* years we find things that have no literal faces but to which poetry can still attribute a "faciality," a power to demand an ethical response—such as, to use two key Wordsworthian locutions, "the face of nature" and "the life of things." This last word, "things," key to Wordsworth's poetic lexicon, does double duty in his verse to denote both vegetable and mineral nature and, more broadly, "all that is." It is to things, and their faciality, that I now turn.

CHAPTER FOUR

The Ethics of Things

In *Lyrical Ballads* and related poems from 1798 to 1802, Wordsworth leads us to reflect on the existential condition of things as a whole, the things that include us. They are things that, in the main, people have not made. Indeed, with respect to things Wordsworth raises an eyebrow at the very idea of "making," whether by man or God. "Have I not reason to lament / What man has made of man?," asks the speaker of "Lines Written in early spring," contrasting the real or apparent pleasure in nonhuman nature to the alienation of human nature, an alienation inscribed in the poem's process of discursive reasoning.[1] "There is nothing," Wordsworth later wrote, "so injurious as the perpetually talking about *making* by God"; "for Heaven's sake . . . say as little as possible about *making*" (letter to Catherine Clarkson, January 1815, *Letters* 3:189). Wordsworth's things are irreducible to making or use, to matter or narrative; indeed, they are uncontainable by any narrow definition of *thing*. Rather, they bespeak the fusion of object and event, matter and energy, human and nonhuman, the categorical and the specific. Wordsworth's things are things without objects, things anterior to and in excess of subject/object dualities.

The nonnarrative fullness of things—a fullness historically figured as their "face" or, in Wordsworth, denominated their "life"—may prevent the ills of fixating on things as mere objects: commodity fetishism, consumerism, environmental devastation. Such ills can, of course, be overstated. Bill Brown, in advancing "thing theory," avoids the moralism of Marxist critique by focusing on the constitutive interconnections between subjects and inanimate objects, individuals and their material things (*A Sense of Things* 5–8). Yet the very distinction between subject and object—as well as between human and nonhuman, material and immaterial—weakens, in ethically and ecologically beneficial ways, when things are thought through in their unmade and nonrepresentational interconnectedness, their minimally personified face or animate life.

As the philosopher Silvia Benso has argued, our contemporary environmental crisis renders urgent an ethical attitude toward "things," a word she uses primarily in Heidegger's sense "of being present-at-hand" or, in her own terms, as an "undifferential" reference to "vegetal, mineral, artificial (and maybe even animal) entities" (xxxii). Heidegger conceives of things in a protoenvironmental way, but he "arrests himself on the threshold of ethics" (xxxvi). Thus, Benso dialectically introduces Emmanuel Levinas, who formulates an ethics without regard for things. Levinas, as we have seen, grounded his ethics on the face-to-face, nonassimilative encounter of one human being with another. Synthesizing Levinas and Heidegger, Benso stakes out an "ethics of things," a model of ecological rather than ego-logical interaction with nonhuman things (or not exclusively human things) in their alterity.[2] To do so, she applies to things not faces but "facialities": "Faces express a specific content, a defined contour, an individuated existence. Facialities invoke the intimation of signification of a face, and yet the vagueness of a cluster of meaning the demarcation of which remains blurred, fluid, porous to a continuous, osmotic exchange between inside and outside that mobilizes boundaries, and therefore definitions. . . . Facialities evoke the possibility of the existence of faceless faces, which, despite their facelessness, are yet endowed with the intimating power of the face to demand an ethical response" (xxix–xxx).

Benso offers a prolegomenon to a metaphysical ethics of things, the grounds we have for benign response to and principled (in-) activity regarding things, particularly the things of nature in their irreducibility to human purposes. It is beyond my present scope to advance this ethics with theoretical rigor—or, bluntly, to address why we ought not to destroy the earth. My more modest aim is, first, to bring to light the prehistory of such an ethics in premodern and early modern language and literature. Pursuing the philology of "thing" allows us to recover, uncannily, the interconnectedness of all bodies and events in the substratum of a term we now often use to designate a more or less alienated object. The "face" attributed to these plenary things by the 3rd Earl of Shaftesbury may partly be understood in Benso's sense as a "faciality," the power to demand an ethical response. Following Shaftesbury, eighteenth-century poets bestowed on natural arrangements a face that could not be fully known but for that reason ought to be revered. Wordsworth passes from the quasi-individuated "face" to the web-like, suprahuman "life" of things, offering a way beyond not only ("Romantic") individualism but anthropocentrism itself and, in Romantic studies, critical initiatives tethered to Cartesian and Kantian models of subject and object.

My second aim, then, is to situate Wordsworth as a pivotal figure in ecological ethics. Wordsworth borrowed from, but gestured beyond, natural religion (as in Shaftesbury) and pantheism (Spinoza) in imagining a joyous affection and nonappropriative stance toward the things of nature. In chapter 2 I examined Wordsworth and the face of the Other that transcends while never being wholly dissociated from its physical contours; here, the faciality of nature seems immanent not transcendent, referring to the divine (or simply the real) in or as nature, or all that is. From a political point of view, the world as it is, as given, is a flawed arrangement subject to revision and capable of perfection: this holds true from the English Jacobin novel of the 1790s through to Marxist-influenced criticism of our own time. From an ecological view, however, the world as it is, or as it would be could we turn back the clock—the "green world"—has an abiding value that is diminished by short-sighted interventions and the depletion of its parts. The problem for ecology is privation or loss, errancy from the way a system ought to work—energy depletion, deforestation, dehydration (or waterway degradation), the loss of genetic and species diversity. Wordsworth was the first poet to give voice to this conservationist ethic and to embody it in practice. In the words of one of his neighbors as recorded by a later Lake District conservationist, the Wordsworth Society member Reverend Hardwicke Rawnsley (1851–1929), Wordsworth "couldn's abear to see faäce o' things altered ya kna."[3] Wordsworth's nature ethic—or ethics deduced from a theory of nature (in ancient philosophy, *phusis*)—was not lost on his Victorian admirers.

The metaphysics of Wordsworth's early "nature poetry," especially *Tintern Abbey*, have been out of critical favor, though the tide is once again turning. Influential New Historicist readings of the 1980s charged *Tintern Abbey* in particular with being a bad-faith or self-subverting effort to evade historical-material realities such as the vagrants, ironworks, and alleged pollution in the Wye River valley of the 1790s (McGann, 86–88; Levinson, *Wordsworth's Great Period Poems* 46–57). Even if the valley had been scarred by pollution and crowded with the dispossessed and unemployed, it does not follow that Wordsworth, in his role of poet, ought to have abandoned lyric thinking in favor of social protest. But in fact Wordsworth's 1798 visit to the Wye River upstream from Tintern Abbey would not have been marred by the ills of a later industrial age: Charles Rzepka ("Pictures of the Mind") scours the historical record to show that in Wordsworth's day the Wye River was not polluted or surrounded by vagrants, that we have no evidence of industrial despoliation in the vicinity of Tintern Abbey, and that Wordsworth could have seen the Abbey from nearly any spot along a downriver approach without seeing the ironworks. Rzepka's is the fullest empiricist confutation of the New Historicist critique of the poet's alleged false consciousness, though preceded by a good many critical inquiries into the argumentative and ideological weaknesses of that critique.[4]

The fundamental oppositions on which the New Historicist critique relies—human and nonhuman, history and nature, freedom and necessity—are already deconstructed in Wordsworth's poetry. Jerome McGann quipped, "Between 1793 and 1798 Wordsworth lost the world merely to gain his own immortal soul" (88): that is, abandoned free political action in history (the world), "merely" to find within himself a spark continuous with God or nature—a pearl, for McGann, of illusory price. But the phrase "*his own* immortal soul" rings false: the Wordsworth of the *Lyrical Ballads* era is not interested in a distinctly human, individuated soul, let alone one that he calls his own. Thus, in "Lines Written in early spring" "human" becomes a delimiting adjective for some larger "soul" or life: "To her fair works did nature link / The human soul that through me ran . . ." (The proper end of life is to "grow / Into souloneness with the Life of things," wrote the Wordsworth-inspired poet Henry Ellison [*Thoughts on Man, Art, and Nature*, ll. 671–72, in *Madmoments* 1:253].) Nor is the cosmos Wordsworth conjures limited to "the world" McGann invokes, a place made by human activity in history. Wordsworth's system of things exceeds human agency, although it does not preclude it. Wordsworth allows that what we do or do not do matters greatly—morals, politics, and history remain central concerns for him—but he stressed, dialectically, that our choices and the outcomes of our actions are limited by and dependent on natural systems of determination. That things go on irrespective of our activity is a fallacy Wordsworth imputes to Rivers, the villain of *The Borderers*, who seeks to evade responsibility for a murder:

> What? in this universe,
> Where the least things controul the greatest, where
> The faintest breath that breathes can move a world—
> What, feel remorse where if a cat had sneezed,
> A leaf had fallen, the thing had never been . . . ? (3.5.83–87)

Wordsworth may have endorsed Rivers's vision of ecological interdependence, which anticipates the "butterfly effect" of chaos theory, but he did not approve of Rivers's concomitant abdication of moral responsibility. We may infer that for Wordsworth the determining system of things—in *The Old Cumberland Beggar* he calls it "the tide of things" (l. 157)—is not incompatible with human and thus historical agency. But neither is it fully answerable to it.[5]

To arrive at a robust sense of Wordsworth's relation to natural things requires that we begin with his relation to words as things, and particularly to the rich and strange word *thing*—a word that appears (in singular and plural forms) 439 times in his corpus.[6] (By comparison, "nature" has 395 occurrences.) Words are a key part of human ecology, if by that phrase we mean "the study of the complex relationships between human communities and their dwelling places" (McKusick 70). Words structure our relations to things just as poets seek to structure our relations to words, even if "strictly," as Heidegger writes, "it is language that speaks" (216). Wordsworth's poetry derives much of its power, Walter Pater cryptically suggested, from the wells of the English language and its "older" literary instantiations: "Those who lived about Wordsworth were all great lovers of the older English literature. . . . He drew something too from the unconscious mysticism of the old English language itself" ("Wordsworth" 137). I will argue that Wordsworth's insight into things is made possible by his receptivity to and delicate evocation of the comprehensive (or perhaps mystical) sense of *thing* that was available at the end of the eighteenth century and that to a lesser degree remains available today.

ASPECTS OF *THING*

Contemporary "thing theory" tends to sideline or ignore the conceptual fullness and recalcitrance of *thing*, which Wordsworth, building on an eighteenth-century poetic heritage and more generally a rich English etymology, so brilliantly conveys. Bill Brown cites Heidegger's contention that "the English word *thing* . . . has preserved the 'semantic power' of the original Roman word *res*, which is to say its capacity to designate a case, an affair, an event" (Heidegger 175). Yet, Brown adds, "I am specifically not deploying an etymological inquiry to delimit and vivify the meaning of things" ("Thing Theory" 5, n.15). Here I would like to deploy precisely such an inquiry, before turning to address what the eighteenth-century poetic career of things, as it culminates in Wordsworth, has to offer our theoretical engagement with them.

Historically, *thing* has a curious fate: it begins by meaning more or less everything but comes in the course of the nineteenth century to signify chiefly one type of thing—the manufactured object or commodity. *Thing* is originally an Old English term, related to the Old German *dinc* and the modern German *ding*. In Germanic tongues, *dinc* (or *ding*) conveys a wide range of meanings, from meeting or assembly (thus the parliament of Iceland is called the *Althing*) through event, case, action, habit, on the one hand, and material entity or object, on the other. J. R. Clark Hall's Old English dictionary defines *thing* (neuter, as one might expect) as—take a deep breath—"creature, object, property, cause, motive, reason, lawsuit, event, affair, act, deed, enterprise, condition, circumstance, contest, discussion, meeting, council, assembly, court of justice, point, respect, sake." Context is all, as readers of *Beowulf* soon discover—Beowulf professes, on arriving in Denmark, "Grendel's thing became known to me on my native turf."[7] This "thing" is not that which Grendel has physically made. It is what he has done, the Grendel act or affair, or, at this point in the poem, a limited version of that act or affair, as much as wafts from Denmark to Beowulf's native Geat-land. All that Beowulf professes to know about Grendel's thing is that the monster has been harassing the feast hall of the Danes. Even here, in a narrative instance that is centuries away from Wordsworth's deliberately vague usage, "thing" designates a narrative that is not fully known and gestures toward the unknowability of larger chains of events. The Dane Hamlet reveals, as it were, the heart of the mystery: "There are more things in heaven and earth, Horatio, / Than are dreamt of in your philosophy" (1.5.175–76).

Old English, and Modern English in its wake, does not delimit *thing* to material object. Indeed, in Old English there is no term, such as *object*, for a material entity (or, as in German philosophy, the nonself mutually constituted in relation to a subject). From this linguistic detail we can boldly surmise that medieval Germanic-language speakers, much like the ancient Romans (whose *res* parallels or informs *thing*), did not in general conceive of material objects in a delimited physical sense, as separate from events, from the constitution and frame of that which is and comes to be, and from the transcendental conditions for knowing what little we can know of systems or stories that exceed our comprehension—in short, as Lucretius put it in his poem on Epicurean enlightenment, "the nature of things" (*de rerum natura*). This etymological fullness of *thing* is captured in the first part of Samuel Johnson's definition of the term in his *Dictionary* (1755): "whatever is." (Heidegger similarly notes that "*thing* or *dinc* . . . denote anything whatever that is in any way" [176].)

However, we can find on Johnson's page the shadow of commodification. Johnson's full definition of "thing" contains a second part that makes *thing* less than *noun*, and alienates humans from things: "Whatever is; not a person." The definition is clearly paradoxical: "whatever is" contains persons. Johnson could have ventured the hypotactic "whatever is, excepting persons," but this is problematic if "whatever is" includes the conditions and events (space, time, the weather) from which personhood is inextricable. It is for us, as the poet Mark Akenside declared in *The Pleasures of Imagination* (1744), "To weigh the moment [importance] of eternal things,/Of time, and space, and fate's unbroken chain,/And will's quick impulse" (pt. 1, ll. 89–91). From these things we cannot be excluded. Johnson is trying to have it two ways, defining *thing* as the all and as the nonhuman only, even while recognizing their incompatibility. The lexicographer takes liberties unavailable to the logician. Johnson presents the rift between humanity and inert or inhuman things that exists by 1755, but it fits badly within the historical *thing*.

Ten years after the first edition of Johnson's *Dictionary* appeared, William Blackstone began publication of his magisterial *Commentaries on the Laws of England* (1765–69), the second volume of which is on "the Rights of Things" or "the *jura rerum*, or, those rights which a man may acquire in and to such external things as are unconnected with his person" (2:1). The Oxford English Dictionary attributes to Blackstone the first clear example of *thing* as "a being without life or consciousness; an inanimate object as distinguished from a person or a living creature" (definition 8b).[8] The OED next adduces from *Barnaby Rudge* (1840) a sentence that mentions "consideration of persons, things, times and places." Dickens's distinction among persons, places, and things now informs the standard multipronged definition of *noun*, but it is significant that for Johnson *noun* is simply "the name of any thing in grammar," a definition that renders noun and thing coextensive. It is tempting to say that between Johnson and Dickens—between the mid-Georgian and Victorian eras—arises commodity fetishism, the severance of manufactured or cultivated objects from human (or, pace Marx, extrahuman) activities and processes and their enshrinement as autonomous, even magical, entities. With industrial modernity, the limited sense of *thing* as a material and noncognitive object, particularly a manufactured object, gains prominence in the word's semantic field.

Wordsworth does not use *thing* in this delimited sense, even when he describes what we are now most apt to call things: the commodities and multitudinous spectacle of the metropolis. Recounting his "Residence in London" in book 7 of the 1805 *Prelude*, Wordsworth reproduces the names and to a degree the looks of things—for instance, "the labouring hackney-coaches, the rash speed/Of coaches traveling far"; "the string of dazzling wares,/Shop after shop" (ll. 165–74, 1805 text)—but his one use of the word *things* has a devisualizing and deobjectifying effect: "The endless stream of men and *moving things*" (158, my emphasis). The phrase is deliberately vague—what are these things? do they not move as men do, or do they include men?—and thus serves as a counterpoint to the protocinematic sweep of the rest of Wordsworth's descriptive catalogue,[9] harking back instead to the "marvellous things" of his boyhood imaginings of the city (108).

Wordsworth uses *things* in a way that blurs distinctions between persons and nonpersons, between entities and events. This usage may reflect, as Pater remarked, "the unconscious mysticism of the old English language itself"—but it also reflects the Stoic convention, evident in early modern literature, of seeing things as a unity sustained by a rational power or spirit. Thus Shaftesbury apostrophizes a world soul in which all things participate and that animates all things: "Sole-Animating and Inspiring Power! Author and Subject of these Thoughts! Thy Influence is universal: and in all Things thou art inmost" (*The Moralists* pt. 3, sec.1, in *Characteristicks* 2:89).[10] Shaftesbury's deity is the Stoic *logos,* the faintly personified rational principle that undergirds and upholds all aspects of the universe—in Spinoza's formulation, with which Shaftesbury may have been acquainted, "that eternal and infinite being we call God, *or* Nature" (*Ethics* pt. 4, *Spinoza Reader* 198).

This deity has no form, but it can nonetheless be seen in the order of nature or, in the catachresis by which this order was also known, the face of things. Shaftesbury claims that "the Face of Things" is always beautiful for those who understand the principle according to which all things work together necessarily, if to us darkly (*The Moralists* pt. 1, sec. 3, in *Characteristicks* 2:18). (Thus, the Stoic must "adapt to all things," a phrase Shaftesbury borrows from the Greek of Marcus Aurelius [*Life* 26].) The face of things is a denominative face, a "thing of nothing," in Hamlet's phrase.[11] It is not a face such as pagans gave their gods, nor the visage of Yahweh, the eternal "I am," which Moses can see just once "face to face, as a man speaketh unto his friend" (Exodus 33:11, King James version).[12] Rather, this face tentatively transforms the indefiniteness of things into a constellation that evokes without representing the Other in whose face Levinas has taught us to see the ground of ethics and divinity. It is, in Benso's terms, more a faciality than a face. Shaftesbury grants things the intimating power of the face and asks us to imagine and love that face, even if it is no more than a name.

The face of things is not Shaftesbury's own locution: it goes back at least as far as Samuel Daniel (1563–1619), who maintained in his verse epistle "To Henry Wriothesley" that the experience of adversity, which alone teaches "the true face of things," is requisite to true happiness (l. 36). But knowledge of the face of things is rarely accorded in English verse. As Yahweh's face is alternately visible and invisible to Moses, so the modern face of things is occasionally revealed but more often shaded or concealed, a challenge to ocular empiricism as well as to the humanist notion that things exist to become objects of human thought. Milton fired the first salvo against representational thinking with regard to the face of things in having Satan's voice tempt the sleeping Eve with a nocturnal landscape designed for human, indeed her, eyes alone:

> . . . now reigns
> Full Orb'd the Moon, and with more pleasing light
> Shadowy sets off the face of things; in vain
> If none regard; Heav'n wakes, with all his eyes,
> Whom to behold but thee, Nature's desire,
> In whose sight all things joy, with ravishment
> Attracted by thy beauty still to gaze. (*Paradise Lost* 5:41–47)

Here the face of things is cloaked in shadow, figuring for the fit reader its incomplete comprehensibility. Conversely, the heavens are assigned eyes that, Satan's voice cajoles, are only for Eve.

In Milton's wake, eighteenth-century poets, largely abandoning the Satanic notion that nature revolves around individuals, took up the cloaked face of things as a metaphor for a posited order one cannot fully know. From Alexander Pope on, the face of things appears and reappears as veiled in night or mist or fog or other pleasing obscurity—not, as in Shaftesbury (or Lucretius), illuminated by philosophy.[13] In Miltonic fashion, poets preferred veiled truth to a white mythology, while assuming, however, that there was indeed a naked face of things, an outward form redolent of an internal rationale, to be hidden. In a physical register, Pope in his *Odyssey* made "darkness cover'd o'er / The face of things" his stock translation of Homer's stock phrase *knephas elthe*, "darkness came."[14]

James Thomson and Thomas Warton played variations on Pope's phrase, giving it metaphysical overtones: darkness "gathers round / To close the face of things" (Thomson, "Summer," ll. 1653–54); "congregated clouds, / And all the vapoury turbulence of heaven, / Involve the face of things" (Thomson, "Winter" [1744], ll. 55–57); "all is silence drear; / And deepest sadness wraps the face of things" (Warton, "The Pleasures of Melancholy" [1755], ll. 151–52). In these last lines from Warton, human subjectivity suffuses a suprahuman order, but it is not clear which element is given the upper hand: either human sadness veils the face of things from only human beings, who are thus alienated from the suprahuman fullness of things, or sadness is imputed to the catachrestic face of things through a humanistic "pathetic fallacy." With the latter possibility we move at once backward, to a Satanic representation of anthropocentric nature, and forward, toward the Romantic trope of mind's sovereignty over the empirical world, if not over things as such.

JOY IN THE ONENESS OF THINGS

It is well known that Wordsworth (sometimes) purveyed this trope of the sovereign mind. Less appreciated is his countervailing rejection of mind's ascendancy over things. "The face of things" or "the face of nature" persists in Wordsworth's poetry, its relation to humanity variously configured.[15] At times Wordsworth is eager to assert human mastery over things, as in the famous Mount Snowdon episode of *The Prelude* book 13 (1805). Wordsworth allegorizes the "huge sea of mist" that, seen from atop Snowdon, obscures the Irish Channel as the mind's "domination" of "the outward face of things," a domination deriving from the self's transcendental priority over nature and the superiority of imaginative "higher minds" to "the grossest minds" (ll. 40–119). But to counterbalance the vertical cast of mind one finds in such a passage, there is the leveling of human and nonhuman, high and low, found, for example, in *The Pedlar* (ms. E), in which the protagonist comes to feel "the pure joy of love" diffused "by the silent looks of happy things, / Or flowing from the universal face / Of earth and sky" (ll. 175–80). In this vision of connectedness, humans might themselves constitute "happy things"; they possess no privilege in the peddler's terrain. Elsewhere Wordsworth throws into doubt even the minimal anthropocentrism of assigning a face to earth and sky. In book 5 of *The Prelude,* the slippage from "the speaking face of earth and heaven / As . . . prime teacher" (l. 12) to the "ghastly face" of a drowned schoolmaster (472), reveals through disfiguration the giving face that constitutes, if not all identity, then at least the identity of God or nature in a Stoic vein.[16]

In the fine ambiguities of Wordsworth's verse, the extrahuman acquires an agency that may or may not derive from or prove comparable with human agency. "I saw the sentiment of being spread / O'er all that moves," Wordsworth claims of his teenage self in *The Prelude* (2:420–21): through one of those busy "of's" that Christopher Ricks has identified as a hallmark of Wordsworth's style (110–25), "the sentiment of being" encompasses "being" as object and subject, referring either to a sentimental apprehension of being, or to being's own "sentiment" or essence (in Johnson's second definition of the term, its "sense considered distinctly from the language"), or to both at once. It is thus impossible to tell whether human sentiment or extraconceptual being—in a further indeterminacy—either "spread" (past and possibly ongoing activity) or "had spread itself" (accomplished act) or "had been spread" (accomplished act of another agent) over a multiplicity of beings (e.g., "O'er all that leaps, and runs, and shouts, and sings, / Or beats the gladsome air"). Wordsworth's style allows for maximal possibilities of interconnection with minimal clarification of who or what is acting or being acted on. He ends his litany to being by subsuming multiplicity into the unity of "one life," but even that unity remains divided among possible agents: "in all things / I saw one life, and felt that it was a joy" (2:429–30). Life, like being, may spread over the poet or spread outward from him. Such puzzlement over where (if anywhere) humans end and nature begins is, the ecocritic Greg Garrard has argued, what "mark[s] romanticism as proto-ecological" (464). But we can find a fully ecological stance, as well as an ethics, in Wordsworth if we understand his ambiguities as denying primacy either to self (the Other's other) or to (things as) the Other.

The issue of this ethics is, for Wordsworth, joy. The bond between (one) life and joy has a human history, which we can trace back to Stoic philosophy: "the mind should know its own self and feel its union with the divine mind, the source of the fullness of joy [*gaudium*] unquenchable" (Cicero, *Tusculan Disputations* 5.25.70). Joy (*gaudium*), strictly distinguished from pleasure (*voluptas*), is the "elation of spirit" the sage finds in "goodness and truth" (Seneca, *Epistles* 59.2)—that is, according to the common Stoic tag, in "living according to nature," both the (rational) nature of the universe and one's corresponding inner nature. Wordsworth knew something of ancient Stoic doctrine since his adolescence (see chapters 3 and 8), though he would study it more concertedly later in life.[17] En route to *Lyrical Ballads,* however, Wordsworth ingested the version of Stoicism found in Spinoza[18]—the author about whom, according to Coleridge, he and Wordsworth were talking in the summer of 1796 (*Biographia* 1:193–97).

The book in question is, most likely, Spinoza's *Ethics,* written in Latin and published posthumously in 1677—a widely circulated and discussed book of the seventeenth- and eighteenth-century "Radical Enlightenment" (Jonathan Israel's phrase) that, as Marjorie Levinson has recently argued, continues to matter for the Romantic poets.[19] The *Ethics'* pantheistic (or ontological monist) view of God and man may be found in a Wordsworth manuscript fragment from February 1799:

[A]ll beings live with God, themselves
Are God, existing in one mighty whole,
As undistinguishable as the cloudless east
At noon is from the cloudless west, when all
The hemisphere is one cerulean blue.[20]

Wordsworth links union-in-God and the unity of nature through a simile ("as undistinguishable as"), and in doing so suggests what Spinoza argues—that God and nature are the same, the one substance of which all things are simply attributes (thus all beings "are God"). Spinoza equates God with the eternal, immutable laws of nature, such as science may discover, and with a universal system of causal necessity, in which every event is predetermined by antecedent events. To know God is to have an "adequate knowledge of the essence of things"—of the necessity of all objects and events (*Ethics* pt. 2, prop. 40, *Spinoza Reader* 141). Possessing a clear conception of this necessity will weaken the irrational power of the passions over us, giving us calmness, rational joy, and, passing beyond passion altogether, beatitude.

Spinoza's impress may be seen in Wordsworth's (and Coleridge's) emphatic use of "joy" as an aspect of the apprehension of God in or as nature. Spinoza, still more than the Stoics from whom he borrowed, stresses the joy of coming to know God. For Spinoza, joy (*laetitia*, which might also be translated "gladness") is a passion "by which the mind passes to a greater perfection"—that is, a greater capacity for self-preservative action; its opposite, sadness, is "that passion by which it passes to a lesser perfection" (pt. 3, prop. 11, p. 161). Although "there are as many species of joy, sadness, love, hate, and the like, as there are species of objects by which we are affected" (pt. 3, prop. 56, p. 184), the best species of joy and love stem, first, from the life of social virtue—rationally seeking "the common advantage of all" (pt. 4, prop. 18, p. 210)—and, finally, from the knowledge of God, "the mind's greatest good" (pt. 4, prop. 18, p. 213). Moving by "intellectual love" toward the knowledge of God—and so to human perfection— occasions "the greatest Joy," and beyond all motion lies the equable state of mind the Stoics designated *gaudium* (rational joy) and Spinoza calls *beatitudo* (blessedness), which is "perfection itself" (pt. 5, props. 24–33, pp. 257–60).[21] Wordsworth echoes Spinoza's metaphysical ascent from passionate dependence on transient objects to an intellectual love and joy in book 13 of *The Prelude* (a passage I examine in chapter 7).

Yet Wordsworth generally echoes Spinoza's joy in the underlying oneness of things without his focus on the joyful understanding of it. Extending the franchise of joy, Wordsworth not only proposes a more generally human ability to intuit (rightly or wrongly) the interconnection of all things but also suggests that things can do the same and thus deserve the respect owed exclusively to human beings in Spinozan and ancient Stoic ethics. "'Tis my faith that every flower / Enjoys the air it breathes," Wordsworth maintains in "Lines Written in early spring"; "the budding twigs spread out their fan, / To catch the breezy air; / And I must think, do all I can, / That there was pleasure there." Thinking is what separates the speaker from the joy of being that he accurately perceives or erroneously projects, as well as what distinguishes these two epistemic possibilities. But for Wordsworth in balked understanding begin responsibilities. The possibility that subrational (even inanimate) things experience joy has ethical consequences for our attitude toward or interaction with them. According to Wordsworth, subrational things (or rational things in subrational moods) are not inferior or accountable to the philosophical mind capable of rational reflection on the one life.

As Wordsworth writes even in the most rationalistic moment of *The Prelude,* inspired by and addressed to Coleridge, human reason can at most "chasten" and "balance"

> the deep enthusiastic joy,
> The rapture of the hallelujah sent
> From all that breathes and is . . . (13:261–63)

Broadly, the sense of these lines is clear: a plenitude of things, not just human beings, rejoices and gives thanks ("hallelujah" means "praise Yahweh," the God of the Bible). But reading more closely entangles us in grammatical and substantive questions. First, is "deep enthusiastic joy" the same as, or in its depth different from, "the rapture of the hallelujah"? Are these two elements of Wordsworth's sentence in apposition, or do they constitute a list, albeit a somewhat slurred one? Maintaining a distinction between the two would reserve deep joy—specifically, the deep joy of participating in God ("enthusiastic" deriving from *en*, "in" + *theos*, "God")—for a group more delimited than "all that breathes and is": presumably, to the Stoic sage whose *gaudium*, deeply rooted in the nature of things, is distinct from any superficial pleasure (Seneca, *Epistles* 23:4–6),[22] and whose thoughts are, in Wordsworth's own phrase, "too deep for tears" ("Intimations" *Ode*). Yet if the two elements of Wordsworth's line are read as synonymous parallelism, then these oppositions of depth and surface, thought and expression, break down, and deep joy as well as rapturous hallelujah belong to "all that breathes and is."

This last phrase raises a second question: is it only things that are and that breathe (that is, complex life forms) that literally or as-it-were praise God, or does this hallelujah come from all that breathes and also (moreover) all that is, inanimate as well as animate? If we follow the allusion of "hallelujah" to its Biblical source, we arrive at the very same question. In Revelation, the only canonical book of the Bible in which "hallelujah" (in its Greek form, "alleluia") appears, St. John the Divine records his vision (or audition): "I heard as it were the voice of a great multitude, and as the voice of many waters, and as the voice of mighty thunderings, saying, Alleluia: for the Lord God Omnipotent reigneth" (19:6). Does this "saying" include the voice of elements and natural forces? "As it were" seems more than analogical here, if less literal than the description of animate waters and lively stones in one of the thanksgiving Psalms: "Let the sea roar, and the fulness thereof; the world, and they that dwell therein. / Let the floods clap their hands: let the hills be joyful together / Before the Lord" (Psalms 98:7–9). Wordsworth's rapturous hallelujah occupies the same uncertain space the psalmist finds between panpsychism and prosopopeia, between a poetry that magically makes things happen and one that records fictions of what never was. Through an art that leads us to suspend judgment on things and their opposites—human/ nonhuman, animate/inanimate, projection/detection—Wordsworth invites us to imagine a nonspecific joy in *widest* commonalty spread.

TINTERN ABBEY AND THE LIFE OF THINGS

Tintern Abbey is Wordsworth's best-known, and perhaps greatest, poetic statement on "all that is." The poet recalls earlier recollections, "mid the din / Of towns and cities," of a previous visit to the Wye River valley, and the reveries these recollections allowed, when "with an eye made quiet by the power / Of harmony, and the deep power of joy, / We see into the life of things" (ll. 47–49). This last phrase is novel: a search of the *Chadwyck-Healey English Poetry Full-Text Database* reveals scant use of "the life of things" before Wordsworth, and Wordsworth's impress on later poetic use of the phrase is clear.[23] With this phrase Wordsworth turns away from the quasi-personified face of things and allows that things can be animated without our seeing them, even minimally, as our selves. If a figural charge adheres to "the life of things," it is that of Aristotle's *energeia* ("animation"), the attribution of activity to (apparently) lifeless things.[24] Yet through the special decorum of Wordsworth's *energeia* any attribution or poetic making seems detection or surmise.

It is through "a sustained movement of surmise," Geoffrey Hartman writes, that Wordsworth "gradually expands into communion" (*Wordsworth's Poetry, 1787–1814*, 27–28). The poet recalls that five years earlier nature, to him, had been a visual and libidinal experience of the lone self, but he has since lost his attraction to nature's (sur)face:[25]

> For I have learned
> To look on nature, not as in the hour
> Of thoughtless youth, but hearing oftentimes
> The still, sad music of humanity . . .

And I have felt
A presence that disturbs me with the joy
Of elevated thoughts; a sense sublime
Of something far more deeply interfused,
Whose dwelling is the light of setting suns,
And the round ocean, and the living air,
And the blue sky, and in the mind of man,
A motion and a spirit, that impels
All thinking things, all objects of all thought,
And rolls through all things. (ll. 89–103)

The culminating lines of this great passage resolve the tension found in Johnson's definition of *thing* as "whatever is; not a person." Here we are distinguished as or among "thinking things," and yet both our selves and the objects we make through thinking are joined in the anteriority and comprehensiveness of "all things." We are things among things, metaphysically, ecologically, participating in a life of things that is nowise reducible to a story we can tell about it.[26]

Wordsworth's insight into thingness relies on an incantation of "things" that conjures the word's own strange, but not inhuman, thingness. Wordsworth's emphatic repetition of the word is illuminated by his 1800 note to *The Thorn*, another poem in *Lyrical Ballads*: words are things we cling to and repeat in "impassioned" states, when "the mind attaches to words, not only as symbols of the passion, but as *things*, active and efficient, which are themselves part of the passion."[27] Wordsworth's theoretical vindication of the repetitions of passionate speech gives to his repetitions in *Tintern Abbey*—"all thinking things . . . all things"—yet another layer of signification: things include words themselves, words that do not entirely represent things but that belong to and circulate among them, especially where those things are passions.

This native language of things is, for Wordsworth, lyrical and not narrative or procedurally philosophical. In the passage from *Tintern Abbey* quoted above, Wordsworth codes his relation to things as intuitive by implicitly contrasting it with what "I have learned." What he has learned, however, is not to hear the music of humanity but only "to look," and "hearing" magically appears, a participle unattached to agency, an activity apart from philosophical education. An ironic relation to narrative accompanies the lyric speaker's next claim— "And I have felt"—but what is felt turns out to be not emotions in time and place, the stuff of the "frantic [i.e., gothic or sentimental] novels" Wordsworth deplored in his 1800 Preface to *Lyrical Ballads,* but rather a disturbing "presence" and joyful, elevated "thoughts" that may or may not be coincident with or equivalent to "a sense sublime" of that which impels all things. Having thus dismantled the time and space coordinates of narrative, and directly after the tolling of "things," Wordsworth faintly parodies the narrative logic of consequence or the philosophical logic of deduction: "*Therefore* am I still / A lover of the meadows and the woods, / And mountains . . ." (my emphasis). "Therefore" is here pseudological, evocative either of premises not to be found or of a narrative development similarly absent.

The life that Wordsworth has sensed beneath the face of things is not answerable to human life or logic. Things do not justify loss and suffering in general, nor in particular—*Tintern Abbey* is neither a theodicy nor, in M. H. Abrams's term, a "biodicy" (*Natural Supernaturalism* 96). Insight into things is, instead, an insight into necessity or impulsion. Objects and events are determined by prior events and objects in a way we cannot fully understand; still, in intimations of order we may find some comfort. It is a comfort like that of music: "the still, sad music of humanity" of *Tintern Abbey* (about which I will have more to say in chapter 5), or, in the words of the Wanderer in *The Excursion,* the music of things which the ear of old age is allowed special access. When "the gross and visible frame of things / Relinquishes its hold upon the sense / . . . how loud the voice / Of waters" (9:64–68); age confers

> Fresh power to commune with the invisible world,
> And hear *the mighty stream of tendency*
> Uttering, for elevation of our thought,
> A clear sonorous voice . . . (9:87–90, my emphasis)

As "the mighty stream of tendency," the life of things emphatically assumes active motion and natural direction. Like a river heard from atop a tall mountain—the Wanderer's conceit—it can be sensed but not comprehended or "envisioned." Eluding the totalizing eye, the stream of tendency figures the *kinēsis* (motion) at the heart of *energeia* (animation)—and of music.

THINGS' CLAIM ON US

In sum, Wordsworth, working with the stuff of the English language, working from Stoic and Spinozan philosophy and from a poetic "face" of world order, wound his way into a lyric apprehension of the life of things, a life that humans, with their passions and actions and words, share almost as equals with other thinking things, other breathing things, and indeed with all things. Some of Wordsworth's Victorian and early twentieth-century readers recognized at least a part of this: in Wordsworth's poems Mill found "pleasure which could be shared in by all beings," and Arnold found "joy in widest commonalty spread." In a 1920 essay titled "Neglected Sources of Joy," W. J. Jupp commends Wordsworth's "vision of the brighter, holier time that shall yet be upon the earth," when all will come to share his "sense of the unity of all existence in the invisible and eternal order, the consciousness that we and all other creatures are at one in that unity" (688–89).

And with this consciousness comes, I would add, an ethical imperative. Wordsworth elaborated on the ethical implications of the life of things—here, other physical things—in a fragment he wrote shortly after *Tintern Abbey*:

> There is an active principle alive in all things:
> In all things, in all natures, in the flowers
> And in the trees, in every pebbly stone
> That paves the brooks, the stationary rocks
> The moving waters, and the invisible air.
> All beings have their properties which spread
> Beyond themselves, a power by which they make
> Some other being conscious of their life . . .
> (ll. 1–8, in *"Lyrical Ballads," and Other Poems* 309)

Wordsworth then nods to the animating world soul of Shaftesbury and the Stoics, and elaborates on the human mind's proper activity in benevolence that is unconstrained by positive law or "negative morality" (l. 73). But what most interests me here are Wordsworth's opening lines on the activity of all natural things and their claims to attention. Instead of anthropomorphizing things, Wordsworth here moves toward "thingicizing" ethics. That is, his ethics of things is grounded in the nature of things and, more particularly, in the claims to (our) conscious attention made by natural things. Though not personified or given a human face, these things still have facialities in Benso's sense. We are bound to them by affection and duty, and imaginatively entertaining their reciprocity—their similar bond to us—may have ethically beneficial consequences. We can apply to Wordsworth Benso's description of her own project: he too "aims at restoring things to a preeconomical horizon of festive appreciation and celebration within which things can be encountered in their facialities and tendered—that is, treated with tenderness—because of the generosity of their self-giving, as if their alterity were a gift" (xxxi).

In Wordsworth's poems, the alterity of animals and of rocks, stones, and trees is often a gift: an ass awakes Peter Bell to his own moral being; the "lonely pair / Of milk-white Swans" give of themselves in *Home at Grasmere* (ll. 248–89); and the "grey stone / Of native rock" provides "the home / And centre" of Wordsworth's schoolboy "joys" (*Prelude* 2:33–36). The whole "circumambient world" is a gift to the villagers of Grasmere:

> [T]hem the morning light
> Loves as it glistens on the silent rocks,
> And them the silent rocks [love], which now from high
> Look down upon them, the reposing clouds,
> The lurking brooks from their invisible haunts,
> And old Helvellyn, conscious of the stir,
> And the blue sky that roofs their calm abode. (*Prelude* 8:54–61)

In all these poems, moreover, the self-giving of mute or insensate things grounds a moral order that humans are censured for breaking or seeking to break. Thus Peter first beats the ass destined to soften his heart (1st ed., ll. 404–535); some resident of Grasmere, Wordsworth fears, may have shot the now-absent swans; the "grey stone" of Hawkshead "was split and gone to build / A smart assembly room," the site of gaudy amusement (*Prelude* 2:38–39). In all these scenarios, things keep on giving so long as they are allowed. Wordsworth's poems kindle in thinking things vigilance toward the things of nature, a reminder of their commonality.

And what of evil—does it or can it exist in a pantheistic (or panentheistic) cosmos? Wordsworth in the later 1790s apparently thought not: things tender only gifts. However, incorporating "There is an active principle alive in all things" into the Wanderer's climactic oration in book 9 of *The Excursion*, Wordsworth deletes his attribution of "a power by which they make / Some other being conscious of their life" and substitutes a short concession that the tendency of *some* things may be *partially* evil or deleterious to *some* others:

> Whate'er exists, has properties that spread
> Beyond itself, communicating good,
> A simple blessing, or with evil mixed . . . (9:10–12)

Wordsworth's—or at least the Wanderer's—cosmic optimism is all the more stunning when set beside the famous Homeric passage to which these lines allude. In the great interview scene at the end of *The Iliad* between a suppliant Priam and a relenting Achilles, Achilles offers this pessimistic consolation to the man whose sons he has killed, whose one son has killed the youth that he himself loved:

> Two urns by Jove's high throne have ever stood,
> The source of Evil one, and one of Good;
> From thence the cup of mortal man he fills,
> Blessings to these, to those distributes ills;
> To most, he mingles both: The wretch decreed
> To taste the bad, unmix'd, is curst indeed . . . (Pope's version, 24:663–68)

For Homer there is no unmixed good: a mortal enjoys either partial good or endures unmixed evil. For Wordsworth, by contrast, things bring unmixed good, "a simple blessing," or at worst good "with evil mixed."

Part of Wordsworth's optimism about things derives from the vagueness of the word *things* as he uses it in his poetry. In the course of the nineteenth century *things* were increasingly understood as nonhuman things, especially manufactured objects. Marx addresses this tide of materialization with his concepts of reification (when human activities turn into alien, fungible things) and commodity fetishism (when made things become our new masters). David Simpson sees Wordsworth's poetry as registering the shock of these processes, particularly of "commodity form as a general principle governing human culture and the human mind" (*Wordsworth, Commodification and Social Concern* 10). Yet Wordsworth's *things* resist commodification. Industrial-era developments did not foreclose a more encompassing sense of things, one that persists to this day in ordinary locutions such as *the way things go* and *thinking about things*. Such things still evince the continuities between entities and events, and blur the difference between subjects and objects in the constitution of those entities and events. More important, they suggest unfathomable systems that we need, perhaps, more than narrative itself. It may be quixotic to think that the vestigial etymological force behind the greeting *How are things?* might help (re-) insert us into a less reified world, one in which human and nonhuman activities are viewed as interanimate with objects, made and unmade. But perhaps this is what literature, and Wordsworth in particular, still has the power to do.

CHAPTER FIVE

Music versus Conscience

Wordsworth listens or recalls listening to sad music and is not saddened:

> For I have learned
> To look on nature, not as in the hour
> Of thoughtless youth, but hearing oftentimes
> The still, sad music of humanity,
> Not harsh nor grating, though of ample power
> To chasten and subdue. (*Lines written a few miles above Tintern Abbey*, ll. 89–94)

Wordsworth's passage poses a fundamental question: what *is* "the still, sad music of humanity," and what does it mean to attend to it? In the course of this chapter I will wind my way to address this question directly, but first I must approach it negatively, because the most striking thing about the still, sad music of humanity—especially as this phrase would have been heard by Wordsworth's original readers—is that it is *not* the still small voice of *conscience*.

Judging by literary accounts, it was not uncommon in the later eighteenth century to withdraw to rural solitude, better to hear this latter voice. Conscience could be understood as God's guiding voice, but it was also his scourge, a harsh punishment for criminal acts. Wordsworth, in his verse of the 1790s and early 1800s, depicted something quite novel: withdrawing to hear not conscience but *music*. The nature of Wordsworth's "music" is complex: in various contexts, it might mean actual music (Wordsworth had a particular fondness for shepherd's flutes), poetic musicality, or the pleasant sounds of natural surroundings. In *Tintern Abbey* music may also be a metonymy for the subject who listens to music, receptivity to music figuring receptivity to human nature. In any case, whether in listening to music or in acting as though one were listening to music, something very different is happening than being guided by voices. Music prompts an affective state that we may call, with Alexander Gerard, "a pleasant disposition of soul" that "renders us prone to every agreeable affection" (64). It is not, like conscience, directive: it does not tell us what to think, feel, or do.

Wordsworth thus stakes out a metaethics that is post-Christian and, to some degree, protopostmodern. Metaethics concern the conditions that allow the ethical to emerge: conscience and the active God or nature that placed it there to be obeyed would be one such condition, but an ear for music seems, prima facie, a very different type of condition. In substituting music for conscience Wordsworth suggests that moral response begins either in music or on the model of our response to music—in attunement to the Other, or the Other as tune. This challenge to an ethics of obedience was one that, especially in the Revolutionary decade of the 1790s, had political as well as theological implications. That Wordsworth was aware of these is implied by his later, semireactionary adoption of a more or less Christian conscience as his supreme value in *The Excursion*—though even here, as I argue in chapter 8, *conscience* as the inner voice of God vies with its etymological root of "knowing together," knowledge arrived at jointly with others in a communicative process. The 1814 Prospectus to *The Recluse* (in *The Excursion* 39) links conscience less to solitude than to "retirement": "subject there / To Conscience only, and the law supreme / Of that Intelligence which governs all" (ll. 20–22). Yet conscience does not appear in Wordsworth's earlier version of these lines in *Home at Grasmere*, ms. B (ll. 959–72), written c. 1800–1806, in which retirement "consists / With being limitless the one great Life." Conversely, this earlier version begins with a reference to music that was later omitted: "On Man, on Nature, and on human Life, / Thinking in solitude, from time to time / I feel sweet passions traversing my Soul / Like Music." Wordsworth's turn to conscience in his later poetry highlights his earlier avoidance of it, setting conscience in dialectical opposition to his tentative assays at an ethical subject shaped by music.

CONSCIENCE

To appreciate Wordsworth's turn from and back to conscience requires our having some historical sense of what the term meant or could mean in the Romantic era. It is, primarily, the English version of the Vulgate Bible's *conscientia*, itself a rendering of St. Paul's Greek concept-word *syneidēsis*: the law written in the heart of the Gentiles, the moral code that all humans possess independently of revelation (see, e.g., Romans 2:14–15). But in Pauline Christianity, references to conscience commonly stress what it *dis*approves. *Syneidēsis* is, in Greek, "an index of moral failings or . . . a moral dissuasive: on this view it never gives positive encouragement: a good conscience [Paul's *syneidēsis agathē*] is a quiet conscience."[1] Theologians have at times construed *conscientia* in a more positive sense—some twelfth-century commentators, for example, equated it with the "image and likeness of God" of Genesis 1:26[2]—but in the sermon and literary traditions Wordsworth knew, "conscience" appears most often in its minatory or punitive aspects. Thus an eighteenth-century English translation of Montaigne's essay "Of Conscience" is rife with references to unforgiving conscience: "Conscience, the Soul's Tormentor"; "the revengeful Furies of . . . Conscience"; "Conscience . . . [that] tortures us sleeping and waking with many racking Thoughts" (2:45–51). Francis Atterbury (1662–1732) preached a sermon on "The Terrors of Conscience," defining this faculty as "the Avenging Principle within us" (4:91). Even the irenic Hugh Blair, whose *Sermons* remained a transatlantic model for moderate clergy well into the nineteenth century, defines "the power of conscience" negatively: "it produces an apprehension of merited punishment, when we have committed evil" (379). It is not surprising, then, to find this notion of conscience in a broadside ballad such as "The Children in the Wood," a poem Wordsworth much admired: "And now the heavy wrathe of God / Upon their uncle fell; / Yea, fearfull fiends did haunt his house, / His conscience felt a hell."[3]

Yet in another context, which Wordsworth also may have known, conscience features not as a ministry of pain but, more positively, as the approbative voice of God. Offering the eighteenth century's most significant philosophical elaboration on conscience, Joseph Butler displays a special (we may call it an enlightened) decorum when he speaks of it as a faculty of approbation, man's "rule of right within himself," which entails the obligation to follow it: "Your obligation to obey this law, is its being the law of your nature. That your conscience approves of and attests to such a course of action, is itself alone an obligation. Conscience does not only offer itself to show us the way we should walk in, but it likewise carries its own authority with it, that it is our natural guide; the guide assigned us by the Author of our nature: it therefore belongs to our condition of being."[4]

Conscience can hasten as well as chasten, and it is in this double sense sometimes associated with the "still small voice" of 1 Kings 19:11–12 that subdues the fire-eating prophet Elijah, rendering him serviceable to God's designs. Conscience becomes, particularly among evangelicals, the "still small voice" of enlightenment for which the Christian should listen in composure and silence, outside the din of the public world and particularly of England's *ancien régime*.

Conscience is granted by Christians an exclusive purchase on natural morality. Thus Cowper satirizes the ethics of the 3rd Earl of Shaftesbury, which equate the moral sense and the sense of beauty, as (alluding to 1 Corinthians 13:1) "tinkling cymbal and high sounding brass / Smitten in vain!"; for "such music cannot charm" the soul where "The STILL, SMALL VOICE is wanted" (*The Task*, book 5, "The Winter Morning Walk," ll. 681–85).

For William Wilberforce—a man Wordsworth admired and to whom he sent as a gift the 1800 *Lyrical Ballads*—that still small voice is the bliss of solitude and prepares the true (as opposed to merely nominal) Christian for virtuous public activity: "Rise on the wings of contemplation, until the praises and the censures of men die away upon the ear, and the still small voice of conscience is no longer drowned by the din of this nether world. . . . Thus, at chosen seasons, the Christian exercises himself; and when, from this elevated region he descends into the plain below, and mixes in the bustle of life, he still retains the impression of his more retired hours" (235). Similarly, Vicesimus Knox asked rhetorically, within a larger satire on the pernicious moral example of "lords, dukes, and East India nabobs": "Can the still small voice of conscience be heard by those who live in the noise and tumult of pleasurable pursuits?"[5] Both "the world" in its Johannine sense, and the particular social world of "the higher and middle classes of this country," as Wilberforce put it, are what the Christian must periodically escape in order that he might return to the practice of charity within them. In William Crowe's loco-descriptive poem *Lewesdon Hill* (1788) the awe-inspiring voice of conscience is what turns the Christian back from retirement. One would never descend the mount of contemplation for "the noisy world," writes Crowe, were it not for "conscience, which still censures on our acts, / That awful voice within us, and the sense / Of an hereafter," which rouse us "to remove, according to our power, / The wants and evils of our brother's state."[6]

More could be said on the career of conscience in the 1790s, but suffice it to say that the concept was a vital and polyvalent one and that Wordsworth, in his poetry before *The Excursion,* almost entirely avoided it. What makes this surprising is his sustained exploration, especially through 1798, of the psychology of crime, guilt, and sorrow,[7] themes that, before and after Wordsworth—from, say, "The Children in the Wood" to Elizabeth Gaskell's *Mary Barton* and Charlotte Brontë's *Jane Eyre* (both 1848)[8]—typically involve a greater or lesser engagement with conscience. In the two cases in which Wordsworth uses "conscience" in the 1790s, he does so with qualifying irony. In the early version of *The Borderers* (1797–99) conscience is a concept that only Rivers, the Iago-like villain, invokes, and he does so with patently evil intention. In act 2, scene 3, when Herbert innocently wakes in the night, impeding Rivers's plan to inveigle Mortimer into murdering him in his sleep, Rivers puts this appearance in a bad light, commenting to Mortimer in an aside: "how comes he here? The nightmare, conscience / Has driven him out of harbour?" (ll. 145–46). The appeal to conscience, the soul's tormentor, is reduced to a conman's trick. In "The Convict" from the 1798 *Lyrical Ballads,* conscience appears as a bona fide torment but as one that might be assuaged by transportation (presumably to Australia) and a moral reformation in nature. The convict's conscience is less consistently torturing than his cell, "the comfortless vault of disease" (ll. 29–32); the poem's speaker offers the convict, in closing, this impotent blessing: "My care, if the arm of the mighty were mine, / Would plant thee where yet thou might'st blossom again" (ll. 50–51).

MUSIC IN LIEU OF CONSCIENCE

Among Wordsworth's greatest innovations as a (semi-) secularizing poet in the Alfoxden and Grasmere years was his transformation of conscience, "the soul's tormentor" and the "still small voice," into inarticulate and nondirective "music." This is sometimes the music or blended sounds of outer nature: e.g., "th' aëreal music of the hill" of *An Evening Walk* (1793 version, l. 436), or the "soothing melody" that begins and ends *The Ruined Cottage,* ms. D (ll. 15, 531–33). Alternatively, this music may be an emanation or abstraction from human nature, "the still, sad music of humanity." Thus, in *Tintern Abbey*— significantly, the poem that follows "The Convict" in the 1798 *Lyrical Ballads*— the tortures of conscience become, in the open air, "The still, sad music of humanity, / Not harsh nor grating, though of ample power / To chasten and subdue." To read this music—*music* both as referent and as the sound of Wordsworth's metrical line—as substitute for conscience is to understand why it is not harsh nor punitive (as conscience was popularly held to be) but nonetheless "chastens" or purifies by making one responsive to and responsible for the Other, outside of a Christian (or monarchist) ethics of obedience or, as Wordsworth called it in an Alfoxden fragment, "negative morality."[9] Music puts one into a responsive *mood,* to use a word that Wordsworth emphasizes in *Tintern Abbey* ("that blessed mood . . . that serene and blessed mood," ll. 38–42): a word that, while referring primarily to a "state of mind as affected by any passion" (Johnson, first definition), relates back to a *modus* or "style of musick" (second definition). Johnson illustrates this sense of the term with a line from *Antony and Cleopatra:* "Give me some musick; musick, *moody* food / Of us that trade in love."

An important feature of the music that Wordsworth invokes in *Tintern Abbey,* and elsewhere, is that even when "sad" it does not sadden. As music, it does not even *express* sadness but, to use the philosopher Peter Kivy's distinction, is *expressive of* sadness, in the way that a St. Bernard's face may be said, quite apart from any inference about its emotional state, to "look sad."[10] The aesthetic response to music is arguably never sadness but always some type of pleasure or exhilaration. Coleridge suggests the argument that Kivy will develop: "If we sink into music . . . we feel ourselves moved so deeply as no object in mortal life can move us except by anguish, and here it is present with Joy. It is in all its forms still Joy" (*Philosophical Lectures* 168). Kivy argues, similarly, that the emotions (e.g., sadness) we hear in pure music do not excite corresponding emotions in us but rather always arouse excitement, wonder, or awe (*Introduction to a Philosophy of Music* 132–34). The sound of sorrow, or sorrow understood as a sound, pleases not because of any theodicy, any belief in providence or in the invulnerability of rationality but simply because it partakes of music.

Wordsworth, while seemingly pleased by sad music, does not specify why it pleases. It may be because, as his friend Coleridge says, music "in all its forms is still Joy." But in the years following *Tintern Abbey* Wordsworth trucked more with a modified Pythagorean-Platonic notion of *harmony:* all exist in a harmonious cosmos and all make sounds that recreate, while music is especially good at recreating, that harmony at an environmental or microcosmic level. The basic creed of inner-as-reflection-of-outer harmony finds clear expression in Akenside's *The Pleasures of Imagination* (1744), in which the man of taste's "tuneful breast enjoys" all sweet sounds and sights (1:586), inwardly attuning him to a well-tempered cosmos:

> . . . for th' attentive mind
> By this harmonious action on her pow'rs,
> Becomes herself harmonious: wont so oft
> In outward things to meditate the charm
> Of sacred order, soon she seeks at home
> To find a kindred order, to exert
> Within herself this elegance of love,
> This fair-inspir'd delight: her temper'd pow'rs
> Refine at length, and every passion wears
> A chaster, milder, more attractive mien. (1:599–608)

The 1805 *Prelude* contains sentiments indistinguishable from Akenside's: "The mind of man is framed even like the breath / And harmony of music" (1:351–52); "The spirit of Nature was upon me here, / The soul of beauty and enduring life / Was present as a habit, and diffused. . . . / Composure and ennobling harmony" (7:736–41). Wordsworth's autobiographical poem expresses as well an enthusiasm for the mathematics and geometry that, from Pythagoras onward, evince the same orderliness that underlies musical harmony (see, e.g., *Prelude* 10:878–904, the poet's turn from Godwinianism to mathematics; 5:49–139, the dream of preserving "poetry and geometric truth"). The geometry-music link provides the eighteenth-century historian of music (and biographer of Samuel Johnson), Sir John Hawkins, with a way of explaining the radical, rather than mimetic, pleasures of music: "in music there is little beyond itself to which we need, or indeed can, refer to heighten its charms. If we investigate the principles of harmony, we learn that they are general and universal; and of harmony itself, that the proportions in which it consists are to be found in those material forms, which are beheld with the greatest pleasure, the sphere, the cube, and the cone, for instance, and constitute what we call symmetry, beauty, and regularity" (1:xx, "Preliminary Discourse"). In *Tintern Abbey* there is of this mathematical-musical formalism (or mysticism) only this foretaste: "While with an eye made quiet by the power / Of harmony, and deep power of joy, / We see into the life of things."

THE MUSIC OF THINGS

For Wordsworth, nonrational (or unconscientious) things contribute and respond to that power of harmony. Animals, birds, flowers, waters, and (in concert with them) stones have song, melody, even "language"—just not, in Wordsworth's phrase, "articulate language." Wordsworth makes a fundamental distinction between human language and the language of all things, and he tends in his early poetry to emphasize attentiveness to the latter as a crucial step in moral education, as well as an abiding source of pleasure. This is the burden of an Alfoxden Notebook entry from January–February 1798, arguably written with *The Ruined Cottage* in mind:

> Why is it we feel
> So little for each other but for this
> That we with nature have no sympathy
> Or with such idle objects as have no power to hold
> Articulate language.[11]

The sympathy Wordsworth here endorses is not the narcissistic identification of eighteenth-century sentimentalism, that which Wordsworth later criticized as "imperious sympathy" (see chapter 3); it is, rather, an empathetic engagement with things that cannot reflect us, that on the contrary unmoor us from our sense of self or human exceptionality. Before we can be ethically open to other humans, responsive to them in their alterity, we need first to open ourselves to idling and inhuman things in a way that habituates us to asymmetrical sympathy. To do this, in turn, we need to be attuned to languages that are not "articulate," that is, literally, composed of distinctive, serial sounds. Johnson's *Dictionary* defines "articulate" as "distinct . . . not continued in one tone . . . that is, sounds varied and changed at proper pauses, in opposition to the voice of animals, which admit no such variety." For Wordsworth, hearing inarticulate languages is not distinct from hearing music: thus, "I heard a Stock-dove *sing* or *say* / His homely tale, this very day."[12] The voices of animals and birds; the sounds generated by the actions and reactions of wind, water, rock, wood; the sound of fiddle music: all these inarticulate languages have a claim to our attention, and this tendering of attention, or tenderness, is the foundation of ethics, the prerequisite to a proper attitude toward other rational beings.

That a musical language abides with doves may not be a novel insight in the canons of poetry, but Wordsworth grants voice to other inarticulate beings and inanimate objects in remarkable ways. In *An Evening Walk*, the elements of nature (are said to) sing to each other, claim one another's attention, give each other pleasure: "While music stealing round the glimmering deeps, / Charms the tall circle of th' enchanted steeps" (ll. 349–50). "All air is, as the sleeping water, still, / List'ning th' aëreal music of the hill" (ll. 435–36). *The Prelude* depicts human presence among inarticulate languages we cannot, or cannot fully, understand: "the ghostly language of the ancient earth" (1799, 2:358); the dry wind that blows "with what strange utterance" (1805, 1:348); "the voice of mountain torrents" carried far into the Boy of Winander's heart (6:408–9); the rocks of Simplon Pass that "muttered close," while "black drizzling crags . . . spake . . . / As if a voice were in them" (6:562–64). It is indeed "mighty sum / Of things for ever speaking" ("Expostulation and Reply"), but they are not speaking wholly, or solely, to us.

Natural music participates in the economy of interchange or gift that, as Alex Dick argues, also characterizes poetry, charity, and Wordsworth's sense of them: they all are more or less useless expenditures that can only be partially recuperated into a system of mutual obligation ("Poverty, Charity, Poetry" 365–96). The poet's song, like the bird's, is in one light always a "waste": and yet, to recall James Thomson's fine line on springtime birdsong, "This waste of music is the voice of love" ("Spring" l. 615). Song is one of the acts of giving that constitutes community. From the auditor's point of view, it provides as well a model of ethics grounded not in reciprocity, justice, or any rational imperative but, rather, on attending to the inarticulate language of other things, including the nonhuman Other, and responding to the Other's very alterity as though it were a gift.

That ethical relations among humans must begin with "idle objects as have no power to hold / Articulate language" is due in large part to the "strife of phrase" that too often divides articulate speakers especially when, as in "Expostulation and Reply" and "The Tables Turned," the topic is books (here, implicitly, of moral philosophy). "Books! 'tis a dull and endless strife, / Come, hear the woodland linnet, / How sweet his music; on my life / There's more of wisdom in it." In *The Prelude,* Wordsworth inveighs, "how vain / A correspondence with the talking world / Proves to the most" (1805, 12:171–73), and proceeds to hoist eloquent speakers with the petard of (their own) Popean rhetoric:

> . . . men adroit
> In speech and for communion with the world
> Accomplished, minds whose faculties are then
> Most active when they are most eloquent,
> And elevated most when most admired. (12:225–29)

Wordsworth's final two lines are garnished with rhetorical figures—the parallelism of the one line flipping into the chiasmus of the next, with zeugma underlying the whole—designed to garner the esteem of others, for *amour propre* is the greatest good of the conversable world. Yet for Wordsworth, conversational wit is the menace of ethics. Wordsworth offers as his ideal silent poets: "men for contemplation framed / Shy, and unpracticed in the strife of phrase." "Theirs is the language of the heavens," he concludes with sublime indistinctness, "the power, / The thought, the image, and the silent joy" (12: 266–71).

THE MUSIC OF HUMANITY

"The still, sad music of humanity" is, of all of Wordsworth's enigmatic phrases, perhaps the most enigmatic, as well as the most provocative. It is something the speaker conjures hearing where "the still small voice" might be—Wordsworth's phrase evokes this Biblical locution—but instead of a concluding "of conscience" we find "of humanity." *Humanity* is a complex word: it means, according to Johnson's *Dictionary,* "the nature of man"; "the collective body of mankind"; or "benevolence, tenderness." The "music *of* humanity" is a strange utterance, not only because of the ambiguities of "humanity," but also because "of" is here, as Christopher Ricks has shown it so often is in Wordsworth's verse, a "busy preposition."[13] The music the speaker of *Tintern Abbey* hears could be *about* humanity, or somehow emanating *from* humanity,[14] or be itself "humane music." How he "hears" it is another question: it could be with "the fleshly ear," as he puts it in *The Prelude*, but it might also, as with the "one song" of nature there, be "most audible then when the fleshly ear . . . / Forgot its functions and slept undisturbed" (1805, 2:431–34). One possibility that can, I think, be discounted is that this is a music *made* by human hands, "music" in its ordinary sense: man-made music would be the music "of (particular) humans," not of mankind as a whole, or tenderness as a quality. Still less is this music, as David Bromwich ventures, "the cry of human suffering and human need" (88). Music by its very nature is not a cry or an appeal. Bromwich himself concedes as much when he adds that the music of humanity chastens the grand rhetorical aims of the French Revolution: "music, we know, is to be listened to, and not taken as a guide to action" (89). Accordingly, we cannot respond to it as we would to a cry for help. We can only listen to it; find in it pleasure or displeasure, agitation or comfort; judge it to be beautiful, or not.

What we cannot do, however, is be saddened by it, even if it is "still, sad music." To arrive at this conclusion depends, I think, on a reader's knowing something about the philosophy of music as it was known in Wordsworth's day—which is, by a happy coincidence, proximate to the philosophy of music in our own day, insofar as one of its leading practitioners, Peter Kivy, worked out his ideas in dialogue with the musical theory of seventeenth- and eighteenth-century Europe. For Wordsworth, as for Kivy, being moved by sadness in music is not being moved to sadness. It is being moved to pleasure, to a general feeling of excitement, by the formal beauty of a music that is expressive of sadness. Music that we perceive as being sad—and, in Wordsworth's case, human conditions or qualities that we perceive as or akin to sad music—do not make us sad but may offer us both pleasure and a finer moral sensibility. Wordsworth lays claim to the poetic theme of a sadness that pleases: "Sorrow that is not sorrow but delight, / And miserable love that is not pain / To hear of" (*The Prelude* 12: 245–47). We linger on the unexpected enjambment, "To hear of": for Wordsworth, whatever is or may be heard—as music, as poetry—can only be received with joy.

In his poetry through 1807, Wordsworth strongly implies that music, even sad music, does not sadden; it only enlivens. The speaker of "The Solitary Reaper," for example, overhears a song in a foreign tongue that seems expressive of sadness ("some natural sorrow, loss, or pain"), but it arouses in the speaker nothing but excitement, wonder, and pleasure. Another example comes from Wordsworth's translations from Virgil's *Georgics*, dating back to his Cambridge years and including portions of the Orpheus and Eurydice story (Virgil, *Georgics* 4:464–527). Wordsworth adds to his translation of the Orpheus story a detail not in Virgil or in Virgil's preeminent poetic translator, Dryden: in Wordsworth alone, when Orpheus sings his "tale of sorrow" for the doubly lost Eurydice, all the forest *rejoices*. Virgil expresses Orpheus's power over brutes and the wilderness: he mourns, *mulcentem tigris et agentem carmine quercus*, "charming the tigers and moving the oaks with song" (*Georgics* 4:510). The line is rendered by Wordsworth freely as "the solemn forest . . . / Had ears to joy":

> For sev'n long moons he sat by [S]trymon's shore
> And sung the [tale] of sorrow o'er and o'er
> High o'er his head as sad the mourner sung
> Aerial rocks in shaggy prospect hung
> The solemn forest at the magic song
> Had ears to joy—and slowly moved along.[15]

What beautiful music or poetry inspires in the listener is wonder or pleasure: the power of music is, for Wordsworth, always halcyon or harmonizing.[16] Its difference from conscience is underscored by the last line of Wordsworth's Orpheus translation, in which the poet's dying cry echoes along the riverbanks, "from [s]till small voices heard on every side" (the line is not in *Georgics* 4.526–27). Unlike the still small voice of conscience they evoke, these voices are not directive, but commemorative, communal, and quietly joyous.

And so is the voice that speaks "the still, sad music of humanity," a sentiment itself part echo, and not fully distinct from the music that conveys it. The music he hears has a counterpart in the musicality—and the slow, impeded movement—of his own language in formulating it: as Wordsworth noted, *Tintern Abbey* merits being called an ode by dint of "the impassioned music of . . . [its] versification."[17] *All art constantly aspires towards the condition of music*. For while in all other works of art it is possible to distinguish the matter from the form, and the understanding can always make this distinction, yet it is the constant effort of art to obliterate it."[18] Wordsworth may not have agreed wholeheartedly with this judgment of Pater's, but he would at least have understood it—and he may have been the first poet in English to be able to do so. To be sure, *Tintern Abbey* has subject matter and morality; it is not defined wholly, like pure music, by its structural and sensual properties. But the poem's subject matter is, at crucial moments, and especially in his lines on "the still, sad music of humanity," left indefinite and subordinate to the rhythms, alliteration, and vowel music of verse. By the 1830s, this aspect of Wordsworth's poetry was recognized and prized, particularly in America. An anonymous essayist on Wordsworth in Richmond, Virginia's, *Southern Literary Messenger* (1837) praises Wordsworth's "eminently lyrical" genius: "There is no poet who seems to have a more exquisite ear for the musical qualities of language, which he selects and combines for his varied purposes, with an instinctive sense of melody and harmony truly admirable" (706). Seven years later Edwin Percy Whipple wrote of Wordsworth for the *North American Review*: "The vagueness and indistinctness of the impression which the most beautiful and sublime passages of his works leave upon the mind is similar to that which is conveyed by the most exquisite music. . . . His description of indefinite emotions and subtile ideas is so expressed as to be heard by the soul, rather than seen by mental vision" (365). Wordsworth's "music of humanity" includes, finally, a self-reflexive glance at the humane music of his own verse.

That is, the music of humanity is not only described but embodied by Wordsworth's lines: they, too, may chasten and subdue, even while giving the pleasure that music gives. Indeed, chastening and subduing, making us tender or humane, would seem to be precisely the ethical aim or "worthy *purpose*" of Wordsworth's most sublime and beautiful verse, and *Tintern Abbey* in particular.[19] Here, by transforming conscience into music, Wordsworth turns an ethics of obedience (thou shalt/thou shalt not) into a less structured responsiveness to the human and nonhuman other, an attitude of beneficence.

The morality of conscience was typically, we have seen, a negative one: conscience served as deterrence from, and punishment of, evil acts and intentions. Wordsworth rid his early poetry of the terrors of conscience and offered instead music, along with aesthetic response more generally, as a source of uplift and consolation. Consolation will always be necessary as long as there are evil and death, and Wordsworth's early poetry abounds in both of these, from the nearly motiveless malignity of Rivers in *The Borderers* through to the evil at the edges of *Tintern Abbey*: those "evil tongues," "rash judgments," "sneers of selfish men," and "greetings where no kindness is" that the speaker holds up to Dorothy in the poem's final movement. But here, as more prominently in *The Ruined Cottage*, critics have been too quick to assume that Wordsworth's consolations for suffering and death imply a theodicy. Cleanth Brooks influentially wrote that sufferings were presented by Wordsworth as, at least in part, "a necessary part of a total pattern, rich and various and finally harmonious" (385–86).[20] However, neither *Tintern Abbey* nor *The Ruined Cottage* clearly invokes any such pattern: in the latter, Armytage simply speaks, in passing, of "the pass-ing shews of being," and then he and the narrator feel the sun and hear birds sing. "The still, sad music of humanity" is quickened, metrically, into "that se-cret spirit of humanity"—"Which, 'mid her plants, her weeds, and flowers / And silent overgrowings, still survived" (ll. 503–6). Death is survived, but not by any individual.[21] Music is the index of, and balm for, the life of the species as it moves onward. Suffering and sadness *may* ultimately be justified by some greater harmony of things—and this is an explanation toward which Words-worth more and more tended. But in his poems of the 1790s, there is also the possibility that, quite simply, music and whatever partakes of music, grounded upon nothing but music itself, is an inherent delight.

THE REPRESSION OF CONSCIENCE

I have so far in this book avoided psychobiography, but it is something that Wordsworth invites in his successive accounts of his father's death in 1783, when the poet was in his fourteenth year. The first of these accounts is from the meditative, loco-descriptive poem Wordsworth drafted in 1787, *The Vale of Esth-waite* (ms. A, ll. 272–48, *Early Poems and Fragments* 446–48); the second account, much revised and highly revisionist, comes in the "Waiting for the Horses" episode of *The Prelude* (11:344–88). The first telling, written when the poet was seventeen, candidly recounts the birth of a punitive, even lethal conscience—called here "a still voice"—in the guilt the boy felt for his father's death. In the second telling, however, this guilt is dismissed as "the trite reflections of mo-rality," and where the "still voice" of conscience once stood, generalizing and deathly, there is the intense singularity of the wind he heard on the day he stood waiting for the horses to bring him home from boarding school to his father's house, on the eve of Christmas holidays, days before his father died on Decem-ber 30. "The bleak music" is that to which he now recurs, and rather than deal-ing death, it proves a fountain of life.

In *The Vale of Esthwaite* there is potential music to be heard in the sound of wind in the hawthorn, but it is not yet realized. Wordsworth's own music here is derivative, the tetrameter couplets of Milton's *Penseroso*, but his sentiment is candid:

One Evening when the wintry blast
Through the sharp Hawthorn whistling pass'd
And the poor flocks all pinch'd with cold

Sad drooping sought the mountain fold
Long Long my swimming eyes did roam
For little Horse to bear me home
To bear me what avails my tear
To sorrow o'er a Father's bier.—
Flow on, in vain thou hast not flow'd
But eas'd me of a heavy load
For much it gives my soul relief
To pay the mighty debt of Grief
With sighs repeated o'er and o'er
I mourn because I mourn'd no more . . .

What arrives on the far side of the poet's guilt for not having mourned for his father upon his death (perhaps for feeling a certain Oedipal satisfaction in that death?), is a "small voice" that sentences the boy to a corresponding death.

Thanks to the voice in whisper sweet
That says we [he and his father's shade] soon again shall meet
For oft when fades the leaden day
To joy-consuming pain a prey
Or from afar the midnight bell
Flings on mine ear with its solemn knell
A still voice whispers to my breast
I soon shall be with them that rest.

It would be easy, and not inappropriate, to indulge a Lacanian reading of this passage. The "still voice" represents, if not the birth, then the ascendancy of the superego, the internalized father whose law is death, the negation of desire, the induction of the subject into a symbolic order that is already, in its reduction of the singular libidinous real into a web of role-playing (including the role of son, of father) and structural interchangeability, a type of death. The young man takes a masochistic pleasure in this "sweet" voice that unleashes his death drive, his yearning for the quiescence of inorganic matter—although this yearning is as much self-pity and poetic self-exhibition as it is real.

The sweetly punishing, self-canceling voice of the introjected father—Wordsworth would have called it conscience—disappears from the elaborated retelling of this Christmas story in *The Prelude*. Here Wordsworth comes closer to specifying the source of his guilt, though it now appears to be different—an inordinate, anxious hope in sublunary things—from what it had before:

indifference or satisfaction at his father's death.[22] What he now implies his sin to have been may be an evasion or repression; what Wordsworth calls it, however, is a trite reflection.

> Ere I to school returned
> That dreary time, ere I had been ten days
> A dweller in my father's house, he died,
> And I and my two brothers, orphans then,
> Followed his body to the grave. The event,
> With all the sorrow it brought, appeared
> A chastisement; and when I called to mind
> That day so lately past, when from the crag
> I looked [for the horses] in such anxiety of hope,
> With trite reflections of morality,
> Yet in the deepest passion, I bowed low
> To God who thus corrected my desires.

The father's death now merely *seems* a chastisement of his anxious hopes in worldly things (the stability of home life, or simply a fine vacation), and the "trite reflections of morality" he entertained at thirteen were, presumably, of the "vanity of vanities, all is vanity" variety, "trust not in things of this earth," or "O God, let thy will and not mine be done." Wordsworth grants dignity to his youthful sense of guilt and self-abasement but nonetheless deems it trite; trite as well is his boyish notion of a punitive father God who "corrects" or mortifies desires for things of this world, "the place in which, in the end," Wordsworth writes elsewhere in *The Prelude*, "We find our happiness, or not at all" (10:726–27).

His interest now is not in the guilty conscience of his adolescence but rather in remembering the singular, numinous aura that objects possessed before his fall into the self-estrangement of conscience or the symbolic order, on that day when he stood waiting for the horses:

> And afterwards the wind and sleety rain,
> And all the business [activity] of the elements,
> The single sheep, and the one blasted tree,
> And the bleak music of that old stone wall,
> The noise of wood and water . . .
> —All these were spectacles and sounds to which
> I often would repair, and thence would drink
> As at a fountain.

"The *single* sheep," "the *one* blasted tree": these objects are not reducible to signifiers or to classes of things (if you've seen one sheep you've seen them all) but unique and irreplaceable, things that can't be substituted or exchanged. This world of charismatic objects is lost to all but memory, but memory feeds on it as on traces of the real, that which can be glimpsed in flashes on the periphery of the symbolic grid. Wordsworth tells a similar story in his 1807 *Ode* (later subtitled *Intimations of Immortality from Recollections of Early Childhood*), where it is a single and singular tree, not reduced to the category of trees, that recalls to him the charisma of the world before the role-playing and substitutions of adult life ("A wedding or a festival, / A mourning or a funeral"):

—But there's a tree, of many one,
A single Field which I have look'd upon,
Both of them speak of something which is gone:
    The Pansy at my feet
    Doth the same tale repeat:
Whither is fled the visionary gleam?
Where is it now, the glory and the dream? (*Poems, in Two Volumes* 272)

In *The Prelude*, the lost world contained as well, or so Wordsworth now hears it, a "bleak music"—but its sound, like the "still, sad music of humanity," is refreshing, purifying. He listens to this bleak music as he did in his boyhood to fostering nature and not, as he did in his adolescence, to the still, deathly voice of conscience.

THE RETURN OF THE REPRESSED

Having raised the banner of conscience in *The Excursion*, Wordsworth extends its dominion into his revisions of the unpublished poetry begun in the 1790s. In the late version of *The Borderers* (1842), the power of conscience earlier only proposed, slyly, by Rivers (here renamed Oswald), is witnessed by a repentant beggar woman: "Pity me, I am haunted;—thrice this day / My conscience made me wish to be struck blind; / And then I would have prayed, and had no voice" (ll. 2217–19). In the early 1790s Wordsworth developed *Salisbury Plain* into *Adventures on Salisbury Plain* by adding to the female vagrant's tale the story of the discharged sailor who robbed and killed a man to feed his family; in *Adventures*, the sailor knows fear and guilt, but only in Wordsworth's later reworking, *Guilt and Sorrow* (1842), does "conscience" explicitly prompt his confession: "'O welcome sentence which will end though late,' / He said, 'the pangs that to my conscience came / Out of that deed. My trust, Saviour! is in thy name!'" (ll. 655–57).[23]

But the acme of Wordsworth's rewriting of his earlier ethic, and the final triumph of logocentric conscience over music, comes in the late ode *On the Power of Sound* (1835), where the effect of music is now analogous to that of punitive conscience. Both offer traumatic access to hypostatized reason and the divine order it reflects, both of which are "terrible" to those who, like criminals and idiots, have acted in its absence:

> As Conscience, to the centre
> Of being, smites with irresistible pain,
> So shall a solemn cadence, if it enter
> The mouldy vaults of the dull Idiot's brain,
> Transmute him to a wretch from quiet hurled—
> Convulsed as by a jarring din;
> And then aghast, as at the world
> Of reason partly let in
> By concords winding with a sway
> Terrible for sense and soul! (ll. 96–105, *Last Poems* 120)

In this stunning passage, music no longer chastens and consoles but rather, like conscience, reveals in a flash the terrible chasm between the *logos* and any mind habituated to moral or intellectual darkness. Wordsworth has wandered far from his earlier adventures in protopostmodern ethics, not to mention from the anarchic glee of his early poem *The Idiot Boy*.

As *On the Power of Sound* continues, the music of things is yoked to praise the divine. Wordsworth revisits the "Deep that calls to Deep across the hills" of *Descriptive Sketches*, and turns it into a similitude for the universal praise of God:

> As Deep to Deep
> Shouting through one valley calls,
> All worlds, all natures, mood and measure keep
> For praise and ceaseless gratulation, poured
> Into the ear of God, their Lord! (204–8)

The ode's last and most striking revision is of Wordsworth's "Intimations" Ode.[24] Whereas the earlier poem tentatively played with "the eternal Silence" as the deeper reality beneath the passing show of phenomenal being, *On the Power of Sound* ends with a ringing endorsement of the Word that sustains and will survive the passing world: "O Silence! are Man's noisy years / Nor more than moments of thy life?" "No!," the speaker emphatically answers, concluding that "Harmony" is inextricable from the divine *logos*: "though Earth be dust / And vanish, though the heavens dissolve, her [Harmony's] stay / Is in the WORD, that shall not pass away" (217–24).

Not to give the older Wordsworth the last word, I close with a brief reflection on the poet's legacy to the Victorian novel. His quondam transformation of the still small voice into the music of nature was not lost on astute readers. In Gaskell's *Mary Barton,* the conventional image of conscience as the punitive law within is offset by a sense that music can console those who suffer or bear witness to moral suffering. Gaskell's narrator takes evident pleasure in dramatizing the effect of "the Destroyer, Conscience" (422) on John Barton, Mary's trade unionist father, who has committed a murder (chapters 34–35). But at one remarkable point in her narration (chapter 22), the narrator distinguishes herself from her titular protagonist as one fortunate enough to attend to nature's healing music. Mary, living in urban Manchester, can find little solace for her suffering in "the outward scene" of "hard, square outlines." The narrator, by contrast, can both sympathize with Mary's plight and find solace for her own uneasiness because she is writing "this lovely night in the country," where "the nearer trees sway gently to and fro in the night-wind with something of almost human motion; and the rustling air makes music among their branches, as if speaking soothingly to the weary ones, who lie awake in heaviness of heart. The sights and sounds of such a night lull pain and grief to rest" (303).[25]

CHAPTER SIX

Captivation and Liberty in Poems on Music

In 1818 Hazlitt called poetry "the music of language, answering to the music of the mind" ("On Poetry in General" 23).[1] Within the next twenty years, as melomania swept across the Atlantic, American readers found the music of language in Wordsworth's stanzas. Let me here single out the anonymous essayist on Wordsworth in Richmond, Virginia's, *Southern Literary Messenger* for December 1837.[2] Setting out to write on Wordsworth's *Sonnets dedicated to Liberty,*[3] he gets waylaid by general considerations of Wordsworth's "eminently lyrical" genius. As an example of Wordsworth's "music-breathing mellifluence," the essay quotes "The Solitary Reaper" in its entirety, asking of it: "Is not this the very music of language? Do not these words float in airy waves, until the sense is charmed and lulled into delicious reverie, as by the 'lascivious pleasings of a lute'?" This last phrase comes from the opening soliloquy of Shakespeare's *Richard III,* in which Richard conjures the once forward-marching figure of "War" who now "capers nimbly in a lady's chamber / To the lascivious pleasing of a lute" (1.1.9–13). The quotation, which appears to drift into our reviewer's reverie, aptly recalls him to a sense of purpose: "But we have been irresistibly seduced into these general remarks. We must now proceed to the more immediate subject of this paper." He then turns, dutifully, toward a discussion of Wordsworth's sonnets, in which the poet is said to "speak with the voice of a sage" in inculcating "the cause of freedom and of man." In short, our Richmond reviewer, having briefly succumbed to the siren call of Wordsworth's music, regains his liberty and turns to his task of praising Wordsworth's sonnets on "an erect and republican spirit."

Emerging from this review is a theme that I'd like to develop in this chapter: the Orphic power of music to seduce and distract—to wring the will of its freedom—in a way that is not incompatible with civic liberty. To flesh out this theme, I focus on three poems from Wordsworth's 1807 *Poems, in Two*

Volumes—in order, "The Solitary Reaper," "The Power of Music," and "Stray Pleasures"—and, more summarily, *The Waggoner,* written in 1806 but not published until 1819. In these poems, and especially in "The Solitary Reaper," "the music of harmonious metrical language"[4] mimics the power of vocal or instrumental music to distract from both meaning and purposeful activity. But music, for Wordsworth, is no mere drug; still less is it a threat to society. Although sound may induce reverie, it nonetheless brings individuals together, apart from an overbusy world. The immersion of musical pleasure serves as a counterforce to the commercial spirit over which Wordsworth, no less than many of his American reviewers, worried. It is a commonplace from Shakespeare's best-known plays of Rome and Venice that the unmusical person is a threat to the state: in *The Merchant of Venice,* for example, Lorenzo, while addressing "the sweet power of music," contends: "That man that hath no music in himself, / Nor is not moved with concord of sweet sounds, / Is fit for treasons, stratagems, and spoils" (5.1.79–85).[5] Wordsworth's concern with the unmusical man is not, however, with the restiveness of faction, but with the restlessness and isolation of economic man. Absorption in melody and rhythm make for solidarity in a present moment that is political insofar as it harkens back to an imaginary past of primitive equality and ahead to a future of equality restored.

Before I elaborate this argument, let me first glance at the metrical structures of Wordsworth's poems on music—their own music, as it were. "The Solitary Reaper" and "The Power of Music" are each based on a type of ballad stanza. "The Power of Music" is written in a form not always recognized as such: the anapestic or iambic-anapestic tetrameter found in eighteenth-century amorous and comedic ballads by, among others, Matthew Prior, Lady Mary Wortley Montagu, and William Blake.[6] Wordsworth experimented with an anapestic ballad stanza of alternating tetrameter and trimeter in "The Convict," published in the 1798 *Lyrical Ballads,* but he settled on a Prior-like iambic-anapestic tetrameter stanza for the comic ballad *The Farmer of Tilsbury Vale. A Character* (published anonymously in *The Morning Post,* 1800) and several poems that appear in the expanded 1800 *Lyrical Ballads:* "Poor Susan," "The Two Thieves," "Rural Architecture," and "A Character, in the Antithetical Manner."[7]

The more familiar type of ballad stanza, with its alternating line lengths of eight and six syllables (and/or four and three stresses) is one that Wordsworth rarely employed in its standard form.[8] He more often modified it for his purposes, as, for example, in "Lines Written in early spring."[9] Wordsworth works both within and against the phonic expectations of the form and does so with a craftsmanship that involves, by his own account, "a more impressive metre than is usual in Ballads" (*Prose Works* 150). The modified ballad stanza of "Lines Written in early spring," a stanza of eight, eight, eight, and then six syllables, draws attention to the last line by having it come up short. The thematic surprises of this poem unfold in stanzas that end on notes of mystery—what are those "sad thoughts"? What "has man made of man?" These successive mysteries unfold in curtailed lines of six rather than eight syllables, so that as we come to the end of each stanza, we have a rhythmic as well as semantic sense of something missing.

This modified ballad stanza returns as the first half of the eight-line stanza of "The Solitary Reaper," where it is followed by two tetrameter couplets. "The Solitary Reaper" is arguably as much about its own stanza-music as about anything else: form here is almost coextensive with content. I quote the poem's first and third stanzas:

> Behold her, single in the field,
> Yon solitary Highland Lass!
> Reaping and singing by herself;
> Stop here, or gently pass!
> Alone she cuts and binds the grain,
> And sings a melancholy strain;
> O listen! for the Vale profound
> Is overflowing with the sound.
> *   *   *   *   *   *   *   *   *   *
> Will no one tell me what she sings?
> Perhaps the plaintive numbers flow
> For old, unhappy, far-off things,
> And battles long ago:
> Or is it some more humble lay,
> Familiar matter of today?
> Some natural sorrow, loss, or pain,
> That has been, and may be again?

Wordsworth's final stanza ends, famously, with a couplet on memory: "The music in my heart I bore,/Long after it was heard no more." "The Solitary Reaper" testifies to the power of metrical arrangement and long vowels ("profound"/"sound"; "flow"/"ago"; "bore"/"more") to distract pleasurably from the very words that formulate a speaker's response to a song in a language (Gaelic) he does not understand. Material signifiers gain aria-like ascendancy over immaterial meanings. For sure, "The Solitary Reaper" is a poem of "semantically rich craft," as Susan Wolfson has shown ("Wordsworth's Craft" 111–13). The careful reader may trace the junctures of sound and sense in the poem's stanza structure: for example, we first stop short on the hexasyllabic line, "Stop here, or gently pass," our progress further impeded by its opening trochee. But thinking through the poem's artifice is only one way into it, and on the poem's own terms it is not necessarily a better path than the one pointed to by the rhetorical question of the *Southern Literary Messenger*: "Do not these words float in airy waves?" As words convert to waves, their very signification is what gets left behind. It is hearing the word "sound" as sound that appears to have attracted Dorothy Wordsworth to the end of the poem's first stanza: she writes, "There is something inexpressibly soothing to me in the sound of those two Lines. . . . I often catch myself repeating them in disconnection with any thought" (*Letters* 1:650). The poem's overflowing sound invites the evacuation of sense. The *Beau Monde* reviewer of Wordsworth's *Poems* of 1807 strikes a chord with his bald assessment: "Solitary Reaper and Stepping Westward are poems both innocent of all meaning" (Reiman, *The Romantics Reviewed* 1:43).

But there is also a false note in this review. "The Solitary Reaper" means at several different levels, and this reviewer helps us to see one of them by adverting to the *sequence* of poems in "Poems written during a Tour of Scotland," a section of *Poems, in Two Volumes* commemorating the six-week tour William and Dorothy took, partly with Coleridge, in August and September 1803. "The Solitary Reaper" is followed by "Stepping Westward," another poem about "a sound," here "Of something without place or bound."[10] It is preceded by "Rob Roy's Grave," a poem still more clearly about the sound of *liberty*. The historical Rob Roy (1671–1734) was, at least as Walter Scott depicts him in his 1818 novel, an honest Scottish drover who, after the royal proscription of his clan, turned outlaw, cattle thief, enemy of Hanoverian troops in Scotland, and friend of the common people. In Wordsworth's poem, Rob Roy waxes philosophic, setting freedom and (as he understands it) natural morality above positive law. He rejects statutory law as an engine of social and inner divisiveness: "What need of Books?/Burn all the Statutes and their shelves/They stir us up against our Kind;/And worse, against Ourselves." Roy derives his own "moral creed" from "the principles of things":

> The Creatures see of flood and field,
> And those that travel on the wind!

With them no strife can last; they live
　　In peace, and peace of mind.

For why?—because the good old Rule
Sufficeth them, the simple Plan,
　That they should take who have the power
　　And they should keep who can.

Roy's creed has a double edge, with two implications for our understanding of *liberty* in the poem—which, when it arrives, Wordsworth places in italics. Within Roy's claim to a natural superiority over those with legal power, *liberty* means negative liberty from the constraints of sanctioned morality ("thou shalt not steal" presumably foremost); and yet, given it is the people who, collectively, have the power, it is also—and this is what makes Roy a popular hero—an assertion of the positive liberty of the oppressed, the liberty to live and to flourish, which may require a redistribution of goods from rich to poor. "Rob Roy's Grave" ends with an image of the faces of the Scottish poor that "kindle, like a fire new stirr'd, / At sound of ROB ROY's name"—that is, at the name of their Robin Hood–like hero, a man whom we are told "didst love / The *liberty* of Man," who "battled for the Right," who protected "the poor man" from the depredation of the rich. The name stirs in herdsmen and reapers sentiments of loyalty and liberty, and in the narrator nostalgia for the old days in hope that they will become the future.

It is not a political future that English reviewers would be apt to endorse, since the Highlands Wordsworth toured were subject to the metropolitan authority, and larger imperial designs, of London. In the first decade of the nineteenth century Scotland presented a dual problem, as the site of both dubious loyalty to the Union, and a possible Napoleonic invasion. Dorothy writes in her *Recollections of a Tour Made in Scotland* (1803): "When we were traveling in Scotland an invasion was hourly looked for, and one could not but think with some regret of the times when from the now depopulated Highlands forty or fifty thousand men might have been poured down for the defence of the country" (171–72). The problem William faced in his poetic "Tour" is thus, as Allen Grossman observes, that of "imagining an adequate (heroic) counterforce [to Napoleon], which in turn brought to mind the implications of the suppression of the clans in Scotland especially after 1745 . . . and the implication also of general . . . economic colonization of the British Isles" (129). In turning to Rob Roy's grave, Wordsworth imagines, with wry distance but not without sympathy, a premodern economy in order to reorient popular solidarity and heroism—a type of liberty not purchased with the loss of power.

The *Beau Monde* reviewer who called "The Solitary Reaper" "innocent of all meaning" did so in relation to what he perceived as the criminal or radical tendencies of "Rob Roy's Grave," the first piece in "Poems written during a Tour in Scotland." The reviewer nervously dismisses "Rob Roy's Grave"—"the strains of this poem might be dangerous if it were not so foolish"—but his judgment nonetheless concedes the danger. And within a poetic sequence no poem is innocent of the dangers that have preceded it. Sound carries, and with it, meaning.[11] For the sequential reader of *Poems, in Two Volumes*, the sound of liberty overflows into the sound of the reaper's song, as well as into the speaker's reflection on time, the unspecified lost thing—call it freedom—"that has been, and may be again."[12] Meaning may retreat in reverie, but like the repressed it always returns. Wordsworth's poems ask us to negotiate between surrender to musical form and the recuperation of meaning both within and between the individual pieces he ordered with care.

The next piece I would consider, "The Power of Music," suggests the social meaning of music's suspension of practical sense. Music here figures as a fiddler who captivates a humble London crowd. In Wordsworth's *Poems, in Two Volumes* "The Power of Music" follows another poem of London life, "Star Gazers," but in his 1815 *Poetical Works* it is placed in the "Poems of the Imagination" after a poem with which it is more closely connected, "Poor Susan" from the 1800 *Lyrical Ballads*. Both "Poor Susan" and "The Power of Music" are written in the ballad stanza of iambic-anapestic tetrameter, a showy meter associated with comic ballads that Wordsworth generally reserved for his lighter compositions and, in the case of these two poems, his treatment of urban themes. "Poor Susan" and "The Power of Music," which may best be described as tragicomic, both address the power of song—the thrush's song or the fiddler's—to distract from the dreariness of labor, poverty, and urban displacement. (Wordsworth's Highland reaper, by contrast, is distracted—as we the readers are distracted—only from her labor, the "reaping" that ever gives way to "singing.")

In an irony that unfolds during the course of "The Power of Music," the street corner fiddler is identified in the poem's opening line as "An Orpheus! An Orpheus!," as though he were an avatar of the legendary pre-Homeric poet with the power to civilize animals or brutal humans. Horace, in his *Ars Poetica*, recounts: "While men still roamed the woods, Orpheus, the holy prophet of the gods, made them shrink from bloodshed and brutal living; hence the fable that he tamed tigers and ravening lions; hence too the fable that Amphion, builder of Thebes's citadel, moved stones by the sound of his lyre" (ll. 391–96,

Loeb translation). The familiarity of Horace's lines is attested by their appearance in the homely verse of William Brimble, described on his 1765 title page as "of Twerton, near Bath, Carpenter":

> Let hist'ry boast fam'd Amphion's powerful call,
> When stones came dancing to the Theban wall,
> Leap'd from their beds right angl'd, smooth and strait,
> And in harmonious order rose in state. . . .
> How Orpheus' power, nor rocks, nor trees withstood,
> But follow'd to his harp a dancing wood;
> How savages of fierceness was disarm'd,
> And from their currents list'ning rivers charm'd. . . .
> Still music's power, unrival'd, stands confess'd,
> And fiercer foes can charm than savage beast.

Brimble thus begins a couplet ballad the narrative of which is largely summarized in its title: "On TWO MUSICIANS of BATH being attack'd by a Highwayman, who, on their presenting a FIDDLE, rode off without his Booty"—the comic twist being that it is not the fiddle's music that deters crime but rather the notorious poverty of fiddlers (*Poems*, 11–13). The mock-Horatian strain of a ballad such as Brimble's—as well as its rude artfulness—may lie behind the opening lines of Wordsworth's poem on music's power:

> An Orpheus! An Orpheus!—yes, Faith may grow bold,
> And take to herself all the wonders of old;—
> Near the stately Pantheon you'll meet with the same,
> In the street that from Oxford hath borrowed its name.

Orpheus is alive and well, not in the Pantheon, the masquerade hall named after the Roman seat of all the old gods,[13] but on the street, among those whose unsophisticated receptivity is offered as something of an ideal:

> What an eager assembly! what an empire is this!
> The weary have life, and the hungry have bliss;
> The mourner is cheared, and the anxious have rest;
> And the guilt-burthened Soul is no longer opprest.

As we saw in chapter 5, music is for Wordsworth, at least through 1806, that which assuages or indeed replaces guilt and the burden of conscience.

The fiddler has a hat for donations, and the sign of the faithful is that they give all they have:

> He stands, back'd by the Wall;—he abates not his din;
> His hat gives him vigour, with boons dropping in,
> From the Old and the Young, from the Poorest; and there!
> The one-pennied Boy has his penny to spare.

The poor boy gives his all to the fiddler, who enchants him for a brief while: the image is like a bell that tolls us back to the New Historicist critique of Romantic writing. This scene invites a Marxist objection not only to "The Power of Music" but also to Wordsworth's larger corpus of poems on the pleasures of sound. Somewhere, someone must, I suspect, have written or lectured on this poem in search of a victim, and from a certain angle victims are here aplenty. The poor boy parting with his coin may seem a comment on art's ability to mystify material relations, to distract the poor from their needs and rights. Music is here the opiate of the masses.[14] Just as the fiddler stupefies his audience with sound, so would Wordsworth stupefy his in poetic numbers, blinding them to revolutionary imperatives.

From a certain point of view these objections are unanswerable. But at least for a moment we might consider a different point of view, which I believe to be Wordsworth's, according to which the blessing of verse as well as violin is precisely the ability to forget about money and the economic base of relations—about "getting and spending," to quote from the 1807 *Poems*' best-known sonnet. Music brings together a community in pleasure that matters more than the material. Music, at least for the audiences *in* and *of* Wordsworth's poem—if not for the fiddler or, arguably, for Wordsworth the professional poet—is not a means (like getting) to an end (spending or amassing); it is, rather, an autotelic activity, an end in itself, the kind of activity ancient Athenians thought of as most perfect (see Hannah Arendt, 206–7). From the standpoint of modern economics, performance is unproductive labor; for the Greeks, it is, along with the autotelic activity of democratic politics itself, the highest human achievement.

In Wordsworth's poem the power of music is lost on a genteel audience that believes only in acquisition. This audience enters Wordsworth's poem as the adversarial figures of the poem's final stanza—though it has been present all along in the poem's early nineteenth-century readership, as well as its contemporary one. The "you" of its final stanza includes us:

> Now, Coaches and Chariots, roar on like a stream;
> Here are twenty souls happy as Souls in a dream;
> They are deaf to your murmurs—they care not for you,
> Nor what ye are flying, or what ye pursue!

The fiddler's street corner auditors don't care, because they alone in this scene are absorbed in present pleasure; all around them, busy worldlings fly from the past or pursue an uncertain future.[15] And, to illustrate that flight through formal means, Wordsworth trots his reader along through the headlong rhythms of anapestic verse. This meter does not, like that of "The Solitary Reaper," reproduce a sense of his lyric speaker's entrancement; instead, it exhibits its own theatrical power to whisk us past the scene it describes. As we come to the end of the poem's comic prance, we are left with a criticism of the pace we've pursued.

Wordsworth's critique is of commerce, luxury, and propulsion itself insofar as these things threaten the bonds that constitute community. The poet's *Southern Literary Messenger* reviewer, writing in 1837—the year of Henry Reed's American edition of Wordsworth, and also of a financial crisis in America—invokes Wordsworth's power to counteract "the progress that luxury has made in these United States," and one feels the weight in this line of "progress" as well as of "luxury." He laments his countrymen's "vain efforts to emulate the ostentation and parade of European society, by which we have impaired our stern republican virtues" (710). In "The Power of Music," the people's temporary trance is hardly stern, but it is a civic event or even a religion: they stand apart, together, in a concentrated present. In contrasting their ritual presence to the *differance* of purposive endeavor, Wordsworth reminds me of an exchange in Boswell's *Life of Johnson*: "'Sir [Boswell addresses Johnson], you observed one day at General Oglethorpe's, that a man is never happy for the present, but when he is drunk. Will you not add,—or, when driving rapidly in a post chaise?' JOHNSON. 'No, Sir, you are driving rapidly *from* something, or *to* something'" (3:5).[16]

Those in chaises and chariots are in one manner like political critics, of either the 1830s or our own day: they look before and after and pine for what is not. Music is now, while politics is always braced in time. But to understand Wordsworth fully is to understand him dialectically, for he too is a politician, not just an ear in a crowd. Some of Wordsworth's nineteenth-century readers saw in his backward glances—to an idealized view of Rob Roy's Scotland, say, or an absorbed crowd passed by on the street—a blueprint for a future that wouldn't need a future: that is, a utopia. To recall Whipple's verdict of 1844: Wordsworth's "England of a thousand years past is the Utopia of a thousand years to come" (383).

The final ironies of "The Power of Music" are political, involving both a transformation of the mythic role of Orpheus's music and the narrator's detached view of the new Orphic role he describes. Traditionally, Orpheus has figured the benevolent ruler who brings order and hierarchy to the base elements of nature. He stands for the ordering power of music, in opposition to music's Dionysian power to whip maenads into a destructive frenzy. But Wordsworth's story is not one of social order imposed by an Orpheus figure on a discordant mob. On the contrary, this Orpheus, or Orpheus-Dionysus hybrid ("he abates not his *din*"), (re)calls his hearers to a once or future state of life and bliss *outside* the social order as it is presently constituted. This Orpheus supplies salubrious retreat from a commercial metropolis that has lost all sense of, to use two of Wordsworth's favorite words, being and breathing:

> That errand-bound 'Prentice was passing in haste—
> What matter! he's caught—and his time runs to waste—
> The News-man is stopped, though he stops on the fret,
> And the half-breathless Lamp-lighter he's in the net!

Yet what the fiddler does to his passersby is what Wordsworth does not do to his reader: immobilize, assuage, and band together ("O blest are the Hearers and proud be the Hand / Of the pleasure it spreads through so thankful a Band"). The poet instead hurries us onward in anapestic strides, imaging successive auditors (the apprentice, the newsman, the lamplighter, et al.), and ending with "pursue!" There is irony, of course, in the apprentice's "time run to waste," for Wordsworth here pictures time redeemed, *kairios* rather than *chronos*; the irony, however, is not entire. The reader of "The Power of Music" is suspended, finally, between content and form, absorption and theatricality, arrest and bustle, civic unity and commercial profit. Our guide through this scene of captivity, who has simulated the liberty of motion, has shown us the freedom that may lie in music's chains, as well as the enchainment of a purely market liberty.

This double paradox—freedom in the captivity of music, slavery in the freedom of markets—is a theme upon which Wordsworth plays variations in two other poems written in 1806, with which I will close this chapter: the mock-epic *The Waggoner*; and the untitled poem beginning "By their floating Mill," later titled "Stray Pleasures," placed two poems before "The Power of Music" in *Poems, in Two Volumes. The Waggoner* might seem, at first glance, to inculcate the prudential self-restraint that befits the marketplace. In this verse tale, Benjamin the Waggoner ends up being fired by his employer for bringing in his wagonload late (and for allowing the master's dog to be bruised by an ass's hoof), the reason for his tardiness being that he has "fallen off the wagon" and spent a good portion of the previous night drinking and enjoying music in a pub alongside a colorful companion he has made on the road. The poem's speaker regrets at the end that Benjamin, once fired, was never replaced, and never again could the people of his district—especially the poor and vagrant, "The lame, the sickly, and the old" (l. 836 [1819 text])—depend upon a covered wagon ride in inhospitable weather. At the sight of travelers struggling in the wind and rain the narrator concludes:

> Then most of all, then far the most,
> Do I regret what we have lost;
> Am grieved for that unhappy sin
> Which robbed us of good Benjamin;—
> And of his stately Charge [his wagon and horses], which none
> Could keep alive when He was gone! (842–47)

Yet what is this "unhappy sin"? It may refer to Benjamin's night in the tavern when he should have been on the road—yet "sin" seems too strong for this moment of surrender, especially when it appears to have been of little consequence (Benjamin delivers his wagonload not too late into the morning; the master's mastiff has a wound that is only superficial). The real sin here seems to be Benjamin's unjustified dismissal or, extrapolating from that, a workplace ruled by capricious masters and enslaved men.

Conversely, what might seem a lure to the weak-willed workman—"a fiddle in its glee / Dinning from the CHERRY TREE [tavern]!" (296–97)—is instead a prelude to the poem's most animated lines, in which Wordsworth vies with his master in the colloquial mock-epic in tetrameter, the Burns of *Tam o' Shanter*:

> Blithe souls and lightsome hearts have we,
> Feasting at the CHERRY TREE!
> This was the outside proclamation,
> This was the inside salutation;
> What bustling—jostling—high and low!
> A universal overflow!
> What tankards foaming from the tap!
> What store of cakes in every lap!
> What thumping—stumping—overhead! . . .
> 'Tis who can dance with greatest vigour—
> 'Tis what can be most prompt and eager;—
> As if it heard the fiddle's call,

The pewter clatters on the wall;
The very bacon shows its feeling,
Swinging from the smoky ceiling! (327–44)

"The fiddle's *squeak*—that call to bliss," the narrator later resumes, is "ever followed by a kiss" (373–74). Channeling Burns, Wordsworth arrives at his most Dionysian description of the joys of drink, music, dance, *erōs*—the power of music setting bodies and lines of verse in buoyant motion. If this is a loss of liberty, Wordsworth's reader cannot but wish: enchain me.

Wordsworth's last great poem of music, "Stray Pleasures," is not quite so capering in its form—a six-line stanza that, from a two-beat opening line, expands into lines of five beats (often with internal rhymes), and then contracts again. Yet the poem emphatically endorses music and the free pleasure, and pleasing freedom, it affords. Music here frees three persons who are "prisoners" to toil; it is also free music, in that it is neither paid nor intended for the group it consolidates.

By their floating Mill,
Which lies dead and still,
Behold yon Prisoners three!
The Miller with his two Dames, on the breast of the Thames;
The Platform is small, but there's room for them all;
And they're dancing merrily. (*Poems, in Two Volumes* 232)

"They dance," we find at the end of stanza 3, "there are three, as jocund as free." Their freedom in gaiety—we must call this a positive liberty—derives from a moral creed not dissimilar to Rob Roy's "they should take who have the power / And they should keep who can":

Man and Maidens wheel,
They themselves make the Reel,
And their Music's a prey which they seize;
It plays not for them,—what matter! 'tis theirs:
And if they had care it has scattered their cares,
While they dance, crying, "Long as ye please!"

The power-to-the-people implication of this stanza—let them take what they need to be free or enjoy freely—passes in the next into a less revolutionary but more utopian register. Here pleasure appears not as booty but rather as undirected gift, one that, as Simon Jarvis has observed, is outside any economy of exchange, "the dissemination of pleasure through its excess" (105):

> They dance not for me,
>   Yet mine is their glee!
> Thus pleasure is spread through the earth
> In stray gifts to be claim'd by whoever shall find;
> Thus a rich loving-kindness, redundantly kind,
> Moves all nature to gladness and mirth.

The "loving-kindness" that circulates "redundantly" (defined by Johnson as "superfluously; superabundantly") seems to need no origin.

Yet the *word* "lovingkindness" has a very specific provenance, one with which Wordsworth could assume his readers' familiarity: it is, as Johnson remarks, "a scriptural word" for "tenderness; favour; mercy." It translates the Hebrew word *hecedh* in the King James Bible, especially in the book of Psalms, where it refers specifically to God's tenderness toward his creatures and is often reinforced through synonymous parallelism by the phrase "tender mercies," as in the verse Johnson uses to illustrate "lovingkindness": "Remember, O Lord, thy tender mercies and thy lovingkindness; for they have been ever of old" (Psalms 25:6; cf. 51:1, 69:16, 103:4). With this charged term we move from *music* as the source of a blind and binding freedom to a principle that lies behind the ideal distribution of music: the energy of *love*. For the psalmist, that love comes from on high, with power and glory, the greatest act of a God held to be most excellent. Wordsworth, for his part, spreads out "rich loving-kindness" along a vertical as well as a horizontal axis. As I will argue in my next chapter, he thought such a gratuitous, freely given love, whether human or divine, to be sublime.

CHAPTER SEVEN

The Moral Sublime

The yearning for infinitude has been, for twentieth-century literary criticism, the defining aspect of the Romantic sublime, the key to what is particularly Romantic about it—especially in the writings of Wordsworth, the touchstone figure for writing on the Romantic sublime. But this criticism, for all its virtues, uniformly ignores the ethics, and particularly the love ethic, that Wordsworth invokes in his sublime writing as in his theoretical writing on the sublime. In the critical literature, "the Romantic sublime" refers, typically without moral reference, to the mind's transcendence of a natural and/or social world that finally cannot fulfill its desire. Revealed in the moment of the sublime is that the mind is not wholly of the world, but this revelation may be triggered by a particular setting in the world. The lonely grandeur of lakes and mountains, or the solemn interior of a cathedral, invite sublime musings, composed in a heightened style that may also be described as sublime or awe-inspiring. Often cited as the epitome of the Romantic sublime is a passage from book 6 of Wordsworth's *Prelude:*

Our destiny, our nature, and our home,
Is with infinitude—and only there;
With hope it is, hope that can never die,
Effort, and expectation, and desire,
And something evermore about to be.
The mind beneath such banners militant
Thinks not of spoils or trophies, nor of aught
That may attest its prowess, blest in thoughts
That are their own perfection and reward—
Strong in itself, and in the access of joy
Which hides it like the overflowing Nile. (*Prelude,* 1805 text, 6:538–48)[1]

At this point in his narrative, Wordsworth has just crossed the Alps unwittingly, failing en route to achieve the grand prospect view he earlier imagined. He turns from his disappointment to praise the imagination as a power superior to any actual experience and to celebrate, in these lines, the soul as fundamentally alien to the world of the senses. Wordsworth expresses a yearning for the infinite, the unbounded, the supersensible; he expresses, as though it were a natural or intuitive aspect of our being, the desire to transcend the limitations imposed on us as finite, historically situated beings. While this yearning evidently has religious roots (particularly Neoplatonic and Augustinian ones), its quasi-secular or at least nonsectarian expression comprises what we now think of as the Romantic sublime. Whether or not this yearning sufficiently characterizes what Wordsworth actually took to be sublime is a question I address in this chapter.

Let me first concede that the desire for transcendence, as an aspect if not necessarily the essence of the Romantic sublime, received widespread expression in and well beyond the British Romantic era. Indeed, the frequency with which authors of the Romantic era invoke the sublime of transcendence has led critics to label it "Romantic"—although its ultimate provenance is in Longinus.[2] (Romantic poets address the sublime in a correspondingly sublime or awe-inspiring style, again following the lead of Longinus, who—as Boileau famously quipped—"in talking of the sublime, is himself sublime.")[3]

Yet Wordsworth did not consider transcendence as a good in itself; rather, it is good only insofar as it leads to or accords with the moral good. For Wordsworth, morality is largely transcendent, in that it rises above the restraints of animal life; but it is also incarnate in the activity of life. Wordsworth suggests this dual nature of morality in his crossing-the-Alps passage. Transcendence is moralized by the elision of "infinitude" with the less abstract, though similarly unbounded, virtue of "hope": hope that transcends definite content, making possible the unpredictable, the new, genesis as opposed to mortality. "With hope it [our home] is, hope that can never die"—although *we* die; hope, raising us above our animal or given condition, makes us, or marks us as, in some sense immortal or transcendent. Hope affords a counterpoint to suffering and death, as well as to the conflation of fact and value (what is and ought to be) elsewhere endorsed by Wordsworth in his antimurmuring, Stoic moods. And yet our home is also with the immanent and at least partly corporeal virtues of "effort, and expectation, and desire," wellsprings of the activity figured here in the crossing of the Alps. Thomas Weiskel, in his influential structuralist-psychoanalytic model of the Romantic sublime (1976), linked the Wordsworthian sublime with a static narcissism, and some feminist critics subsequently characterized that narcissism as masculine and domineering. Athwart these perspectives I discover in Wordsworth a sublime of moral relations, particularly of love as an overcoming of self. This sublime love ethic, key to *The Prelude* (and earlier suggested in *Tintern Abbey*), implies a politics as well, as I suggest in the conclusion to this chapter.

MORALITY TRANSCENDENT AND IMMANENT

In Wordsworth, transcendence is related, and finally subservient to, the *moral sublime*. To emerge as a fully moral being, one transcends one's narrow self-interest, or even the vital instinct of self-preservation. To do these things requires great effort, and this effort, as well as the moral activity it enables, are sublime. Such a conception of the moral sublime was vital to the intellectual world that Wordsworth inhabited. Joseph Priestley, the scientist, Unitarian preacher, and political radical much admired in the 1790s by Wordsworth, Coleridge, and Lamb,[4] argued that sublimity is not confined "to the ideas of objects which have sensible and *corporeal* magnitude" (the Alps, the ocean, and so forth): "*Sentiments* and *passions* are equally capable of it, if they relate to great objects, suppose extensive views of things, require a great effort of the mind to conceive them, and produce great effects. Fortitude, magnanimity, generosity, patriotism, and universal benevolence, strike the mind with the idea of the sublime. We are conscious that it requires great effort to exert them; and in all cases when the mind is conscious of a similar exertion of its faculties, it refers its sensations to the same class" (Lecture 20, "Of the Sublime," 154).

The end to which exertion aims matters to Priestley (as it will to Wordsworth); his idea of "great objects" is not that of the sublime's progenitor, Longinus. Longinus, who had a heroic or aristocratic notion of greatness, illustrates his postulate that "sublimity is the echo of a noble mind" with the example of Ajax in the *Odyssey* (11:543–67): "How grand . . . is the silence of Ajax in the Summoning of the Ghosts, more sublime than any speech!" (section 9). In the scene to which Longinus alludes, Ajax, summoned from Hades, proudly refuses to speak to Odysseus because he is still angry with him for having been awarded the armor of Achilles, armor he considers his due. The scene concerns, in short, the sublime of the grudge. Whereas Longinus praised a heroic pride that would neither remit nor complain, Joseph Priestley in "Of the Sublime" praises as the most sublime sentiment, the noblest exertion of all, "the prayer of our Saviour upon the cross, in behalf of his persecutors, *Father, forgive them, for they know not what they do*" (155, quoting Luke 23:34). Priestley has shifted allegiance, within the discourse of the sublime, from heroic greatness to Christian goodness, personal excellence to universal love—or, in Wordsworth's formulation, from "spoils and trophies" (such as Achilles's armor) to "thoughts / That are their own perfection and reward." Thus the protagonist of Wordsworth's *The Borderers* can say to the man who has led him to perdition—looking back to Ajax, but siding finally, and strenuously, with Christian ethics—"There are men / Who with bare hand would have plucked out thy heart / And flung it to the dogs.—But I forgive thee" (5.3.247–49).

For Kant, whose thinking on ethics and aesthetics would also come to influence Coleridge and Wordsworth, moral activity rises to sublimity not so much through the exertion it requires or the consequences it produces but through its transcendence of "the inconstancy of external things." Kant's most sublime thing is to act according to fixed principles:

> But what if the secret tongue of the heart speaks in this manner: "I must come to the aid of that man, for he suffers; not that he were perhaps my friend or companion, nor that I hold him amenable to repaying the good deed with gratitude later on. There is now no time to reason and delay with questions; he is a man, and whatever befalls men, that also concerns me." Then his conduct sustains itself on the highest ground of benevolence in human nature, and is extremely sublime, because of its unchangeability as well as of the universality of its application. (*Observations on the Feeling of the Beautiful and Sublime* 65)

There is always in Kant, to whom I will repeatedly return, a flavor of the ancient Stoic, opposing the mind (to again quote Wordsworth) "strong in itself" to the vagaries of fortune and chance, and what strikes him as sublime is what the Stoic would call sagacity. Wordsworth also entertains the moral agent's sublime inviolability in *The Prelude*, even as he admits a large degree of moral luck in his own moral and poetic formation.

But before turning to *The Prelude*, I would touch upon one last steppingstone to that philosophical song, the blank verse of Mark Akenside. A poetic expatiation on the prose aesthetics of Shaftesbury and Addison, *The Pleasures of Imagination* argues that human beings love the grand and the novel because we are made in God's image and intended by God strenuously to ascend the heights of virtue to become as he is. Humanity's impatience with limits shows us that it is our destiny not to be limited by nature but to act as unconditioned moral beings, and so fulfill our divinely appointed *telos*. Akenside's moral ascent, if not always his implicit theology, echoes through Romantic writing:

Say, why was man so eminently rais'd
Amid the vast creation; why ordain'd
Thro' life and death to dart his piercing eye,
With thoughts beyond the limit of his frame:
But that th' Omnipotent might send him forth
In sight of mortal and immortal pow'rs,
As on a boundless theatre, to run
The great career of justice; to exalt
His gen'rous aim to all diviner deeds;
To chase each partial[5] purpose from his breast;
And thro' the mists of passion and of sense,
And thro' the tossing tide of chance and pain,
To hold his course unfalt'ring, while the voice
Of truth and virtue, up the steep ascent
Of nature, calls him to his high reward,
Th' applauding smile of heav'n? (1:151–66)[6]

Akenside seems close to Kant; it is possible to imagine Kant writing Akenside's lines on humanity's impartial truth and virtue (should Kant have written verse, and in English). In both there is a universalizing abstraction, a debt to the philosophical style of the Stoics. (Wordsworth by middle age inclined toward moral writing in this manner, e.g., in the Wanderer's hymn to God in nature: "Duty exists;—immutably survive,/For our support, the measures and the forms/Which an abstract Intelligence supplies;/Whose kingdom is, where Time and Space are not" [*Excursion* 4:73–76].) Like Kant, Akenside praises actions rather than actors, and for both authors those actions appear more or less inaccessible: Akenside is inclined to locate praiseworthy moral activity in the classical past (the "Genius of ancient Greece!" is the "nurse divine/Of all heroic deeds and fair desires!" [1:565–70]), while Kant admits the empirical possibility that no truly virtuous (i.e., morally motivated) action has ever been performed.

Wordsworth's achievement in *The Prelude* lies in *personalizing* such a moral philosophy, grounding abstract moral activity in individual, more or less particularized life. I say "more or less" advisedly, as *The Prelude* everywhere exhibits a tension between presenting, on the one hand, a general story of the mental and moral development of mankind (the Enlightenment project) and, on the other, a unique history of his own wayward, accidental development as a poet of nature (the Rousseuvian confessional project).[7] A closely related tension in the poem lies between Wordsworth's claims to having arrived, in the years his narrative covers, at what he calls in the "Intimations" *Ode* "the philosophic mind"—one that rises above chance, luck, the inconstancy of external things—and his narrative of having been shaped as a poet and moralist by certain nonreproducible interventions of nature, chance, and history. Thus on one hand he asserts a mind "Strong in itself, and in the access of joy / Which hides it like the overflowing Nile"; a mind secure, at the conclusion of *The Prelude,* from the "revolutions" (in both senses of that term) of history, having become:

> A thousand times more beautiful than the earth
> On which he dwells, above this frame of things
> (Which, 'mid all the revolutions in the hopes
> And fears of men, doth still remain unchanged)
> In beauty exalted, as it is itself
> Of substance and fabric more divine. (13:447–52)

Yet at odds with this philosophic description of mind—or seen alongside it in what Seamus Perry calls Wordsworth's "double focus"[8]—are Wordsworth's hymns to the "one life" that involves all things and thinking things (see chapter 4), as well as his praise of the "numerous accidents in flood or field" (*Prelude* 1799, 1:280) that shaped his own moral education.

However much Wordsworth may speak, like an ancient sage, of having attained intellectual imperviousness to outer circumstances and (to borrow Bernard Williams's terms) "incident luck," he also presents himself as a creature of "constitutive luck" and corporeal grounding.[9] This conflict is due, in good measure, to Wordsworth's vexed attitude toward philosophy itself, which is, *in bono,* the aim and end of *The Prelude* and, *in malo,* the Godwinian force that nearly extinguishes the poet's imaginative existence. Inasmuch as *The Prelude* is a crisis autobiography, its crisis lies in the poet's attempt, in the early course of the French Revolution and then in his turn to Godwin, to subordinate ethics to politics and particularly to an abstracting conception of political justice. The poet's therapeutic cure comes through recollecting how nature (or, less metaphysically, the sensory environments of the Lake District) taught him, or how he imagines it teaching him, morality in the first place.

Morality, then, is for Wordsworth partly immanent in nature. Reviewing his childhood, the poet regains trust that nature can teach by accidents (1805 *Prelude* books 1, 2, 5, 11–12), a repudiation of his earlier attempt, under Godwin's sway, to transcend "accidents of nature, time and place" (10:822).[10] The main moments of growing up, "being fostered alike by beauty and by fear" (1:306, with Wordsworth clearly borrowing Akenside's aesthetic teleology), involve the fear, regret, and perhaps, as David Collings argues (130–37), the masochistic pleasure the boy feels in stealing birds' eggs, trapped birds, and a boat. In all these incidents, elements of the environment either rise up (a craggy steep) or foreground themselves (loud winds, "low breathings" [1:330]) *as if* chastening (as well as exciting) the errant boy. Inasmuch as "nature," or the aesthetic evaluations we feel drawn to make of nature, edify, they do so without saying, as in a requirement ethic, "thou shalt not," and without clearly rising to unconditional laws (e.g., do not steal). Rather they suggest, within specific contexts, certain hypothetical imperatives: when to let be, when to respect the endeavors or self-preservative instincts of other beings.

Finally, the "spots of time" to which Wordsworth recurs in book 11 teach, if they teach anything, to attend to others, including other things, in themselves, in their imaginative strangeness and stark singularity: "The single sheep, and the one blasted tree, / And the bleak music of that old stone wall," a music that, as I've argued earlier (chapter 5), silences the trite moralizing of conscience. The ethics that Wordsworth gleans from nature is not transcendent but radically immanent, and as such sits uneasily (or skeptically) alongside the ideal of moral exertion Wordsworth shared with Priestley and that of moral transcendence he learned from Akenside and perhaps, at a later stage, Kant.

After the 1805 *Prelude,* Wordsworth grew more Kantian (and/or Stoic) in his moral thought. The debt of his fragmentary essay "The Sublime and the Beautiful" (probably written between 1806 and 1812) to Kant's mature aesthetic in his *Critique of Judgment* has been well analyzed by Raimonda Modiano, who traces the movement of Wordsworth's essay away from the sublime of natural form and toward the Kantian sublime of supersensible reason. Modiano recognizes that for Kant sublimity belongs exclusively to the mind, in its ability to think a supersensible totality, although the mind comes to recognize its powers only after an unsuccessful imaginative effort "to encompass nature's magnitude ('the mathematical sublime') or to resist its might ('the dynamical sublime')" (17). But one Kantian note that Modiano misses in Wordsworth is his relation of reason to morality. In "The Sublime and the Beautiful," sublimity requires that the fears produced by absolute power "terminate in repose . . . & that this sense of repose is the result of reason & the moral law" (*Prose Works* 2:355). "The moral law" is new to Wordsworth's lexicon—this is not how the poet imagined his boyhood tutelage by fear in *The Prelude*. Here, though characteristically vague, he seems to imply that without the assurance that reason and law govern God as well as the world, there could be pleasure neither in the idea of God as power nor in those worldly prospects commonly deemed sublime ("a precipice, a conflagration, a torrent, or a shipwreck" [*Prose Works* 2:354]).

For the later Wordsworth—the poet, say, of *Ode to Duty*—the moral law appears to be a necessary condition of the sublime, or at least of the theological sublime. I do not venture to say whether or not Kant would agree. Conversely, however, for Kant beauty and sublimity can contribute to the necessary conditions for morality: "the beautiful prepares us for loving something, even nature, without interest; the sublime, for esteeming it even against our interest (of sense)."[11] That which is to be esteemed—the moral law—cannot technically, in Kant's system, be the object of an aesthetic judgment (because such judgment involves indeterminate, not determinate, concepts). Nevertheless, Kant treats our response to the moral law as analogous to our response to the sublime: once we recognize the moral law as the source of the good and the guide to our duty, we are filled with an awe (of "the moral law within") comparable to our awe in response to the natural world without ("the starry skies above"). Kant writes, "if we judge aesthetically the good that is intellectual and morally purposive (the moral good), we must present it not so much as beautiful but rather as sublime" (*Critique of Judgment*, 132).

LOVING: MOUNT SNOWDON AND *TINTERN ABBEY*

After this excursus into Wordsworth's later, Kantian turn in thinking about the moral sublime, I return to the end of *The Prelude*—and, moving back further, to *Tintern Abbey*—in light of the moral ascent motif we saw in Akenside. Akenside figured ascent in purely metaphorical and metaphysical terms: "the voice / Of truth and virtue, up the steep ascent / Of nature, calls him to his high reward." Wordsworth, far more concretely, offers another route to true love in the mist-shrouded ascent of Mount Snowdon (*Prelude* book 13). The climb begins, significantly, in the place where all ladders start, the turbulent joy of the animal heart:

> Thus did we breast the ascent, and by myself
> Was nothing either seen or heard the while
> Which took me from my musings, save that once
> The shepherd's cur did to his own great joy
> Unearth a hedgehog in the mountain-crags
> Round which he made a barking turbulent. (ll. 20–25)

This glance at dog joy—distanced through Miltonic inversion ("a barking turbulent") and something close to (mock-) epic elevation—symbolically marks the beginning of humanity's ascent over the animal and toward the apotheosis of mind. And yet it serves too (an otherwise gratuitous detail) as a materialist counterpoint and ground to the mind's supersensible musings.

Once the poet attains the mountaintop, he sees a "huge sea of mist" (42) that covers all but a glimpse of the expansive sea below as an image of the creative/ divine mind that transforms the world it perceives and "feeds upon infinity" (70). Critics since Geoffrey Hartman (*Wordsworth's Poetry, 1787–1814* 60–69) have found in this image a partial reconciliation of the transcendent mind and the natural world it inhabits and transforms. But for Wordsworth, the aim and end of the mind made aware of its powers is not simply contemplative but some-how moral, involving "truth in moral judgments; and delight / That fails not, in the external universe" (ll. 118–19). The philosophical reader may wish that Wordsworth had elaborated on what comprises a "true moral judgment," but Wordsworth is never so analytic.

As a moralist he prefers to echo with a generality itself sublime the Christian love ethic announced in Paul's first Epistle to the Corinthians, "Though I speak with the tongues of men and of angels, and have not charity [love], I am become as sounding brass, or a tinkling cymbal" (13:1).[12] Wordsworth's meditation on his moral apprenticeship under "sublime and lovely forms" ends with his learn-ing to love, and with loving as the most sublime act:

> From love, for here
> Do we begin and end, all grandeur comes.
> All truth and beauty—from pervading love—
> That gone, we are as dust. (13:149–52)

The sublime and beautiful in nature lead beyond themselves to a moral senti-ment, "pervading love," that is itself the final cause of the sublime: "from love . . . all grandeur comes, / All truth and beauty." Thus, for Wordsworth, love turns out to be a necessary condition of the sublime (as well as all aes-thetic and veridical judgment), even as the experience of sublimity awakens us to our moral being. This insight is not to be passed over lightly. Love is neces-sary for aesthetic evaluation, because to value is to love. It is necessary as well for philosophy, as the very etymology of that word makes clear (*philia*, "love," + *sophia*, "wisdom"). Without love there can be no good, since the good is an evaluative term by which we orient our desire (and effort, and expectation). Without love there could be no music—to recall another of Wordsworth's keywords—because only love makes music of what would otherwise be mere sound, noise, or tinkling cymbal. "All this waste of music is the voice of love," wrote Thomson, not least because love's voice must call forth music from the wasteland.

Wordsworth immediately continues to describe a ladder of love, in the tradition of Diotima's discourse in Plato's *Symposium* and the ascent from interpersonal (brotherly) love (*philadelphia*) to impersonal love (*agapē*) in the Biblical second Epistle of Peter (1:7):[13]

> Behold the fields
> In balmy springtime, full of rising flowers
> And happy creatures; see that pair, the lamb
> And the lamb's mother, and their tender ways
> Shall touch thee to the heart; in some green bower
> Rest, and be not alone, but have thou there
> The one who is thy choice of all the world—
> There linger, lulled, and lost, and rapt away—
> Happy to thy fill; thou call'st this love,
> And so it is, but there is higher love
> Than this, a love that comes into the heart
> With awe and a diffusive sentiment.
> Thy love is human merely: this proceeds
> More from the brooding soul, and is divine.
>   This love more intellectual cannot be
> Without imagination, which in truth
> Is but another name for absolute strength
> And clearest insight, amplitude of mind,
> And reason in her most exalted mood.
> This faculty hath been the moving soul
> Of our long labour [i.e., *The Prelude*] . . .
> And lastly, from its progress we have drawn
> The feeling of life endless, the one thought
> By which we live, infinity and God.
>   Imagination having been our theme,
> So also hath that intellectual love,
> For they are each in each, and cannot stand
> Dividually. (ll. 152–88)

Imagination allows for higher love by acting as a sympathetic lens into impersonality: that is, into the value of other beings and things we cannot (fully) know, things and persons not connected to and thus personalized for us by the bonds of family, *erōs,* or friendship. Imagination gives us access to things unseen and perhaps, were it not for imagination, inexistent, a prime example being the "one life" the poet recalls feeling when first at seventeen years old,

> To unorganic natures I transferred
> My own enjoyments, or, the power of truth
> Coming in revelation, I conversed
> With things that really are . . . (*Prelude* 2:410–13)

At the end of *The Prelude,* the individual who cultivates imagination and intellectual love is promised a "joy" that, although independent of circumstance, shall nonetheless (however paradoxically) be completed or "perfected," socially and ethically, by "all that friendship, all that love can do" (13:198–204).

The impersonal love ethic Wordsworth espouses has—in its exertion, universality, and unspecificity—an aspect more sublime than the everyday "acts of love," i.e., charity as alms-giving, recounted in *The Old Cumberland Beggar,* or, in *Tintern Abbey,* "that best portion of a good man's life; / His little, nameless, unremembered acts / Of kindness and of love." It recalls, rather, the sublime sentiment of benevolence and forgiveness that Priestley found in the prayer of the crucified Christ—a sentiment much expanded on in a poem dedicated to Priestley (as "Patriot, and Saint, and Sage"), Coleridge's *Religious Musings* (1797), subtitled "Written on the Christmas Eve of 1794." The poem, which Wordsworth admired,[14] lauds "th' oppress'd good Man [Christ], / What time his Spirit with a brother's love / Mourns for th' Oppressor" (ll. 11–13). "Lovely was the Death / Of Him, whose Life was Love!" (28–29), Coleridge pronounces, and then explains the proximity of death (of the self) and love (via God, of all):

> From HOPE and firmer FAITH to perfect LOVE
> Attracted and absorb'd; and center'd there
> GOD only to behold, and know, and feel,
> Till by exclusive Consciousness of God
> All self-annihilated it [the soul] shall make
> GOD its Identity: God all in all!
> We and our Father ONE! (39–45)

"'Tis the sublime of man," Coleridge continues, in a landmark expression of the Romantic moral sublime, "Our noontide Majesty, to know ourselves / Part and proportions of one wond'rous whole! / This fraternizes man, this constitutes / Our charities and bearings" (125–29). The philosophical conclusion of *The Prelude*—which Wordsworth referred to, simply, as "the poem to Coleridge"

(*Prelude* ix)—elaborates on the theological ethics of *Religious Musings* in a less theocentric, more humanistic manner.

Along with *Religious Musings,* the close of *The Prelude* recalls as well *Tintern Abbey,* an earlier poem of a "sense sublime / Of something far more deeply interfused" (ll. 96–7), and the love it engenders:

> Therefore am I still
> A lover of the meadows and the woods,
> And mountains; and of all that we behold
> From this green earth; of all the mighty world
> Of eye and ear, both what they half-create,
> And what perceive; well pleased to recognize
> In nature and the language of the sense,
> The anchor of my purest thoughts, the nurse,
> The guide, the guardian of my heart, and soul
> Of all my moral being. (103–12)

The intuition of transcendent or immanent order is not an end in itself but rather consubstantial with morality—the grand close of this sinuous verse paragraph is "moral being"—and, specifically, with love. What draws me back to *Tintern Abbey* at this point in my argument is a desire to show that the poem's final turn, in its fifth and last verse paragraph, is not so much a fall from religious musing into narcissism—Wordsworth finds a mirror in his sister Dorothy—as a reinscription of divinity *within* the relationship of fraternal ("philadelphian") love, whereby William and Dorothy each, alternately, shepherd the other.

This argument goes against the grain of a widespread critical distaste for the final movement of *Tintern Abbey*. Critics tend to find in the poet's tributary lines to his sister Dorothy both an unappealing condescension and a waning of the lyric intensity (and intense abstraction) found in the poem's earlier rhapsodies to nature and the motion and spirit that impel all things. These charges intertwine in John Barrell's influential 1988 essay, "The Use of Dorothy: 'The Language of the Sense' in 'Tintern Abbey.'" Wordsworth here employs words, Barrell argues, as (borrowing a phrase from Donald Davie) "fiduciary symbols," the meanings of which (e.g., "influences," "powers," "thoughts") are not evident but must be taken by the reader upon trust (*Poetry, Language and Politics* 137–67). In influential eighteenth-century theories of language, including David Hartley's, what guarantees the meaning of the abstract words that derive from the reflection of the mind upon itself—words that Wordsworth piles up in syntactic complexity—is the semantically and syntactically simpler "language of the sense," or of concrete objects, that underwrites it: e.g., "the meadows and the woods, / And mountains." Barrell's essay, in its final turn, accuses Wordsworth of using Dorothy to represent that "language of the sense" and his own abstract distance from it; of arresting her own development toward a language of fiduciary symbols and propositional syntax in order to give a ground to his own. Barrell's conclusion, however, rings false: first, because Dorothy does not speak (reveal her own language) in the poem; and second, because she is in no other way, her "wildness" notwithstanding, associated by the poem's speaker with the "language of the sense" (although an inquirer into the historic Dorothy's scenic journals might be able to make such an association). Both languages are Wordsworth's own, the dual register of his own style.

The language Dorothy *is* associated with in the poem—that which marks her surprising entry into the poem—is that of the King James Bible. Through a Biblical idiom Dorothy appears as the other-as-God, indeed the other whom we're first meant to think is God. Wordsworth conjures this identification by introducing his sister via an allusion to a pastoral psalm, the well-known Psalm 23, "The Lord is my shepherd," specifically to verse 4: "Yea, though I walk through the valley of the shadow of death, I will fear no evil: for thou art with me; thy rod and thy staff they comfort me." After the speaker of *Tintern Abbey* has heard "the still, sad music of humanity," and been moved by "a sense sublime / Of something far more deeply interfused" in all things, he turns to a presence that walks beside him, one that would seem at first to be God (or some person of the triune God):

> Nor, perchance,
> If I were not thus taught, should I the more
> Suffer my genial spirits to decay:
> *For thou art with me,* here, upon the banks
> Of this fair river; thou, my dearest Friend,
> My dear, dear Friend, and in thy voice I catch
> The language of my former heart, and read
> My former pleasures in the shooting lights
> Of thy wild eyes. Oh! Yet a little while
> May I behold in thee what I was once,
> My dear, dear Sister! (ll. 112–22, emphasis mine)

Why does Wordsworth wait seven lines between the King James Bible phrase "thou art with me"—referring here to an unidentified "thou" whose presence has not been anticipated in the first 115 lines of the poem—and the identification of that "thou" as his sister? I think he intends by the force of his allusion to make his readers infer that this "thou" is the Lord, and then Jesus-as-Friend, and only gradually disabuse them of this inference: "thy wild eyes" is the first sign that this reading is probably awry. By the time we discover that those eyes belong to his sister, she has been invested with the office and splendor of the Lord of Psalms. She emerges as a new shepherd or comforter, at once naturalized and numinous.

That the poem's speaker turns in the following lines to comfort his comforter, indemnifying her against the prospect of future ills, registers a final irony with respect to the Psalm we've had in mind, a final deconstruction of the hierarchical relation between shepherd and sheep, lord and servant. The speaker here assures his sister that a feminized nature (no longer the Lord of Hosts) can (in this valley of the shadow of death) quell the fear of evil or, as he puts it,

> so impress
> With quietness and beauty, and so feed
> With lofty thoughts, that neither evil tongues,
> Rash judgments, nor the sneers of selfish men,
> Nor greetings where no kindness is, nor all
> The dreary intercourse of daily life,
> Shall e'er prevail against us, or disturb
> Our cheerful faith that all which we behold
> Is full of blessings. (127–35)

Wordsworth's "evil tongues" that shall not prevail come, textually, from Milton's proem to book 7 of *Paradise Lost*: "More safe I sing with mortal voice, unchang'd / To hoarse or mute, though fall'n on evil days, / On evil days though fall'n, *and evil tongues;* / . . . yet not alone, while thou [the epic muse Urania] / Visit'st my slumbers Nightly" (ll. 24–29). Wordsworth imagines into being similarly evil tongues and times, as proof of what he and Dorothy can withstand as long as they stand firm in their religion of love-in-nature. And to underscore that theirs is a religion and a calling, Wordsworth's catalogue of negations ("neither . . . nor . . . nor . . . nor")—of all that will not render them apostate—is modeled, as Michael Vander Weele argues (24), on a Pauline passage concerning the perseverance of the saints in the love of God: "Who shall separate us from the love of Christ? . . . For I am persuaded, that neither death, nor life, nor angels, nor principalities, nor powers, nor things present, nor things to come, nor height, nor depth, nor any other creature, shall be able to separate us from the love of God, which is in Christ Jesus our Lord" (Romans

8:35, 38–39). Wordsworth deploys scriptural allusion in crafting his opposi-tional (or complementary) religion, elevating alternately the other (as the good shepherd) and the self (as nature's prophet) to the perch of lovingkindness God alone once occupied. Alluding to Dorothy first as his Lord, and then cast-ing her as one who (as a younger version of himself) needs shielding from evil, Wordsworth expresses their mutual friendship and love through oscillating asymmetries, turning the rigid verticality of theological ethics into a seesaw.[15]

THE DIVINIZING SUBLIME, THE SAPPHIC SUBLIME, AND *LAODAMIA*

I trust I've shown Wordsworth's proximity to eighteenth-century British writ-ing on the sublime, with its ethical and theological concerns, as well as—to re-trieve an earlier thread of this chapter—to Kant's writings on the sublime, which are, again, closely related to his writings on morals. What I hope to do now is reformulate the critical paradigm of "the Romantic sublime," working ultimately toward a broad revisioning of the sublime in the Romantic period,[16] and immediately toward a framework with which to accommodate Words-worth's *Laodamia* (1815), a work recognized in its day as "Pindaric" (that is, sub-lime) in its "current of rich and bright thoughts" and "vigour."[17]

Till now, criticism on the British Romantic sublime has neglected, even in its numerous glances and side glances at the Kantian sublime, the degree to which the sublime and morality are intertwined. For the later twentieth cen-tury, the seminal work on the Romantic sublime was Thomas Weiskel's *The Romantic Sublime: Studies in the Structure and Psychology of Transcendence* (1976, reissued 1986). Subsequent criticism on the Romantic and post-Romantic sub-lime has drawn heavily upon it, more often than not accepting its main points (especially those about Kant) uncritically.[18] While it is a brilliant work, the time has come to look beyond it, toward elements of the sublime that it has ob-scured: two I would emphasize are first, the sublime's relation to ethics, and second, its deep roots in Longinus and his reception over time. Weiskel con-cedes that there might be an "ethic of sublimity" only to dismiss it as total alien-ation from the world, a suicidal posture (44–48)—a dismissal which involves a curious flattening of his source for this "ethic," Schiller's essay *On the Sublime*. Schiller, developing Kant's notion of moral autonomy, takes freedom from external determination to a metaphoric extreme in writing that when con-fronted by death a man can "by a free renunciation of all sensuous interest . . . *kill himself morally* before some physical force does it" (208, emphasis mine).

Schiller's emphasis, however, is not on suicide but on morality's preeminence over individual life. Indeed, his larger argument is that the sublime is properly a feature of morality, "the absolute moral capacity which is not bound to any natural condition" (201).

For Weiskel, Wordsworth embodies the mainstream of the Romantic sublime, which he calls (after Keats) the "egotistical sublime" or, alternatively, the "positive sublime." This facet of the sublime involves perceiving all things as an extension of, or subservient to, the self. Its psychoanalytic equivalent, according to Weiskel, is primary narcissism. By contrast, the "negative" sublime involves losing oneself, either in supersensuous reason (Kant's mathematical sublime) or in attempted empathy with an external object (e.g., Keats's effort to merge with the nightingale of his great ode). Psychoanalytically, the negative sublime (at least in its Kantian mode) mimics the child's response to Oedipal anxiety, turning away from its attachment to sensible objects and toward an (paternal) ideal of totality and power that it then internalizes (83).

There are various problems with this schema: one might question the usefulness of Weiskel's psychoanalytic framework, and I have already questioned the validity of designating the Wordsworthian sublime as egotistical. Still, Weiskel's antinomy between a positive and negative sublime holds up quite well. This is so in part because the sublime has always been constituted by antinomies. Thus Longinus presents the sublime as both a rhetorical mode and as a feature of the natural world—the grandeur and danger embodied, for example, in the ocean and in volcanoes (section 35). In another antinomy, the rhetorical sublime derives from inspiration (the sublime speaker possessed by a god) but also from craft (the sublime is a skill that may be acquired). But we have yet to appreciate the antinomy in Longinus between—to retroject Weiskel's categories—a positive and a negative sublime. Longinus holds, on the one hand, that the sublime "lifts [great writers] near the mighty mind of God" (section 36)—the sublime as apotheosis. And yet he implies, on the other hand, that the sublime involves—in Sappho's poem, "*phainetai moi*," quoted and preserved for us by Longinus (section 10)—an entire loss of self, a loss that begins by standing *apart* from one who seems a god (it is the man who sits by the speaker's beloved that "seems to me equal to the gods" in the poem's opening line)[19] and ends in the speaker's ecstasy, "near to death," inspired by the sound of her beloved's voice. Sappho's speaker, led beyond the senses ("I see nothing with my eyes, and my ears thunder"), unites with a dehumanized current of organic life, turning "*chlōrotera*"—the Greek comparative adjective here being variously translated as "paler," "greener," or "moister" than grass.

Here is the Loeb translation of Sappho's linguistically challenging poem:

I think him God's peer that sits near you face to face,
And listens to your sweet speech and lovely laughter.
It's this that makes my heart flutter in my breast.
If I see you but for a little, my voice comes no more
And my tongue is broken.
At once a delicate flame runs through my limbs;
I see nothing with my eyes, and my ears thunder.
The sweat pours down: shivers grip me all over.
I am grown paler than grass, and seem to myself to be very near to death.

Longinus praises Sappho's poem (in a judgment that was often echoed in the eighteenth century)[20] for unifying in "one body" (*hen sōma*) the contradictory sensations of erotic love—burning, shivering, etc.—although the poem, at least in the fragmentary state in which he reproduces it, expresses self-fragmentation or annihilation more than (as the Loeb translators render Longinus's Greek) "an organic whole" or "a single whole" (199–201).

What, then, is the Longinian sublime—the divinization, or the negation, of the self? It may suffice to say that Longinus exhibits a talent for dualism, one bequeathed to later aesthetics. This particular antinomy, however, was regarded as a problem in eighteenth-century British aesthetics. For if the sublime *must* display the power of a god-like mind—as in the line from Genesis that Longinus adduces, "God said, let there be light; and there was light" (section 9)—then "he seems to me equal to the gods" cannot (at least in its content) be a sublime poem. Longinus may have erred in calling it one. According to this logic, the influential rhetorician Hugh Blair labels Sappho's poem not sublime but "merely elegant," while Lord Kames calls it "beautiful"—a term, after Burke, designating the antithesis of the sublime. "Beautiful it is undoubtedly," writes Kames, "but it cannot be sublime, because it really depresses the mind instead of raising it."[21]

This theoretical problem identified in eighteenth-century aesthetics was resolved in practice by the British Romantics, who develop what Weiskel will call the positive and negative sublime from a conceptual antinomy already apparent in Longinus. Following Longinus, the Romantics recognize not only a sublime of self-elevation but also one of self-loss. And the label "Sapphic sublime" is more apt for a good many Romantic lyrics than Weiskel's capacious "negative sublime" (anything able to fit both Kant and Keats is a wide berth indeed).[22]

Consider, for example, Shelley's lyric "To Constantia," which, like Sappho's poem, concerns a loss of self in response to hearing a beloved's voice (here accompanied by music):

> My brain is wild, my breath comes quick,
> The blood is listening in my frame,
> And thronging shadows fast and thick
> Fall on my overflowing eyes,
> My heart is quivering like a flame;
> As morning dew, that in the sunbeam dies,
> I am dissolved in these consuming extacies.

Wordsworth never wrote anything so Sapphic himself, but he does dramatize the antinomy of a self-dissolving and a divinizing sublime in *Laodamia*. The story behind his poem is based on a variety of classical sources: John Lemprière's important *Classical Dictionary* [1788] cites Virgil's *Aeneid* 6, Ovid's *Heroides* epistle 13, and the Augustan mythographer Hyginus. It concerns Protesilaus, the Greek whose ship was first to land on the shores of Troy and who, trusting the prophecy that the first hero to leap from the ships would be slain, chose to confront Hector and die by his hands. The gods of the underworld allow him three hours to visit his grieving widow, Laodamia, in his native Thessaly (Wordsworth, for dramatic effect, whittles these hours down to what seems a few minutes), and when he again departs Laodamia commits suicide. In Wordsworth's poem, Laodamia is as ardent as Sappho's speaker, assaying repeatedly—and impossibly—to embrace Protesilaus's shade, enchanted by his appearance: "Redundant are thy locks, thy lips as fair / As when their breath enriched Thessalian air" (ll. 59–60).[23] Laodamia stands apart from the man who seems to her a god, able only to hear his voice; Protesilaus admonishes her, philosophically, to bridle her passions in anticipation of the "equable and pure" happiness that awaits her in Elysium.

Yet *Laodamia*, as Wordsworth originally published it, proves far from didactic, the type of Stoic sermon it more closely resembles after 1827 revisions, without ever fitting Christopher Wordsworth's image of the poem as teaching "the subordination of what is sensual to what is spiritual, and the subjection of the human passions to the government of reason" (2:66). In 1815, and to some degree after Wordsworth's later revisions, the poem vindicates neither the dissolving Laodamia nor the "god-like" Protesilaus. Rather, it attenuates the antinomy that would seem to separate them—a key antinomy, as I have been arguing, of the Longinian sublime.

It does this, first of all, by presenting Protesilaus as incoherent (this hits the mark better, I think, than attributing the incoherence to Wordsworth's presentation). He is given as much to passion as to philosophy, preaching, with Homer, the self-devotion of the heroic ethos and, with Plato (and Coleridge), self-annulment in the higher love. Compare his account of his heroic death (first quotation) with his sage advice to the passionate Laodamia (second):

> "Thou know'st, the Delphic oracle foretold
> That the first Greek who touch'd the Trojan strand
> Should die; but me the threat did not withhold:
> A generous cause a Victim did demand;
> And forth I leapt upon the sandy plain;
> A *self-devoted Chief*—by Hector slain." (42–47, my emphasis)

> "Learn by a mortal yearning to ascend
> Towards a higher object:—Love was given,
> Encouraged, sanctioned, chiefly for this end,
> For this the passion to excess was striven—
> That *self might be annulled*; her bondage prove
> The fetters of a dream, opposed to love." (145–50, my emphasis)

The seeming paradox here might be resolved by appeal to gender difference: self-devotion is good for heroes, self-annulment good for wives. But any such simple opposition is undermined by the ironies with which the poem abounds. First, Protesilaus's self-devotion *is* self-annulment: in choosing glory (the tale he will become), he chooses death. But the self he was he can be no more, for him at least (as distinct from his tale's auditors), amidst the "happier beauty" of Elysium, a world without conflict (104). Second, whether or not on the ladder of love, Laodamia's self, at least her earthly self, *is* annulled: with Protesilaus's departure, she dies (Wordsworth glosses over the immediate cause of her death). But does even this death annul her self, or keep it alive, in the Elysium that she too enters? And is she, too, "self-devoted"? Her erotic devotion to her dead husband may or may not count, in Protesilaus's terms, as self-devotion that must be overcome by a higher love.

A final question: which spouse's moral attachments, finally, are more virtuous, strenuous—and sublime? Wordsworth, in 1815, calls it a draw, admitting both heroic-philosophic husband and erotic-suffering wife into heaven.

> He through the portal [to the underworld] takes his silent way—
> And on the palace-floor a lifeless corse she lay.

> Ah, judge her gently who so deeply loved!
> Her, who, in reason's spite, yet without crime,
> Was in a trance of passion thus removed;
> Delivered from the galling yoke of time
> And these frail elements to gather flowers
> Of blissful quiet amid unfading bowers. (156–63)

Laodamia's unreasonable passion, be it self-devotion or self-annulment, is here rewarded alongside the equally ambiguous ethics of her husband.

Yet Wordsworth's evenhanded concession to the competing demands of the Sapphic and the heroic sublime met with stern opposition from a surprising source—Mary Wordsworth, the poet's wife. According to Benjamin Robert Haydon, Mary persuaded Wordsworth that he had given Laodamia *"too lenient a fate* for loving her Husband so *absurdly."*[24] By 1820 Wordsworth drafted this new ending:

> By no weak pity might the Gods be moved;
> She who thus perished not without the crime
> Of Lovers that in Reason's spite have loved,
> Was doomed to wander in a grosser clime,
> Apart from happy Ghosts—that gather flowers
> Of blissful quiet 'mid unfading bowers.

This belated punishment of Laodamia might seem a clear case of reason's triumph over erotic devotion, as well as Mary's cool conquest over her husband's Sapphic sympathy, were it not accompanied in Haydon's diary by the following circumstance: "While Wordsworth repeated this [revised stanza] in his chaunting tone, his wife sat by the Fire quite abstracted, moaning out the burthen of the line, like a distant echo. I never saw such a complete instance of devotion, of adoration." Sappho may have been evicted from Wordsworth's poem but not from his parlor. Like Ovid's Echo, attenuated with desire, Mary becomes a distant echo of her Narcissus-like husband's words; like the speaker of Sappho's *phainetai moi* she sits at a remove from the enchanting sounds enjoyed at greater proximity by another (here, Haydon). Like Laodamia, Mary might seem to love her husband to the loss of self—and yet, as with Laodamia, her self-loss may also be, paradoxically, self-devotion. The stanza she chants is, after all, one that she persuaded her spouse to write.

THE ETHICS AND POLITICS OF THE SUBLIME

If *Laodamia* had earlier been inducted into the canon of sublime literature, it would have been subject to interrogation by two post-Weiskel schools of criticism: New Historicism and feminism. The first of these would have rooted out its (mystified) political-historical commitments; the latter would have judged it according to its representation of Laodamia, of course, but also according to its amenability to a normative feminist ethics of care.[25] At the risk of oversimplifying, let me venture this binary: the New Historicism politicized, while feminism "ethicized," the sublime. New Historicism, which I'll consider first, deconstructed the opposition between individual transcendence and, the occluded term that becomes primary, the historical and political conditions the individual seeks to transcend. For New Historicists, political and economic events are the "real" beneath the superstructure of art, what really matters; at moments they inspire awe. Thus for Ronald Paulson many of the seemingly apolitical but emotionally charged episodes of *The Prelude* (e.g., dreaming of a deluge, recalling a father's death) are an allegorical coming to terms with the sublime of the French Revolution (248–75). Alan Liu reads Napoleon and the course of his wars with England as the real if unconscious historical referent of Wordsworth's apostrophe to the Imagination in book 6 of *The Prelude*, a reading that has the virtue of accounting for Wordsworth's curious imagery of "usurpation," "banners militant," "spoils or trophies," and—a contested terrain in the Napoleonic wars—"the overflowing Nile."

One could presumably extend such a reading to *Laodamia*, with Protesilaus a "happy warrior" stand-in for Admiral Nelson (a hero Wordsworth much admired), or the imperatives of English empire, and Laodamia a metonymy for the domestic attachments that must be taught to bend rather than break before a new cult of honorable bloodshed. In anticipation of such a reading, David Simpson grounds the Romantic sublime of transcendence in the industrialism and territorial conquest of the early nineteenth century: "The connection between an aesthetics of infinitude and an historical experience founded in expansion (coded positively as 'progress') is so obvious as to seem trite, but we have hardly begun to follow through its implications" ("Commentary: Updating the Sublime" 246).

As crucially as the New Historicism revised our understanding of the Romantics, it left one of Weiskel's earlier assumptions unshaken: namely, that the ethical is structurally unnecessary to any discussion of the Romantic sublime. In deconstructing the opposition between the individual and the political, New Historicist critics established a new opposition between the political (the privileged term) and the (parasitic) ethical; with political and/or economic causes in the ascendant, the ethical—the realm of moral value as it pertains to oneself and one's relations to others—is reduced to a superstructural illusion or ideological screen. Fredric Jameson did much to set the agenda for the New Historicism when, in *The Political Unconscious* (1981), he opposed history and "collective life" to "the purely individualizing categories of ethics" (116). Jameson argues "that only the [Marxist] dialectic provides a way for 'decentering' the subject concretely, and for transcending the 'ethical' in the direction of the political and the collective" (60). Seeing Christian eschatology as a sign or "type" of secular historical process, Jameson imagines an apocalyptic future in which "the collective" will be free from all necessity, be it natural, material, or ethical (281–99). I would argue, however, that Jameson's is an irreducibly ethical vision, oriented toward (as he sees it) a future good; history can no more be uprooted from ethics than ethics can be uprooted from history. But in the absence of a strong argument for the inextricability of ethics and politics—one that might be derived, incidentally, from Longinus, who at the end of his treatise interweaves ethical and political conditions for sublime literature—the New Historicist demotion of ethics has largely been unchallenged in the post-1980s discussion of the Romantic sublime.[26]

The feminist approach to the sublime is, by contrast, an ethical one, although its practitioners tend not to challenge explicitly the priority given to political and economic causes by a regnant New Historicism. Anne K. Mellor's 1993 *Romanticism and Gender* ushered into Romantic studies the concept of a "feminine sublime." Mellor opposes to the sublime of Kant and Wordsworth, which she associates with "masculine empowerment" (85), a feminine sublime in which nature is not transcended but rather salvaged as a space for joy in God and the other, adducing this latter mode in works by Ann Radcliffe, Helen Maria Williams, Susan Ferrier, and Sydney Owensen. In the last two authors Mellor loosely associates the feminine sublime with a Celtic sublime and associates both with "human morality. . . . For Ferrier, as for Morgan, the experience of a sublime landscape should produce a sense of participation in a human community" (103). While I approve of Mellor's impulse to reconcile ethics and aesthetics—an impulse Mellor shares with other canny advocates of a feminine sublime[27]—I cannot endorse a simple dichotomy between an immoral masculine and a moral feminine sublime.[28]

My own interest lies in suggesting the fundamental ethical concerns of Wordsworth in his sublime poems and passages, which do not prove masculine in any simple, antique, or "Protesilean" way but, rather, more closely resemble feminist ethics in their emphasis on face-to-face relations, the response to vulnerability, and conditioned or (in Kant's terminology) "hypothetical" imperatives (i.e., what we ought to do is not wholly independent of nonmoral motives or the particular circumstances in which we find ourselves). The contrastive justice-view of morality (a view that blurs ethics and politics)—everyone ought to be rewarded or punished according to merits or demerits that are or ought to be clearly known—that feminist ethicists seek to decenter is also, as we have seen (in chapter 2), one that Wordsworth sidelined with his turn from Godwin in the mid-1790s and in his pioneering poetry of interpersonal encounter. He reintroduces justice-morality in his revisions to *Laodamia* only at the urging of his wife, and even here Laodamia is not punished for her positive culpability but only for being, in excusing litotes, "not without crime." Wordsworth evidently cares for Laodamia, even while banishing her from paradise.

"Wisdom doth live with children around her knees" is the advice the poet offers to magistrates who, unlike the grievous "Buonaparte," would be "wise and good."[29] Wordsworth's sublime is rooted, on the one hand, in the admirable expenditure of love freely tendered to the supplicant child; on the other, in the infant's own imaginative creation of a coherent world, a mental process or coming-into-being ("something evermore about to be"), anterior to the need for "spoils or trophies," or "aught / That may attest its prowess." Both aspects of the sublime originate, for Wordsworth, in the dyadic relationship of infant and mother. Edmund Burke, in his empiricist theory of the sublime and beautiful, classified love and female form itself under the latter category and described the effects of all beautiful objects and relations to be enervating or narcotic, in contrast to the bracing effects of the sublime.[30] Wordsworth, by contrast, treats maternal love not as beautiful and relaxing but as commanding and organizational. There is a "discipline of love," and the child is, in all senses of the term, its "subject": subjected to it, he becomes an agent or subject through it.

> Blessed the infant babe—
> For with my best conjectures I would trace
> The progress of our being—blest the babe
> Nursed in his mother's arms, the babe who sleeps
> Upon his mother's breast, who, when his soul
> Claims manifest kindred with an earthly soul,
> Doth gather passion from his mother's eye.
> Such feelings pass into his torpid life

> Like an awakening breeze, and hence his mind,
> Even in the first trial of its powers,
> Is prompt and watchful, eager to combine
> In one appearance all the elements
> And parts of the same object, else detached
> And loth to coalesce. Thus day by day
> Subjected to the discipline of love,
> His organs and recipient faculties
> Are quickened, are more vigorous; his mind spreads,
> Tenacious of the forms which it receives
> In one beloved presence . . . (*Prelude* 2:237–55)

Love is an active power that *attaches* parts ("else detached") into wholes, and the child to a world of integral forms and objects he partly brings into being ("his mind . . . / Creates, creator and receiver both," 271–73), making it in a phenomenological sense "his world." Love, in Wordsworth's telling, has the sublime power of the God of Genesis to create a world, albeit not *ex nihilo* but rather from elements that coalesce because irradiated by love, "one beloved presence."

The spark that illuminates a world comes from the "mother's eye" in an originative face-to-face encounter. This primal dyadic encounter will continue on as the ground of Wordsworth's moral being, even as a quasi-personified, feminized "nature" replaces the mother whom Wordsworth lost at a young age, and even as other Others enter his purview on the public roads. ("Nature," like mother before her, "hath a power / To consecrate—if we have eyes to see—/ The outside of her creatures, and to breathe / Grandeur upon the very humblest face / Of human life" [12:282–86].) The disorientating effect London has upon him, as Wordsworth recounts in book 7 of *The Prelude*, derives precisely from the relative unavailability of isolated face-to-face, one-on-one encounters of the type he could rely on in his native Westmorland, "where if we meet a face / We almost meet a friend" (12:141–42). In London, the dyadic "face to face" gives way to a sequential and dehumanizing "face after face":

> Here, there, and everywhere, a weary throng,
> The comers and the goers face to face—
> Face after face—the string of dazzling wares
> Shop after shop . . . (171–73)

The easy slide from "face after face" to "shop after shop," along with the following catalogue of shop signs, make the urban face seem a commodity like anything else, lifeless, fungible, deprived of uniqueness or aura. Wordsworth makes no attempt to totalize or transcend this seeming infinity of faces, as Ezra Pound would in Paris some hundred and odd years later:

> The apparition of these faces in the crowd;
> Petals on a wet, black bough. ("In a Station of the Metro")

Wordsworth does not unify or metaphorically reconfigure the city. He instead winds his way through it with a cataloguing eye, in a gentler-than-Juvenalian mode, until it leads him to a scene recalled, in a later reconsideration of London ("that vast abiding place," 8:837), as the everyday sublime, centered on the mother's eye, although here it belongs to a man:

> 'Twas a man,
> Whom I saw sitting in an open square
> Close to the iron paling that fenced in
> The spacious grass-plot: on the corner-stone
> Of the low wall in which the pales were fixed
> Sat this one man, and with a sickly babe
> Upon his knee, whom he had thither brought
> For sunshine, and to breathe the fresher air.
> Of those who passed, and me who looked at him,
> He took no note; but in his brawny arms
> (The artificer was to the elbow bare,
> And from his work this moment had been stolen)
> He held the child, and bending over it
> As if he were afraid, both of the sun
> And of the air which he had come to seek,
> He eyed it with unutterable love. (8:844–59)

Unlike the "infant babe" passage, here the perspective assumed is not the infant's but the mothering man's—or, more precisely, the perspective of the narrator/Wordsworth eyeing the man who eyes the child with what seems like "unutterable love." At each remove in this chain (and we may add our own remove as readers from the narrator's presentation), the other is not reduced to a finite magnitude, a comprehensible object, but rather granted an unknowable "infinity," in a Levinasian sense. The sublimity of the man's apparent love ("this one man," his nonfungible singularity insisted upon) increases with the opacity of his relation to the child: the narrator scrupulously calls it "*a* sickly babe," "*the* child," never "*his* child." Familial love thus shades in Wordsworth's lines into the more broadly interpersonal or even impersonal. The scene causes us to revise our reading of the earlier "Blest the infant babe" passage—for here, maternity proves a structural not a biological position—even as it recalls compositionally earlier scenes of male mothering: the shepherd Michael who cares for his infant Luke with "female service" (*Michael* l. 164); the farmer Walter Ewbank who cares for his two orphaned grandsons with "a mother's heart" (*The Brothers* l. 237).[31]

My announced framework in this section is the ethics and politics of the sublime, and if I've demonstrated the love or care ethics that abides in Wordsworth's poetry—hopefully to the satisfaction of feminist readers, and to the confusion of any proposed antinomy between masculine and feminine sublimes—I have yet to uncover a politics of the sublime in Wordsworth. Indeed, by insisting on Wordsworth's ethics of interpersonal encounter, even in his poetry on London, I may seem to concede his aversion to the very ground of politics in the *polis*, in the organization of human beings in mass. Yet I believe that a politics is suggested in at least some of Wordsworth's poems of encounter, and I will use here as my test case the blind beggar episode of *The Prelude* book 7.

This beggar, as part and emblem of London life, marks a crisis point for Wordsworth. Here is the Other who cannot be welcomed, who forecloses the possibility of dialogue by revealing to the narrator that all we know of one another *and of ourselves* are dead letters that advertise rather than explain. Here is the Other who cannot be assisted, both because he embodies in himself the misery of masses and because he repulses the speaker as a figure for his own self-blindness, stultifying the autobiographical and moral project of *The Prelude*. And here, where ethics reaches its limit, is where an unimaginable horizon— "another world"—comes into play.

>   'twas my chance
> Abruptly to be smitten with the view
> Of a blind beggar, who, with upright face,
> Stood propped against a wall, upon his chest
> Wearing a written paper, to explain
> The story of the man, and who he was.
> My mind did at this spectacle turn round
> As with the might of waters; and it seemed
> To me that in this label was a type
> Or emblem of the utmost we can know
> Both of ourselves and of the universe,

And on the shape of this unmoving man,

His fixèd face and sightless eyes, I looked,

As if admonished from another world. (7:610–23)

The end of Wordsworth's paragraph—which is also the end of his world—arrives with two unsettled and unsettling questions: admonished to do or refrain from doing *what*, and from *what* other world? Presumably, the narrator is admonished that *something* must be done for the man (his name, in London, is legion) whose face imparts no passion, dispels no torpidity—that is, who cannot be engaged ethically, who falls outside any compass of love. The force of this end-of-the-line face is apocalyptic, destroying the world Wordsworth created through his mother's love just as the "flood of waters" destroyed Noah's world (Genesis 6:17), "the mighty waters" destroyed the Egyptian army (Exodus 15:10), and "the floods of great waters" destroy the unconverted soul (Psalms 32:6). The other world that newly orients Wordsworth is, anagogically, the new heavens and new earth of Revelation. Politically, it is "the Utopia of a thousand years to come" that Whipple foresaw in Wordsworth, "when universal benevolence will prevail upon the earth." Yet, as William Galperin notes, Wordsworth is admonished not from another world but "as if . . . from another world." The new earth, or political utopia, may simply be a different way of looking at this world, in its materiality and shared everydayness, without the strictures of "my world"—"more a matter of perspective than a matter of either fact or imagination."[32] Still, it remains a sublimely undefined place in or from which wrongs can be rectified, and needs alleviated, when these things cannot be done by individual love and exertion, however sublime.

CHAPTER EIGHT

Independence and Interdependence

In February 1805, shortly before Wordsworth completed *The Prelude,* his be-
loved brother John died in the wreck of his merchant ship, the *Earl of Aber-
gavenny.* John's death was a severe blow, and more blows would follow: 1812, a
particularly difficult year in Wordsworth's personal life, saw the fraying of his
relationship with Coleridge and the death of two of his youngest children,
Catherine, not yet four years old, and Thomas, six. These biographical traumas
inform, in part, his 1814 poem, *The Excursion*—the poem that was, to many of
Wordsworth's late Georgian and Victorian admirers, his supreme achieve-
ment.[1] *The Excursion* is a poem that, in its moral thinking as well as its poetic
style, provides a remedy to loss and a prophylactic against further loss. Philo-
sophically, it inculcates a stoic ideal of independence: independence from for-
tune's wheel, immoderate passions, "partial purposes" (to recall Akenside's
phrase), and irrational attachment to those we love.

The poem's *Stoic aesthetic,* as I shall call it, variously aims at a refinement and
correction of feeling and a displacement of feeling by immutable *duty*—a word
with new prominence in Wordsworth's moral lexicon. In the character of the
Solitary, Wordsworth represents the ills of uncorrected feeling: the Solitary
suffers from an undue dependency on other persons and an inordinate hope in
institutions to provide what he cannot provide for himself. Wordsworth, far
from becoming "a slave"—as Mary Shelley famously quipped upon reading *The
Excursion (Journals* 1:25)[2]—remains passionately committed to the analysis
and poetic endorsement of true freedom. Yet alongside the premium *The Excur-
sion* places on independence, it impresses as well the interdependency of all
things, including literary things: its dialogic framework assumes the importance
of intellectual exchange and shared knowledge; its stylistic reliance on the gen-
eral and commonplace bespeaks its own debts to earlier literatures, classical
and neoclassical, Chaucerian and Miltonic.

This chapter, which culminates in a reading of *The Excursion,* begins with a preliminary consideration of the Stoic aesthetic Wordsworth developed in the first decade of the nineteenth century, along with readings of two poems key to that development: *Resolution and Independence* and *Ode to Duty.* This development, as I call it, has been less generously dubbed "Wordsworth's anti-climax" by twentieth-century critics who see in the poet's work after his "great decade" (1797–1807) a precipitous decline of imaginative and expressive power.[3] The partial recuperation of Wordsworth's post-1807 poetry inaugurated by William Galperin in *Revision and Authority in Wordsworth* (1989), and extended by critics including Mark Canuel and Sally Bushell, involves more an ideological than a poetic defense: appreciated for its communitarian leanings, including its consolidating, allegedly nonsectarian use of religion, Wordsworth's later poetry is seen to deconstruct the individualistic Romantic humanism (or "Romantic ideology") that, arguably, comes into being less in Wordsworth's poems of the great decade than in post-Victorian criticism of those poems. This revisionist history of Wordsworth's career strikes me as crucial, although its ethical-political model of community versus individual is finally too broad to accommodate the nuance of Wordsworth's achievement. While his later work, stylistically as well as thematically, does have a strong communitarian aspect, it also advances the Stoic— and liberal—inviolability of the individual. In this and the following two chapters, I attend to the finer details of what Wordsworth accomplished, ethically as well as stylistically, in the poetry he wrote from his thirties to his late seventies.

A STOIC AESTHETIC

What did Wordsworth think he was doing in his writings of the first decade of the nineteenth century? A short answer would be: better conforming to Stoicism, specifically to the civic-minded Roman Stoicism of Cicero and Seneca and their modern heir, Shaftesbury. Conversations with Coleridge about Kantian ethics would influence Wordsworth as well, but as with prior conversations about Spinoza, postclassical philosophy interests Wordsworth chiefly as a way of filling in certain blanks or of clarifying uncertain passages in his ancient sources (e.g., how can God and nature be one? What is the moral law, and what might motivate us to obey it?). Throughout this book I have intermittently traced Wordsworth's Stoic debts, from *The Cumberland Beggar* and *The Discharged Soldier* to *Tintern Abbey,* emphasizing the affective state of rational joy associated with, on the one hand, the habitual practice of benevolence and, on the other, the perception of the unity of things (the one life, the unity of God and nature, the causal necessity of all physical events). Since "whatever is, is right" at the level of eternal nature if not of political arrangement (albeit the two levels are not always easily extricable), there is magnanimity in not murmuring against one's condition—a magnanimity on display in Wordsworth's sonnet on the African woman exiled from France (chapter 3).

"Independence" and "independent" play substantial and positive roles in Wordsworth's poetic lexicon, especially as his ethics come to accord more fully with Stoicism. "Dependent," by contrast, is rare, and "dependency" (singular or plural) is used *only* of humanity's relation to "godhead": "Man," "instinct [imbued]/With godhead," acknowledges "dependency sublime" (*Prelude* 8:640; cf. "our sublime dependencies" of *The Excursion* 5:240). The phrase implies that dependency on anything less than a God of which we instinctively feel ourselves to be part is not sublime but servile. And yet from this one good dependency—on the God immanent in (or identical to) all things—there follows the good of *interdependence,* a word Wordsworth does not use (although the OED traces the term back to Coleridge) but that nonetheless provides a useful middle term between the independence Wordsworth applauds and the dependence he conspicuously reserves for God alone. In the cosmos as Wordsworth understands it, at least until his conversion to orthodox Christianity (Jesus first enters his poetry in the late 1820s), all things are interdependent. Nothing can come of nothing: nothing (not even God) stands alone, nothing controls its own being, nothing is self-established.

Yet dependence on particular others—others who, like us, suffer and die—is eschewed in Wordsworth's poetry. As Nancy Yousef has shown, Wordsworth largely (though incompletely) conceals in his quasi-autobiographical *Prelude* his actual dependence on others, including his parents, presenting himself as developing in solitude, organically and as if botanically, from "fair seed-time" (1:305) to poetic flourishing (*Isolated Cases* 117–21).[4] I believe that this concealment, however, has less to do with Wordsworth's anxieties about social dependency, or even his cryptomisanthropy—however real these facets of Wordsworth's personality may be—and more to do with the heuristic goal of making his readers imagine, counterintuitively, what moral independence might feel like, an independence complemented only by "dependency sublime" and one's interdependence with energies less personalized, and more comprehensive, than mother and father, sister and brother.

Such a goal is implied in a letter of 1802, written to the Glaswegian student John Wilson, in which Wordsworth lays claim to a modified Stoic program for poetry: "You have given me praise for having reflected faithfully in my poems the feelings of human nature. . . . But a great Poet ought to do more than this [,] he ought to a certain degree to rectify men's feelings, to give them new compositions of feeling, to render their feelings more sane, pure, and permanent, in short, more consonant to nature, that is, to eternal nature, and the great moving spirit of things" (*Letters* 1:355). In advancing what we may call a Stoic *aesthetics*— in Hegel's sense, a "science of sensation, of feeling"[5]—Wordsworth elaborates two well-known tags of classical antiquity: the Stoic credo "live according to nature,"[6] and the Stoic-inflected lines of Virgil's beginning *felix qui potuit rerum cognoscere causas* (*Georgics* 2:490f.), "happy he who can know the cause of things," which are rendered by Dryden: "Happy the man, who, studying nature's laws, / Thro' known effect can trace the secret cause; / His mind possessing, in a quiet state, / Fearless of fortune, and resigned to fate!" (*Georgics* 2:698–701).

The aesthetics Wordsworth announces to Wilson is not out of keeping with that announced in his Preface to *Lyrical Ballads,* where morality is taught not directly, by precept or obvious example, but indirectly, by enlightening the understanding and ameliorating the affections (*Lyrical Ballads* 745). But here the affections are purified, in a more clearly Stoic way, by being brought into conformity with eternal nature and the spirit of things. The phrase "Stoic aesthetic" is not necessarily oxymoronic: despite the doctrine of *apatheia* (literally, being without *passions*) that plays less a role in Stoic doctrine than in anti-Stoic diatribe, Stoics, especially Roman Stoics, do not aspire to be without *affect.*[7] In Greek, the most common Stoic term for a "proper feeling" or "good emotion"—that is, one that accords with reason and hence with nature—is *eupatheia* (Graver, "Disturbed with Joy" 51–52). Wordsworth, after *Lyrical Ballads* (and certainly after "The Power of Music"), has little more sympathy for irrational passions than the Stoics did. In his letter to Wilson and throughout his career, however, he does emphasize *feelings*—a term associated with touch, the senses, and sensibility as well as with perception in a broad sense—in a way that no ancient Stoic, or even Shaftesbury, would. To conform one's *feelings* to "nature" (or, via one's art, the feelings of others) rather than, simply or immediately, conforming one's *life* or *mind,* is Wordsworth's signal modification of his Stoic inheritance.

THE BLESSINGS OF INDEPENDENT DOMESTIC LIFE

Independence, for Wordsworth, is an ethical concern and a condition that might be fostered by art. It is also, however, an economic and civic condition rooted in the soil and laws of Britain—not in "eternal nature" but in the property arrangements of Westmorland as Wordsworth knew it. Independence in this terrene sense is compromised not by public (parochial, neighborly) aid or assistance, for nothing stands alone, but by physical constraint, relocation, and/or deprivation of property. Thus the Cumberland beggar and the discharged soldier are, their reliance on others notwithstanding, relatively independent—if less so than the small landowners (most notably Michael), peddlers, waggoners, and leech gatherers that later enter Wordsworth's poetic imagination as Stoic avatars, men who are economically as well as ethically self-reliant. It is with special reference to *Michael* that Wordsworth wrote in 1801 to Charles James Fox, MP, enclosing a copy of the 1800 *Lyrical Ballads*. Addressing Fox's "sensibility of heart," Wordsworth regrets that "the bonds of domestic feeling among the poor . . . have been weakened . . . [or] entirely destroyed" by "workhouses, Houses of Industry, and the invention of Soup-shops &c, &c." He focuses on an octogenarian couple that could retain their independence if supported in their own house:

> I have two neighbours, a man and his wife, both upwards of eighty years of age; they live alone; the husband has been confined to his bed many months and has never had, nor till within these few weeks has ever needed, any body to attend to him but his wife. She has recently been seized with a lameness which has often prevented her from being able to carry him his food to his bed; the neighbours fetch water for her from the well, and do other kind offices for them both, but her infirmities encrease. She told my Servant two days ago that she was afraid they must both be boarded out among some other Poor of the parish (they have long been supported by the parish) but she said, it was hard, having kept house together so long, to come to this, and she was sure that "it would burst her heart." I mention this fact to shew how deeply the spirit of independence is, even yet, rooted in some parts of the country. These people could not express themselves in this way without an almost sublime conviction of the blessings of independent domestic life. If it is true, as I believe, that this spirit is rapidly disappearing, no greater curse can befall a land. (*Letters* 1:314)

The loss of independence involved in being "boarded out among some other Poor of the parish" continued to concern Wordsworth, and in *The Excursion* he represents it as fatal. In book 2, the Poet and the Wanderer, arriving in the valley where the Solitary lives, encounter a funeral procession: they at first mistakenly think that the Solitary himself has died, till the Solitary arrives to apprise them that the funeral was for a seventy-year-old man, a "homeless Pensioner" lodged with a poor "Housewife" who used him as "her Vassal of all labour." He died from exposure to a storm when "at her bidding, early and alone, / . . . [he] clomb aloft to delve the moorland turf / For winter fuel" (*Excursion* 2:764–816). Such is the peril of being boarded out, a dependency akin to vassalage. The Solitary's tale helps to explain the fear of dependence that motivates, and finally deforms, other economically precarious characters in *The Excursion*: Margaret and her husband during the economic downturn of 1794–95 (1:566–595); the "Unamiable Woman" who grows avaricious and envious in response to an early experience of "dire dependence" (6:739). The "independent happiness" that the Solitary praises involves freedom not only from the besetting passions of baroque poetry ("defeated pride," "love with despair," etc.) but also, concretely, from the instability of property: "prosperity subverted, maddening want" (3:379–89). Moral independence is, for Wordsworth, related to some measure of *economic* independence—with *economy* carrying its etymological force of "household or domestic management."

RESOLUTION AND INDEPENDENCE

I will return to *The Excursion* later in this chapter, specifically to its keen psychological portrait of the Solitary as a man who, for all his talk of independent happiness, evinces an undue dependency on others. First I want to retrace the path by which Wordsworth worked his way to *The Excursion*. The poem in which he first dramatizes the threat of dependency and his aspirant turn to Stoic discipline is *The Leech gatherer*, composed in 1802, and retitled *Resolution and Independence* when published in 1807 (*Poems, in Two Volumes* 123–29). The poem is a response to Coleridge's *Dejection: An Ode* (itself a response to the opening four stanzas of Wordsworth's "Immortality Ode"), and one may perceive the shadow of Coleridge in the poet, dependent on others and heedless of himself, whom Wordsworth's speaker fears himself to be:

> My whole life I have liv'd in pleasant thought,
> As if life's business were a summer mood:
> As if all needful things would come unsought
> To genial faith, still rich in genial good;
> But how can He expect that others should
> Build for him, sow for him, and at his call
> Love him, who for himself will take no heed at all? (ll. 36–42)

Critics have seen *Resolution and Independence* as Wordsworth's declaration of independence from earlier flesh-and-blood influences on his poetry: for Paul

Magnuson (308–17), that influence is Coleridge, seen as heading down the same path of "despondency and madness" that consumed Thomas Chatterton and (allegedly) Burns; for William Heath, it is his sister Dorothy and her eye for scenic detail (quoted in Wolfson, *Romantic Interactions* 175).

But reading the poem as a paean to poetic independence limits it unduly, for it is as much about interdependence as it is about self-authorship. The leech gatherer the speaker admires is independent, as the poet wishes, and in the end resolves, with God's grace (dependency sublime), to be. The leech gatherer is not swayed by irrational passions ("the fear that kills," l. 120); not reliant on a particular flesh-and-blood other; indeed, he does not even have the house or permanent abode the speaker fears losing (the old man "hous[es], with God's good help, by choice or chance," l. 111). But the leech gatherer also acknowledges the interdependence of things or what Wordsworth calls, in a rich phrase from *Home at Grasmere,* their "kindred independence" (ms. B, l. 461).[8] The leech gatherer's living depends on a variety of separate yet interrelated factors: leech populations, environmental conditions, and medicinal demand. "Yet still I persevere," he says, "and find them [leeches] where I may" (l. 133). His independent happiness is integrated into the life of things.

The poet's own integration into a literary history in which nothing comes of nothing—but yet in which no one author can be said to depend unilaterally on another—is announced by the recondite stanza form Wordsworth employs in his poem, the "rhyme royal" of Chaucer's *Troilus and Criseyde* (an extract of which Wordsworth translated into Modern English in late 1801). "Indeed," writes Charles Mahoney, "the Old Man [leech gatherer] is represented as speaking as if sent from the distant past to remind the persona of the virtues of rhyme royal," its stateliness and gravity (31). The leech gatherer, for Mahoney, embodies, even as he is embodied in, the formal pleasure of verse that overbalances Wordsworth's vocational pains—which included in 1801–2 trying to write his poem to Coleridge (later known as *The Prelude*), along with insomnia and other somatic complaints.

Yet form recalls that which has been written in it. Wordsworth's choice of rhyme royal implicates his poem in a dialogue with other poems that employ this distinctive form, and these poems taken together comprise a type of ethical forum on love, the loves that exalt as well as those that depress a person. The extract from *Troilus and Criseyde* Wordsworth translated concerns erotic love and the suffering it entails. Troilus, separated from Criseyde by the turns of the Trojan War, is "as one that standeth between hope and dread" (*Translations* 59, *Troilus and Cresida* l. 112). His passionate state is akin to the speaker's of *Resolu-*

tion and Independence, who also feels the demand for another's love ("and at his call / Love him") as a dangerous dependency. *Resolution and Independence* alludes as well to a more recent poet who, impersonating a fifteenth-century poet ("Rowley") in the line of Chaucer, also used rhyme royal: Thomas Chatterton, "the marvellous Boy, / The sleepless Soul that perish'd in its pride" (ll. 43–44). Chatterton's "An Excelente Balade of Charitie" (1777), which proceeds (like *Dejection: An Ode*) from sun to storm, is a Good Samaritan parable, a poem on Christian love (*caritas*) as alms-giving, or the duty to help one's fellow in need. With this poem *Resolution and Independence* has a complex relation. Reversing the trajectory of "Balade of Charitie" and *Dejection,* Wordsworth's poem concerns the sunny morning *after* a storm: it is a poem set at a moment not of crisis but rather of preparation. What it prepares the speaker for is twofold: first, to profit from the leech gatherer's example, and second, to *recognize* the other, or give to the other by an act of recognition. This is the disinterested (but not, in a narrow sense, charitable) love ethic that underwrites Wordsworth's poem—as it does his earlier poems of encounter, stretching back to *The Discharged Soldier.*

Physically, Wordsworth's speaker gives the leech gatherer nothing, because the old man wants nothing: he is the "happy man" of ancient philosophy, of Virgil's *Georgics* and Horace's *Odes,* the man of few and simple needs, internally free from fortune's wheel, if externally bound to environmental conditions. The poet's ethical imperative is to emulate the leech gatherer but also not to erase who he is in his difference from the poet: it is to see him, and within the discipline of form to convey him, clearly. He asks, "How is it that you live, and what is it that you do?" (125). The poet's ethical imperative is to listen for an answer, to attune himself to the other's life and activity, and to tame the metaphoric fancy that flickeringly turns the man into "a huge stone" or "a sea-beast," "one whom I had met with in a dream." As Noel Jackson suggests, the narrator's final turn in the poem is toward a particularized and abiding vision of the leech gatherer as he is: "In my mind's eye I seem'd to see him pace / About the weary moors continually" (136–37). Is this an imaginative abstraction or a view of the man in his concrete existence and difference? Jackson sees it as the latter, via the former: "In reifying the leech-gatherer as an object of aesthetic wonder, then, the poet produces a sense of his particularity that might otherwise be lost in an exchange of fellow-feeling" (159). The poem's final turn is a step toward the goal of not looking through or down upon, neither incorporating nor assaulting the other—the sorts of abuse that tempt the poem's speaker, and that are heightened to brilliant comic pitch in Lewis Carroll's parody, "Upon the Lonely Moor" (1856).[9]

By the end of the poem Wordsworth's speaker aspires—with great difficulty—to "give to God and Man their *dues*" (105). This ideal of doing one's *duty* to God and others, religious in form but unspecified in content, will hereafter impress itself strongly on Wordsworth's poetry. Duty enters Wordsworth's moral lexicon as a Stoic-inspired corrective to the supererogatory limitlessness of a Christian (or post-Christian) love ethic. Ironically, however, Wordsworth remains loath to delimit what our duties are. The drama of *Resolution and Independence* lies in a triangulated conflict between an implied duty to oneself (to provide, to persevere, without dependence); an implied duty to the other (here, to see and record without distortion); and an undutiful inclination, which sparks poetry itself, to imaginative drift and the defacement of the other through metaphoric extravagance. The speaker's first impulse is to see the man before him as a stone or sea beast; the progress of the poem is toward seeing the other as one who lives, does, and can justify his doing. The poem concludes, "I'll think of the Leech-gatherer on the lonely moor": such a thought will, its speaker hopes, moor him to a sense of what is due to self and others.

GLIMMERS OF DUTY, AND WHERE THEY COME FROM

In Wordsworth's *Ode to Duty* (composed 1804–6, *Poems, in Two Volumes* 104–7), duty categorically takes the place of the corporeal leech gatherer as a guide to Stoic independence. It is lauded in the poem as the ground of freedom from "vain temptations," "strife," and "despair" (ll. 7–8). It is desired, even as it is (somewhat paradoxically) opposed to "the weight of chance desires" (38);[10] the desire for duty, as a bulwark of stability and repose, is the desire to end all desires. Duty, "Stern Daughter of the Voice of God!" (1), makes one independent precisely through sublime dependency on a God one cannot see but whose voice propagates an intermediary that is law to us.

What Wordsworth's speaker can no longer rely on, ethically, is his own sensible heart, feelings undisciplined by law. He implies, however, that such heart-reliance was once his and that it might be recuperated communally in a utopian (or angelic) future:

> Serene will be our days and bright,
> And happy will our nature be,
> When love is an unerring light,
> And joy its own security.
> And bless'd are they who in the main

This faith, even now, do entertain:

Live in the spirit of this creed;

Yet find that other strength [duty], according to their need.

Among those so blessed are Wordsworth's younger self, who felt love "an unerr-
ing light" and "joy its own security," both in *The Prelude* and, with greater sim-
plicity, in the Alfoxden poem "It is the first mild day of March" (*Lyrical Ballads*
63–64):

Love, now a universal birth,

From heart to heart is stealing,

From earth to man, from man to earth,

—It is the hour of feeling.

*   *   *   *   *   *   *   *

Some silent laws our hearts may make,

Which they shall long obey;

We for the year to come may take

Our temper from to-day.

"Laws" here emerge spontaneously, through love, from the heart, and it is the
heart (not the person, not the will) that just as spontaneously obeys it. The heart
is wholly unconstrained by anything outside itself or, as Rousseau phrases it in a
compatible fantasy of sentimental freedom, "the yoke of any duty" (*le joug d'aucun
devoir*, 117).[11] Duty's subordination to (if not supercession by) the sensible heart
was commonplace in sentimentalist ethics of the later eighteenth century. Hugh
Blair, in one of his widely read *Sermons* (1777–1801), expressly prefers charitable
actions that "flow from the sensibility of a feeling heart" to those performed
"from a principle of duty."[12] This preference is chastened rather than reversed in
the *Ode to Duty*. Wordsworth's early image of self-legislation as heart-legislation,
periodically renewable, abides as a once and future kingdom in his later poem,
but here center stage is assumed by an allegorical depiction of Duty as an exter-
nal force, at once stern and (toward the dutiful action) smiling:

Stern Lawgiver! yet thou dost wear

The Godhead's most benignant grace;

Nor know we any thing so fair

As is the smile upon thy face . . . (49–52)

The speaker of *Ode to Duty* courts duty gingerly, however, and not without
backward glances:

I, loving freedom and untried;

No sport of every random gust,

Yet being to myself a guide,

Too blindly have reposed my trust:

Resolved that nothing e'er should press

Upon my present happiness,

I shoved unwelcome tasks away:

But thee I now would serve more strictly, if I may.

"If I may" may simply be an expletive inserted to fill out the final alexandrine demanded by Wordsworth's disciplined stanza (this ode has the formal regularity of Horace, not the perceived irregularity of Pindar). But I find the phrase to be more than that, either a note of polite deference ("may I follow you, Duty"?) or one of blunt uncertainty ("if I am able or have power to do so"). This tonal uncertainty reflects a crucial question about duty in general: is it inherently motivating (can personified Duty motivate one to do one's duty) or must a will or motive separate from duty intervene to make one do one's duty (is it up to me to try to follow Duty's edicts)?

The more fundamental question broached by the *Ode to Duty* is a practical, and again unanswered, one: what *is* one's duty, and how can one know it? Duty is never defined, nor is the reader informed what it enjoins. A lesser poet—or a requirement ethicist—would have explicitly told us what to do. "Fear God, and keep his commandments: for this is the whole duty of man": this injunction from the end of Ecclesiastes (12:13), echoed and elaborated in many a pre-1800 poem and devotional manual, has imperative force and relative clarity (one needs only to determine which of the numerous Hebraic commandments pertain). Wordsworth, however, while stressing duty's power and desirability, refuses to anatomize its nature. Though he equates it with the astronomic power that "dost preserve the Stars from wrong" (55), this equation seems declarative but is, rather, metaphoric (Jarvis calls it "performative" or "optative," 20–21).[13] Duty thus appears not as whatever it is but as a constelled image of cosmic order and renewal: "And the most ancient Heavens through Thee are fresh and strong" (l. 56). In the strength of this alexandrine, poetry pays tribute to itself, leaving duty without its due. "Duty," elaborately apostrophized, is defaced through metaphorical extravagance—Wordsworth does to duty what he had earlier done, in flashes, to the leech gatherer, dissolving its specificity into a congeries of images.

Wordsworth's curiously empty or undutiful evocations of duty are worth remarking both because they are many and because they made an impression.

Matthew Arnold, as I noted in my introduction, praised Wordsworth for showing us "the joy offered to us in the simple primary affections and duties." But what are these primary duties? For most moralists, they begin with children's obligation to parents: on this point the Biblical commandments (Exodus 20:12) accord with the Stoic "offices" or duties delineated in Cicero's *De Officiis* (or, as it was translated in 1798, *Essay on Moral Duty*).[14] An oddity of Wordsworth's canon is that while it contains some exempla of dutiful parents or caregivers (in *Michael*, in *The Brothers*, in the "mothering" London laborer of *The Prelude*), it contains no dutiful children: even the long-suffering Emily of *The White Doe of Rylstone* is not an image of filial piety. Years later, contemplating the 1839 portrait painted of his own long-suffering daughter, Dora—her father's helpmate and amanuensis until her late marriage in 1841—Wordsworth contrasts her image's air of discontent with an unspecified better time, when Dora "lived thankful for day's light, for daily bread, / For health, and time in obvious duty spent" (*Last Poems* 332). This "obvious" begs the question of what her duty is, conjuring, moreover, possible opposites such as unobvious, obscure, uncertain duty, the kind Wordsworth himself pioneered in his poetry of encounter and that seems now to wear Dora down.

Beyond being "obvious," what are our duties? What is their content? Wordsworth in his poems isn't saying, but his intellectual biography provides two sources that are at least marginally relevant: ancient, especially Stoic, virtue ethics, and Kant's (so-called deontological, or law-based) ethics. Wordsworth derived his knowledge of the first primarily from Cicero's *De Officiis*, which he most likely studied by the time he was fifteen (Wu, *Wordsworth's Reading, 1770– 1799*, 28–29). Ben Ross Schneider (70–76) makes a strong case that Wordsworth read it at Hawkshead Grammar School, finding in his schoolboy poem *Lines on the Bicentenary of Hawkshead School* (*Early Poems* 354–61) an evidentiary catalogue of Cicero's four virtues: wisdom, justice, courage, and decorum. Cicero called the duties entailed by these virtues *officiis*, singular *officium* (a Latin term for the duties engendered by one's social role), translating the technical Greek Stoic term *kathekon*, or "appropriate action" (action in accordance with reason and nature). Wordsworth clearly has Cicero's duties and their preeminently social nature in mind when he uses the English term "offices," as he does in his letter to Fox about the octogenarian couple for whom neighbors "do . . . kind offices." A Roman Stoic context to *Ode to Duty* is supplied when, in 1836, Wordsworth gives the poem an epigraph from Seneca on how to identify the perfectly (and opposed to partially and thus imperfectly) virtuous man; to quote in translation the whole of a sentence Wordsworth gives in part: "he has always been the same, consistent in all his action, not only sound in his judgment but trained by habit to such an extent that he not only can act rightly, but cannot help acting rightly" (*Moral Epistles* 120:10).

The immediate context of *Ode to Duty,* as Stephen Gill points out (*William Wordsworth* 227), also includes the poet's 1803 conversations with Coleridge about Kant's *Groundwork for the Metaphysics of Morals.* Kant, unlike Wordsworth's Stoic sources, draws a sharp division between duty and desire, one that Wordsworth appears, less sharply, to maintain: "I feel the weight of chance desires:/My hopes no more must change their name,/I long for a repose which ever is the same" (37–40). For Kant, the only moral motivation we have is acting from duty, and not merely in accordance with duty. Duty is rational and not *caused* by anything in the world; the only truly moral act (if one has ever been performed) is one that proceeds entirely from a purely moral motive, and not from any phenomenal cause such as desire, passion, or a mercenary obedience to worldly authority. Thus moral activity—motivated entirely and exclusively by duty—frees us from desire, passion, and the turbulence of the world. Only in morality are we autonomous agents. The freedom Kant endorses is one authorized, or we might say "chartered," by reason alone—and as such is the very opposite of the "uncharter'd freedom" of which Wordsworth complains in his ode (37).

The Kantian soupçon of *Ode to Duty* flourishes in Wordsworth's later essay on moral self-education, "Reply to 'Mathetes'" (1809–10). Here we find lines that could have been written by Kant himself:

> He [the appropriately self-educated person] will not long have his admiration fixed on unworthy objects; he will neither be clogged nor drawn aside by the love of friends or kindred, betraying his understanding through his affections; he will neither be bowed down by conventional arrangements of manners producing too often a lifeless decency; nor will the rock of his Spirit wear away in the endless beating of the waves of the World: neither will that portion of his own time, which he must surrender to labours by which his livelihood is to be earned or his social duties performed, be unprofitable to himself indirectly, while it is directly useful to others: for that time has been primarily surrendered through *an act of obedience to a moral law established by himself,* and therefore he moves then also along *the orbit of perfect liberty.* (*Prose Works* 2: 24, my emphases)

The twin notions Wordsworth expresses here—that the moral law must be self-legislated and that only in obeying this self-legislated law are we free—can derive only from Kant, whose conception of morality is, as Jerome Schneewind maintains, "something new to the history of thought" (483). Kant's "astonishing claim," Schneewind continues, "is that God and we can share membership in a single moral community only if we all equally legislate the law we are to obey" (512). This claim, argues Schneewind, reconciles two strands of early modern moral philosophy: natural law theory (there is a moral law that governs God as well as us—this was the Stoics' view) and its opposite, theological "voluntarism" (God, whose will is unlimited by any prior law, wills morality into being—this was the view of Luther). For Kant, contra the voluntarists, there *is* a nonarbitrary moral law; yet, akin to the voluntarists, it is one we are free to legislate for ourselves, as God does. A law one imposes on oneself is, moreover, one that contains within it a motive to obey. And it is this purely rational, non-causal motive that makes us autonomous or free: free from material causes, from determination by anything other than our rational nature. Wordsworth appears to have understood at least the broad outlines of Kant's mature moral philosophy, offering his own version of it in "Reply to 'Mathetes.'"

In a salient passage of *The Excursion,* Wordsworth suggests his familiarity with another aspect of Kant's moral philosophy: the distinction (rooted in seventeenth-century natural law theory) between perfect and imperfect duties (*Metaphysics of Morals* 38–48). A perfect duty, such as "do not commit suicide" or "do not lie," must be followed unconditionally and unexceptionally; an imperfect (or, as Kant also calls it, "meritorious") duty, such as "cultivate your talents" or "help those in need," admits a context-bound latitude (that is, a degree of uncertainty) to its practice. The Wanderer of Wordsworth's poem draws a consonant distinction between "primal [perfect] duties" and "charities," seeing in one the constancy of the stars and in the other the therapeutic, though transient, beauty of flowers:

> The primal duties shine aloft—like stars;
> The charities that soothe, and heal, and bless,
> Are scattered at the feet of Man—like flowers. (9:237–39)

Thus Wordsworth distinguishes between Stoic and Kantian duties, ascendant since *Resolution and Independence,* and the "charities" or impersonal love (*caritas*) enshrined in *The Prelude,* giving both their due in *The Excursion.*

IMPERSONAL STYLE

By the time Wordsworth writes *The Excursion* impartiality has become not only his creed but also a limitation of his style. He increasingly courts an impersonal style that corresponds to the ethic of impersonal love he announces at the end of *The Prelude* and, more succinctly, in the first book of *The Excursion,* in lines originally written for *The Pedlar* (ms. E, written 1803–4). A style and ethics of impersonality converge in this description of the Wanderer in his youth, when he traveled as an itinerant peddler of small wares—and attained Stoic sagacity:

> Spontaneously had his affections thriven
> Upon the bounties of the year, and [he] felt
> The liberty of Nature; there he kept
> In solitude and solitary thought
> His mind in *a just equipoise of love.*
> Serene it was, unclouded by the cares
> Of ordinary life; unvexed, unwarped
> By *partial bondage.* In his steady course
> No piteous revolutions had he felt,
> No wild varieties of joy and grief. (1:380–89, my emphases)

A torrent of negatives—"unclouded," "unvexed," "unwarped," "no piteous revolutions," "no wild varieties"—indicate the Wanderer's exceptionality: being clouded, vexed, and so forth are by strong implication the experiential (though not the moral) norm. The grammatical privatives that express the Wanderer's exceptionality also suggest his impersonality: what sets him apart is a lack of the perturbations that characterize most persons (indeed, that make them "characters" in a literary sense). And this impersonally described man correspondingly loves impersonality. Because of his emphatically *im*partial love—because he doesn't *invest* too much in any one person—he "could *afford* to suffer / With those whom he saw suffer" (1:399–400), an economic judgment on the Poet's part that serves as prelude to the Wanderer's pleasurable tale of Margaret's misery and her ruined cottage.

In *The Excursion* Wordsworth, to a large degree, eschews the eccentricity and Orphism of his earlier verse; he eschews as well metaphor and the mind that would play God among external things. This, of course, is why we like his later style less than his earlier style: it is less literary, more philosophical. In Wordsworth's late style the communal "we" stages its triumph over the personal "I"—perspectives held in creative tension through *The Prelude*, a tension that makes Wordsworth's semiautobiographical poem his greatest achievement. Wordsworth's late style incorporates a host of elements that convert the poet from "a man speaking to men" (Preface to *Lyrical Ballads* 751) to "men speaking through a man." He inclines toward the commonplace (that which has often been thought), the classical, the essayistic, dialogues of multiple speakers, and short, pithy sayings or apothegms that sound familiar.

The Excursion is filled with marmoreal utterances that seem translated from a dead language, offered not in first-person singular but the first-person plural (for example, "we live by admiration, hope and love," 4:760). Wordsworth also gravitates toward the third-person impersonal (the *on* of French or *ille* of Latin) in hortatory locutions that follow the famous Virgilian formula *felix qui* ("happy he who") or the Horatian *ille potens sui / laetusque deget* ("he is master of himself and will live joyously who," *Odes* 3.29, ll. 41–42): for example, "Happy is He who lives to understand!," "and He / Is a still happier Man, who, for those heights / Of speculation not unfit, descends" (4:334–59). The formula also works in the third-person plural ("Happy . . . They who gain / A panegyric from your generous tongue!," 8:84–85), and through the impersonal use of verb infinitives: "Far better not to move at all than move / By impulse sent from such illusive Power [i.e., baptismal vows]" (5:317–18).

Geoffrey Hartman aptly calls *The Excursion* "a Romantic commonplace book" (*Wordsworth's Poetry* 317), a digest of quotations and ideas gathered from Wordsworth's reading and earlier writing. This commonplace book approach is another aspect of the triumph of the "we" over the "I," a sort of collaborative writing with past authors in perpetuation and pursuit of shared knowledge. Wordsworth not uncommonly builds his characters' speeches by accretion, like the author of a medieval *summa*, with the point culled from one authority balanced by a counterpoint from another, their apparent differences giving way to an implied unity. The character of the Poet offers a wonderfully condensed example of this process. His farewell to the spot where the Solitary had retreated from the world is built upon the antithetical parallelism of two literary references:

> How vain, thought I, is it by change of place
> To seek that comfort which the mind denies;
> Yet trial and temptation oft are shunned
> Wisely . . . (5:18–21)

The first thought that comes to the Poet is an oft-repeated classical adage found, for example, in Seneca (who attributes it to Socrates): "Why do you wonder that your travels do not benefit you, when you carry yourself around with you?"[15] This thought is then complicated by a reminiscence of Adam's prelapsarian exhortation to Eve:

> Seek not temptation, then, which to avoid
> Were better, and most likely if from mee
> Thou sever not: Trial will come unsought. (*Paradise Lost* 9:364–66)

The Poet's train of thought is thus less an inert digest of commonplaces than the act of digesting them, bringing them alive through interaction with one another, in a respected classical (and essayistic) mode.

Wordsworth's style waxes classical in and after *The Excursion,* but also neoclassical—that is, proximate to the poetic styles of Akenside and Edward Young. A little-appreciated irony of Wordsworth's career is that the poet who writes in the waning years of the eighteenth century is, in his poetry of encounter, epiphany, and the closely observed particular, the herald of poetic modernity, while the nineteenth-century Wordsworth increasingly writes as an eighteenth-century author. Paradoxically, however, even this turn away from modernity evinces, in its ambivalence, Wordsworth's modernity, in a form shared by Diderot, Schiller, Jane Austen, the later Byron, Matthew Arnold, and Lionel Trilling—authors half, or more than half, attracted to the rebellious or amoral energy of character (in, for example, Rameau's Nephew, Charles de Moor, Mortimer, Henry and Mary Crawford, Don Juan) they would nonetheless sacrifice on the altar of morality, or at least contain within the moral form of comedy. Even the Stoic aesthetics that Wordsworth espoused as a protest against a de-eternizing modernity, which might seem a historical dead end, have a brilliant second life in Zbigniew Herbert, in poems that conjure the harmonies of Roman Stoicism half-lovingly, if tragicomically, amidst a twentieth-century European history that has no place for them.[16]

KNOWING TOGETHER IN *THE EXCURSION*

Of the five main characters in *The Excursion,* the Solitary—introduced third, after the narrating Poet and the Wanderer—is to most modern readers the most appealing.[17] (The Pastor, introduced fourth, will strike readers as too homiletic, certainly by his final, eschatological speech in book 9, and the Pastor's wife, fifth and last, is underdeveloped, which is unfortunate, given the tang of her glancing skepticism toward the Wanderer's idealism [9:457–73].) The Solitary is the metaphysical rebel of the drama, the one the other characters attempt, unsuccessfully, to bring back into the Christian fold.[18] He has a brooding, Hamlet-like quality, mixing sensibility and misanthropy, solitude and sociability. Indeed, he is the only character of *The Excursion* who seems at all to *be* a character, rather than a mouthpiece for Wordsworth's philosophizing. He is also the character with by far the richest history, which consists precisely of *partial* attachments (to wife, to children, to the French Revolution) and of their sundering by death and disillusion. We are attached to the Solitary by his attachment to others, and by a moral skepticism that seems earned. In the dialogic structure of *The Excursion* he is a salutary counterweight to the sagacious independence of the Wanderer.

The Excursion is, as critics have rightly acknowledged, a "dramatic poem" (Bushell 59), indeed a philosophical dialogue akin to Cicero's *Tusculan Disputations*, built upon "the exchange of formal speeches" (Graver, "The Oratorical Pedlar" 95).[19] What this form presupposes is the interdependence of community and the importance of *knowing together*—the root meaning of the Latin *conscience*, and one that Wordsworth may have found in Seneca's *Moral Epistles*.[20] That the Solitary does not, by the poem's end, come to shared knowledge with his interlocutors—that consensus is not achieved—does not so much discredit *conscience* as show it to be an ongoing project, a dialogue interminable. *The Excursion* is not the reactionary work that Laurence Lockridge finds it to be: "Wordsworth's mental retreat from the ethical" into religious consolation (248). Rather, it is an open-ended work that, built upon an ethics of intellectual exchange, throws any conclusion, or ultimate consolation, into question.[21]

As attractive as the Solitary is to the modern reader, and as crucial as he is to the dialogic structure of *The Excursion*, Wordsworth asks us to judge him, and the judgment the poem leads us to make—the conscience it would have us share—is critical, if not uncharitable. The Solitary *lacks independence*: dependent on others in a negative way, his character is partly crafted to show the need for (to revert to key terms of *The Prelude*), "liberty and power" (11:183). With the Wanderer the Solitary agrees in theory that "independent happiness" is the proper end of life (*Excursion* 3:388)—he even offers, as the Wanderer does not, an explicit defense of ancient Stoicism and Epicureanism against the Poet's inaccurate derogation of these sects of philosophy (3:336–410). But the Solitary goes on to entertain the possibility that such happiness has been "perhaps obtained by none" (3:413). He then recurs to the danger of the *seemingly* happy life, which can always be subverted by chance or accident, and urges his listeners to live in hope not because hope is a good, or a virtue (as it had certainly seemed in *The Prelude*), but because it is a vengeful deity that will, in pagan manner, wreak havoc on those who slight her: "slighted Hope will be avenged; and, when / Ye need her favours, Ye shall find her not; / But, in her stead—fear— doubt—and agony!" (3:465–67). One senses he speaks from experience.

The Solitary's problem is that he is too dependent on fortune's wheel or, in a technical sense, *unhappy*: that is, servile, buffeted by the "wild varieties of joy and grief" the Wanderer has managed, philosophically, to avoid (1:389). He has a vertical cast of mind, one that depends on powers (short of God), and is overawed by "glory."[22] The throne he sees, in his vision at the end of book 2, may be the glory seat of God, but God or his Lamb are not, as in the Book of Revelation (19:16–22:6), upon it. Instead, the Solitary's vision centers on an empty throne, a symbol of authority, without content, sought for its own sake. The Solitary's vision begins, like the Mount Snowdon vision of *The Prelude* book 13, with the clearing of mountain mist, but here what is revealed is not a vision of the mind's interaction with nature; it is the transcendent power of "a mighty City," "Glory beyond all glory ever seen" (2:862, 870).

> Right in the midst, where interspace appeared
> Of open court, an object like a throne
> Under a shining canopy of state
> Stood fixed; and fixed resemblances were seen
> To implements of ordinary use,
> But vast in size, in substance glorified;
> Such as by Hebrew Prophets were beheld
> In vision . . . (2:896–903)

But Hebrew prophets never stood in awe of "canopy of *state*," of glorified "implements": the Solitary's vision involves a love of power, of glory, for its own sake, regardless of ends (implements for what? a state ruled how?).

With similar self-abjection, the Solitary describes his late wife as his "earthly Providence, whose guiding love / Within a port of rest had lodged me safe" (3:573–74). After the deaths of her two children, her loss to grief and illness was, or so the Solitary tells us, a loss of illumination, of "pure glory":

> O heavy change!
> Dimness o'er this clear *Luminary* crept
> Insensibly;—the immortal and divine
> Yielded to mortal reflux; her *pure Glory*,
> As from the pinnacle of worldly *state*
> Wretched Ambition drops astounded, fell
> Into a gulph obscure of silent grief,
> And keen heart-anguish—of itself ashamed,
> Yet obstinately cherishing itself:
> And, so consumed, She melted from my arms;
> And left me, on this earth, disconsolate. (3:678–88, my emphases)

The Solitary's lament for his wife would be a pure, if extravagant, one were it not for its intrusive simile comparing his wife's decline from glory to the political fall of "Wretched Ambition." The simile only makes sense if we concede the Solitary's passive-aggression, his hatred of his wife as the converse of his deification of her. As a psychologist, Wordsworth has never been keener or more subtle.

At this point in his life story, it is hardly surprising that the Solitary transfers his restless veneration onto the promise of the French Revolution. Critics often read the Solitary, in his Revolutionary zeal, as a stand-in for his author, but Wordsworth's account in *The Prelude* of his own early enthusiasm for the Revolution has nothing of the Solitary's vertical and dependent cast of mind. The Solitary bows before the glory seat of the Revolution as he had, earlier in the poem, marveled at the celestial city carved from mist:

> From the wreck [of the Bastille]
> A golden Palace rose, or seemed to rise,
> The appointed Seat of equitable Law
> And mild paternal Sway. The potent shock
> I felt; the transformation I perceived,
> As marvellously seized as in that moment
> When, from the blind mist issuing, I beheld
> Glory—beyond all glory ever seen,
> Confusion infinite of heaven and earth,
> Dazzling the soul! (3:722–31)

The Solitary's desire for "mild paternal sway"—he later calls for "Saturnian Rule" (3:764)—is far from being a republican one. Rather than a hope for liberation and self-legislation, and despite a passing tribute to "The Tree of Liberty" (3:730), the Solitary's fantasy is that the Revolution will supply every want:

> Be joyful all ye Nations: in all Lands,
> Ye that are capable of joy be glad!
> Henceforth, whate'er is wanting to yourselves
> In others ye shall promptly find . . . (3:737–40)

The economy the Solitary here conjures is clearly an impossible one: for where is the surplus coming from? Who are these "others" who shall provide for every lack in all lands? Where are, in Blake's terms from *The Marriage of Heaven and Hell* (plates 16–17), the "prolific" to provide for all these "devourers"?

The Solitary, at the end of his tale, inadvertently discloses his central moral fault and the source of his present misanthropy:

> Enough is told! Here am I—Ye have heard
> What evidence [of human greatness] I seek, and vainly seek;

What from my Fellow-beings I require,
And cannot find . . . (9:964–68)

Wordsworth, in his 1845 final revisions to the poem, deleted this last line ("And cannot find") and added in its place the more pointed phrase:

And either they have not to give, or I
Lack virtue to receive . . .

In either version, the Solitary thinks only of his own needs and requirements. He imagines only receiving and, in the New Testament injunction Wordsworth asks us to hear in his 1845 revision, "it is more blessed to give than to receive" (Acts 20:35). Coleridge had turned this line to advantage: "O Lady! we receive but what we give" (*Dejection: An Ode* 47). The Solitary, however, would only receive, not give. He seeks only to fill perceived lacks in himself, not recognizing that what he most crucially lacks is autonomous agency. (He is, in Kant's term from *Groundwork for the Metaphysics of Morals,* "heteronomous.")

Thus when the Solitary deplores, at the end of the poem, the condition of the dependent "multitude" (9:141), he ironically speaks as well of his own state:

On themselves
They cannot lean, nor turn to their own hearts
To know what they must do; their wisdom is
To look into the eyes of others, thence
To be instructed what they must avoid . . . (9.144–48)

The Solitary, erroneously thinking himself above the people, in actuality embodies their problem—without having, like them, the extenuating circumstance of being economically dependent. Despite his economic independence (the Solitary does not work), he is a figure for the masses that, lacking self-determination, pose a political threat for being too readily manipulated. The older Wordsworth grew, the more he worried about populist and popular agitation (a worry shrilly expressed in his 1833 poem *The Warning*); the Solitary is his character study of the political as well as ethical danger of dependency.

The Solitary reveals his shortcomings by his own words. The Wanderer, by contrast—the Solitary's would-be savior and his effective foil—has his shortcomings revealed by the dialogic form of *The Excursion,* his main fault being a certain deafness to other people, particularly to the Solitary. The Wanderer's independence, although laudable in theory, comes to seem, in practice, like unresponsiveness. He lacks a sense of the interdependence that, for Wordsworth, undergirds independence. Ethics begins in listening, in making one-self available, through discourse, to the needs and concerns of the other. The Wanderer, for all his Stoic patina, falls short as an ethical ideal, because he does not listen.

The main thing he seems unable to hear is religious doubt, a serious problem, since his goal is to convert a doubter. The Solitary makes clear that he lacks faith. While sailing to America (where, after his disappointment in the French Revolution, he seeks, again unsuccessfully, an authentic utopia), the Solitary had turned to the Bible, but "faith was wanting" (3:873). Nonetheless, the Wanderer's "replies" to the Solitary all rest upon the presupposition of (an Arminian and panentheistic) faith and a hope built upon that faith. Thus he tells him that he must believe that his family is "glorified" in death because "Hope,—below this, consists not with belief / In mercy. . . . / Hope,—below this, consists not with belief / In perfect wisdom . . ." (4:190–94). Built upon a fine anaphora, this is wonderfully rhetorical, but it also, logically, begs the question—that is, it assumes the very thing the Wanderer is trying to prove (the dead must be sainted or else God wouldn't be the sort of deity that sanctifies the dead). It also assumes in the Solitary the very hopes and beliefs of which the Wanderer is trying to convince him.

The Wanderer evidences a similar fallibility later in the poem, finding nourishing hope where it does not appear, in the Pastor's tale of a gold-digging shepherd who finally, after twenty years, finds gold and then "die[s] of joy"—the Pastor's euphemism for his drinking himself to death in apparently avaricious exultation (6:245–53). Deaf to the moral complexity of the tale he has heard, the Wanderer chimes in, presumably for the Solitary's benefit, with further praise of God, who gives "the guiding vein of hope" (6:268). This uncritical trust in hope as an unconditional good is especially curious, given the tale with which the Wanderer begins *The Excursion,* that of Margaret, the abandoned wife who dies amidst her ruined cottage, worn down by "torturing hope" (1:948). This is not the reasonable form of pursuing the good, Cicero's *voluntas,* or "rational wishing," that the Stoics approved but resembles what they sought to uproot, irrational hope or desire (*libido*).[23] To distinguish true from false hope seems an effort *The Excursion,* and in its first book the Wanderer himself, asks us to make, but it is a distinction to which the Wanderer grows oblivious as the poem progresses.

The Wanderer and the Solitary represent inverse vices, deafness and enslavement to others, which to some degree conjoin in the Solitary, because the flip side of his radical social dependency is his misanthropic seclusion and retreat from discourse. *The Excursion* helps us learn to be better listeners or readers (via, in part, the negative example of the Wanderer), attuned to the interdependencies of dialogue form. It also teaches independence from the passions that hamper rational, ethical, and indeed dialogic activity: excessive and un-self-critical reliance on glorified others (the Solitary); irrational hope and desire (found to varying degrees in Margaret, the Solitary, and the shepherd-gold miner). Dialogue is itself, as the Stoics argued, a form very like conscience, whereby we examine ourselves and our own arguments from a position outside ourselves: thus the advice to turn inner monologue into dialogue; to divide oneself; to see oneself in a mirror; to see oneself as another would impartially see one. Wordsworth knew all this from Shaftesbury, who famously distilled what he saw as the central wisdom of the ancients: "That we had each of us a Patient in our-self, that we were properly our own Subjects of Practice; and that we then became due Practitioners, when by virtue of an intimate Recess we cou'd discover a certain duplicity of Soul, and divide ourselves into two Parties" (*Soliloquy* 1.2, in *Characteristicks* 1:93). Greek literature is the work, Shaftesbury continues, of "well-practis'd Dialogists" from Homer and the Tragedians to Socrates and Plato (*Soliloquy* 1.3, in *Characteristicks* 1:105). The saving grace of *The Excursion* is its "ancient" dialogism, without which it would be only a chain of monologues, offered without irony.

CONSCIENCE VERSUS MUSIC, ROUND TWO

Without its dialogic structure, its project of knowing together, *The Excursion* would offer nothing but a self-contained and typically oppressive form of *conscience*, the term and concept Wordsworth had so studiously avoided in his pre-1807 poems. "Conscience" arrives in the Prospectus to *The Recluse* as a parallel to "the law supreme / Of that Intelligence which governs all," replacing Wordsworth's earlier references in *Home at Grasmere* to "the one great Life" and, thinking upon it, the "sweet passions traversing my Soul / Like Music" (see chapter 5). The Wanderer also professes belief in "the law / Of Conscience; Conscience reverenced and obeyed, / As God's most intimate Presence in the soul" (4:225–27). Conscience is here not a product of human discourse but rather an inner attunement to God's law.

The problem with conscience, as the Solitary suggests, is that it can be "out of tune," deceived, and too easily assuaged. Thus he describes with irony the woman who, having sent out her dependent, the "homeless Pensioner," for winter fuel in inclement weather, rejoices upon his being brought home alive:

"Great shew of joy the housewife made, and truly / Was glad to find her con-
science set at ease; / And not less glad, for the sake of her good name, / That the
poor Sufferer had escaped with life" (2:921–24). ("He lingered three short
weeks," the Solitary concludes, "And from the Cottage hath been borne to-day"
[928–29].) The woman *shows* joy in the old man's recovery, but the joy she
feels—or so it seems to the Solitary—comes from a conscience too easily qui-
eted, and a reputation hypocritically preserved. Whether or not we believe the
Solitary—he is not, after all, omniscient, and his allegations may reflect his own
misanthropy as much as or more than the housewife's state of mind—he at
least raises the possibility that inner conscience might be deficient and in need
of communal or dialogic development. Being cleared by one's conscience, in
short, is not necessarily the last word on one's innocence. Conversely, then, the
accusations of inner conscience may not be as final as they seem, for example,
to the Solitary himself, upon whom, on his voyage to America, "with a fever's
strength" did "conscience prey" (3:857–58).[24]

Thus the bite of conscience, as *The Excursion* imagines it, is to be assuaged
by dialogue, if at all; seemingly gone is Wordsworth's earlier belief that the
nonpunitive force of music might take the ethical place of conscience. Signifi-
cantly, among the many churchyard characters whose lives the Pastor recalls,
the only one deemed capable of "the pure bond of independent love" (7:451),
who seems to have found his place in life among "the assembled spirits of the
just, / From imperfection and decay secure" (7:469–70),[25] is the one who can
hear no music: "a gentle Dalesman . . . / From whom, in early childhood, was
withdrawn / The precious gift of hearing. . . . / And this deep mountain Valley
was to him / Soundless, with all its streams" (7:417–22). Here perfection is
attained by inner conscience and Holy Writ, without, as the Pastor remarks at
the close of the Dalesman's epitaph, the "composing" effect of music (or, we
may add, of dialogue):

> —And yon tall Pine-tree, whose composing sound
> Was wasted on the good Man's living ear,
> Hath now its own peculiar sanctity;
> And, at the touch of every wandering breeze,
> Murmurs, not idly, o'er his peaceful grave. (7:494–98)

"The good Man's *living ear*" is richly ambiguous, referring at the simplest level
to the ear of the man while he was alive but suggesting more broadly that the
good man (any good man) with an ear alive to the Word of God needs no other
sounds ("He that hath an ear, let him hear what the Spirit saith unto the

churches" [Revelation 2:7, 2:11]). In the tale of the deaf Dalesman, the Word heard in silence matters more than compositions of music. And for those who can in a literal sense hear, the Poet who narrates *The Excursion* recommends the Wanderer's articulate voice above any music. To the Wanderer "the general ear / Listened with readier patience than to strain / Of music, lute, or harp,—a long delight / That ceased not when his voice had ceased" (8:605–8).

And yet, in dialogic counterpoint to this elevation of *logos* over music, the poem also relates the Solitary's despondency to his neglect of his musical powers. When the Wanderer and Poet enter the Solitary's cottage, they find "instruments of music, some half-made, / Some in disgrace . . . dangling from the walls" (2:696–97). Wordsworth's association of ethics with music is not wholly silenced in *The Excursion,* nor is his association, most clearly expressed in "The Power of Music," of music and civic solidarity. Like the fiddler of that earlier poem, the Solitary is an Orpheus figure; however, whereas "The Power of Music" showed an Orpheus in his civilizing (and decommercializing) glory, *The Excursion* evinces a tragic Orpheus silenced by the death of his wife and children. "Like Eurydice," writes Kevis Goodman, "the Solitary's family and his civic ideals recede like a puff of smoke in thin air—in spite of (or is it because of?) his clutching at shadows" (115).[26] For Goodman (116–23), the Solitary's sullen apathy as a bereaved survivor (an apathy ironically related to the approved Stoic *apatheia* of the Wanderer) is a betrayal of his debt to history, to the dead that lie buried around him and of whom the Wanderer and Pastor would in books 5–7 remind him.

I would add that his neglect of music is a betrayal of the living as well, those whom, Orpheus-like, he may have had the power to entrance and unite or, at least, enliven with stray gifts of pleasure. In this betrayal—in the disgraced, dangling instrument deprived of use—one can perhaps see Wordsworth's own critical self-reflection on his lost, or renounced, Orphic powers. He had earlier recited ballad meters aloud in a "*chaunt,*" as Hazlitt remarked, "which acts as a spell upon the hearer."[27] Leaving behind his art of enchantment, he built *The Excursion* upon unadorned blank verse, an art of dialogue and the commonplace, in which few birds sing.

CHAPTER NINE

Surviving Death

Wordsworth's poetry from *The Excursion* onward is concerned, almost obsessively, with death, continuities between the living and the dead, and the question of what it might mean to live beyond one's death. The Christian religion has, of course, clear doctrinal answers to this last question. Wordsworth does not. It is difficult, if not impossible, to say if and when Wordsworth arrived at an orthodox belief in personal immortality among the resurrected dead in the kingdom of heaven. Some have found the expression of such a belief as early as the 1807 "Intimations" *Ode*; strictly speaking, however, this poem is not about immortality but rather is an intuition of prenatal existence.[1] The speaker of the poem concludes only that death holds a special pathos, and perhaps a vague promise, to "an eye / That hath kept watch o'er man's mortality."

My contention in this chapter is simply this: that either alongside or in lieu of a belief in personal immortality, Wordsworth offers in his later poetry an ethical vision of *im*personal immortality. This last phrase may at first seem paradoxical, but it is readily explained with reference to the Stoic ethics I examined in chapter 8. Whoever is truly impartial—possessing, like the Wanderer, an "equipoise of love . . . unwarped by partial bondage"—will not set her personal interests above those of the community; rather, the interests of the community will become her interest. And insofar as the individual identifies her own good with communal good, she ensures a kind of continuing life within the life of the community that survives her, especially as it progresses toward the greater good.

This basic concept of self-preservation through self-transcendence is familiar to a variety of religions, including Judaism, Buddhism, and Christianity. Inaugurating the last of these, Paul writes of the believer's need to cast off his self, to "die unto himself," and live in Christ: "I live; yet not I, but Christ liveth in me" (Galatians 2:20). Substitute *humanity* for Paul's Christ, and one has the keystone of John Stuart Mill's "Religion of Humanity": I live, and yet not I, but humanity lives in me. Mill, who confessed in his *Autobiography* to finding in Wordsworth's poems "a source of inward joy," may also have found suggested in them the doctrine of impersonal immortality he sets forth in *The Utility of Religion* (composed between 1850 and 1858). This essay, too little regarded, deserves to be quoted at some length:

> that because life is short we should care for nothing beyond it, is not a legitimate conclusion; and the supposition, that human beings in general are not capable of feeling deep and even the deepest interest in things which they will never live to see, is a view of human nature as false as it is abject. Let it be remembered that if individual life is short, the life of the human species is not short; its indefinite duration is practically equivalent to endlessness; and being combined with indefinite capability of improvement, it offers to the imagination and sympathies a large enough object to satisfy any reasonable demand for grandeur of aspiration. If such an object appears small to a mind accustomed to dream of infinite and eternal beatitudes, it will expand into far other dimensions when those baseless fancies have receded into the past. (106)

Hoping that in time everyone will be "capable of identifying their feelings with the entire life of the human race," Mill turns to the importance of education and offers Cicero's *De Officiis* (itself a source for Wordsworth's Roman Stoicism) as an example of "how ardent a sentiment, in favourable circumstances of education, the love of country has become" (106–7). He then advances "a morality grounded on large and wise views of the good of the whole, neither sacrificing the individual to the aggregate nor the aggregate to the individual, but giving to duty on the one hand and to freedom and spontaneity on the other their proper province" (108). "To call these sentiments by the name morality," Mill avers, "is claiming too little for them. They are a real religion. . . . the Religion of Humanity" (109). He concludes: "if the Religion of Humanity were as sedulously cultivated as the supernatural religions are . . . all who had received the customary amount of moral cultivation would up to the hour of death live ideally in the life of those who are to follow them" (119).[2]

Mill's insights in part derive, as I hope to show in this chapter, from a reading of Wordsworth. Wordsworth, in turn, was acquainted with what would become one of Mill's key suppositions—that one can be just as interested in the future life of another as in one's own future life—through his conversations with the young William Hazlitt. Hazlitt, who met Wordsworth and Coleridge in May 1798, was by his own account eager to discuss moral philosophy, and by his own account his great metaphysical discovery (made in 1794, at age sixteen) was that *we have no natural concern for our future selves*. We are connected to our present selves by sensation and to our past selves by memory, and both of these faculties are self-centered; however, we are (or, Hazlitt fudges, ought to be) disinterested with regard to futurity, because the faculty with which we project a future self, the *imagination*, is the same that enables us to enter into other selves. In the future, self and other are the same. Hazlitt writes, "in defence of the natural disinterestedness of the human mind,"

> The objects in which the mind is interested may be either past or present, or future. These last alone can be the objects of rational or voluntary pursuit; for neither the past, nor the present can be altered for the better, or worse by any efforts of the will. It is only from the interest excited in him by future objects that man becomes a moral agent, or is denominated selfish, or the contrary, according to the manner in which he is affected by his own *future* interest, or that of others. . . . The imagination, by means of which alone I can anticipate future objects, or be interested in them, must carry me out of myself into the feelings of others by one and the same process by which I am thrown forward as it were into my future being, and interested in it. I could not love myself, if I were not capable of loving others. Self-love, used in this sense, is in its fundamental principle [of imagination] the same with disinterested benevolence. (*Essay on the Principles of Human Action* 1–3)[3]

We need not assume that Wordsworth either fully comprehended or concurred with Hazlitt's moral philosophy; indeed, as Stephen Gill notes, it is probable that Wordsworth imagines the bookish Hazlitt as his adversary in the anti-intellectual early poems, "Expostulation and Reply" and "The Tables Turned" (*William Wordsworth* 138–39). Nonetheless, he had some acquaintance with Hazlitt's ideas from 1798, and he claims to have read the copy of the *Essay on the Principles of Human Action* that Hazlitt sent him in 1805 (Wu, *William Hazlitt* 104). The proof is in the pudding: Wordsworth's later meditations on death and available futurities bear the impress of Hazlitt's philosophy.

The Hazlitt figure of "Expostulation and Reply" chides the poem's narrator for being an Adamic egoist, neglectful of both past and future: "You look round on your mother earth / As if she for no purpose bore you; / As if you were her first-born birth, / And none had lived before you!" Yet after his brother John's death in 1805, William became acutely conscious of those who had lived, and died, before him, and he worried over the purpose of it all. Death became for him not an existential concern (anxiety over the extinction of consciousness) but specifically a moral problem. His well-known letter to Sir George Beaumont of March 12, 1805, in the aftermath of John's shipwreck, examines death as a threat to goodness. If it treats alike the good (John) and the wicked, then the universe appears to have no moral structure; if God is the governor of this universe, then he appears in it to be amoral, immoral, or at least less moral than human beings are; and if there is nothing beyond this life to rectify its ills, then the structure of reality offers a disincentive to virtue. Wordsworth worries that this is indeed the case:

> Why have we a choice and a will, and a notion of justice and injustice, enabling us to be moral agents? Why have we sympathies that make the best of us so afraid of inflicting pain and sorrow, which yet we see dealt about so lavishly by the supreme governor? Why should our notions of right towards each other, and to all sentient beings within our influence differ so widely from what appears to be his notion and rule, if everything were to end here? Would it be blasphemy to say that upon the supposition of the thinking principle being destroyed by death, however inferior we may be to the great Cause and ruler of things, we have *more of love* in our Nature than he has? The thought is monstrous: and yet how to get rid of it except upon the supposition of *another* and a *better* world? (*Letters* 1:556)

Wordsworth arrives, as though unwillingly, at the tentative supposition that morality will be vindicated in a better world: it alone dispels a monstrous thought about an unloving God.

Yet Wordsworth's final query ("how to get rid of it except") frames this supposition as *faute de mieux,* the lack of a better way to solve a quandary. What would a better way be? Presumably, it would be one that does not compromise his belief, recently inscribed in the 1805 *Prelude,* that problems must be solved "not in Utopia," "But in the very world which is the world / Of all of us, the place in which, in the end, / We find our happiness, or not at all" (10:723–27). But then, nothing that Wordsworth writes to Beaumont necessarily compromises this belief. He plays with Beaumont, and perhaps with himself, a double game, never specifying what kind of better world he has in mind: is it a new Jerusalem come down from heaven, or the purely natural world that Mill later imagines, improved in historical time through the moral progress of mankind?

Similarly ambiguous is the "thinking principle" that must survive death if morality is to stand: does this mean personal identity or, as it more clearly seems, the principle of thought that all beings share? This weighted possibility opens the way for thinking about futurity à la Hazlitt and Mill: the thinking principle will survive as long as humanity does, and we will live (up to the hour of death) in the lives of those who follow us. Hope and faith in moral progress in this very world may also be read in Wordsworth's following lines to Beaumont on his brother's exceptional virtue—"he walked all his life pure among many impure . . . thinking and living only for others"—which conclude, gnomically, "So good must be better; so high must be destined to be higher" (1:556).

Wordsworth concludes this philosophical part of his letter with a block quotation from Edward Young's *Night Thoughts on Life, Death, and Immortality* (7:205–17), a 10,000-line poem of Christian apologetics in which a skeptic is decisively converted to orthodoxy (unlike the Solitary of *The Excursion*). However, Wordsworth quotes from the poem's pointed queries, not from its (plentiful) assurances. "Dream we, *that* luster of the moral world [i.e., the virtuous person]/Goes out in stench, and rottenness the close?" If rottenness is the dream, what is the reality? A scrupulous avoidance of Christian consolation characterizes Wordsworth's writings until his decisive turn to orthodox faith in his final decades. It is only in 1845 that Margaret of *The Ruined Cottage,* her tale retold in *The Excursion,* is given "the unbounded might of prayer" and a "soul/Fixed upon the cross, that consolation . . . /For the meek sufferer" (*Excursion* p. 75; see also Gill, *William Wordsworth* 415–17).[4]

In 1805, Wordsworth is concerned less with the immortality of personhood than with what will become of us, collectively: in the questions he asked Beaumont, "why have *we* a choice and a will"; "why have *we* sympathies"? The drift of his thought is that we survive by being *we,* an abiding, future-oriented collective: a "we" that on balance feels corporate and anonymous not distributive (the "we" that means "each of us," "any of us," "one"). Wordsworth found two ways to figure this collective, the first in the image of the *river,* an abiding form despite its fluctuating constituency. With Aristotle, and against Heracleitus, Wordsworth believes that you can step into the same river twice—or indeed, an infinite number of times.[5] Second, Wordsworth embodies the collective that lives beyond its members in the *institutions* that endure in historical time, including folkways, religion, and empire (seminally, Roman empire in its Virgilian guise). Thus after writing his 1820 sonnet sequence *The River Duddon,* he writes his *Ecclesiastical Sketches* (later retitled *Ecclesiastical Sonnets*), episodes from the history of the church in England (later extended to include the Anglican communion in America). This work, with its appreciation for the medieval church and its ceremonies, made Wordsworth a favorite and even an alleged prophet of the High Church Oxford Movement (1833–45), and the friend of its purveyors John Keble, John Henry Newman, Frederick Faber, and the American bishop George Washington Doane.[6]

Yet as recent critics have argued, Wordsworth shows little if any interest in *Ecclesiastical Sketches* (or in *The Excursion*) with church *doctrine;* his interest, rather, lies in preserving the Church as a preservative and ameliorative social institution.[7] Wordsworth followed *Ecclesiastical Sketches* with several poetic sequences crafted around tours of places where, once again, the past abides: Italy; Germany and the Lowlands; Scotland and the borders, which for Wordsworth preserve both Roman and Celtic, imperial and mythic, pasts. If individual life is short, the life of institutions and human environments is long, and the future continuous with the past.

THE RIVER AND "LIFE CONTINUOUS"

The river that courses toward imagined boundlessness is Wordsworth's central analogue for the tendency of (unindividualized) "Reason" or life to anticipate its infinite extension. In the first of his *Essays upon Epitaphs,* published in *The Friend* (1810) and later appended to book 1 of *The Excursion,* Wordsworth writes:

> Origin and tendency are notions inseparably co-relative. Never did a child stand by the side of a running stream, pondering within himself what power was the feeder of the perpetual current, from what never-wearied sources the body of water was supplied, but he must have been inevitably propelled to follow this question by another: "Towards what abyss is it in progress? what receptacle can contain the mighty influx?" And the spirit of the answer must have been, though the word might be sea or ocean, accompanied perhaps with an image gathered from a map, or from the real object in nature—these must have been the *letter,* but the *spirit* of the answer must have been *as* inevitably,—a receptacle without bounds or dimensions;—nothing less than infinity. We may, then, be justified in asserting, that the sense of immortality, if not a co-existent and twin birth with Reason, is among the earliest of her offspring . . . (*Prose Works* 2:51)

The least interesting things about the river, to Wordsworth or his child stand-in, are its "image" and objective being; its interest, rather, lies in its power to incite the mind to reflect on its own origin and tendency, the deep truths that are imageless. Such a river recurs in a speech by the Wanderer, who traces the sense of immortality (again, apparently impersonal) to the pagan's reflection on the river to which he has brought a votive offering:

And doubtless, sometimes, when the hair was shed
Upon the flowing stream, a thought arose
Of Life continuous, Being unimpaired;
That hath been, is, and where it was and is
There shall be,—seen, and heard, and felt, and known,
And recognized,—existence unexposed
To the blind walk of mortal accident;
From diminution safe and weakening age;
While man grows old, and dwindles, and decays;
And countless generations of Mankind
Depart; and leave no vestige where they trod. (*Excursion* 4:749–59)

In the Wanderer's litany of sensuous apprehension, "Life continuous" is impeded by emphatic parataxis, "seen, and heard, and felt, and known, and recognized" (remembered). This sensory list cannot be taken entirely literally, however, as the future ("there shall be") is, as Hazlitt observed, something that exists only imaginatively, not pertaining to the individual who perceives and remembers. But the spirit of the Wanderer's claim is clear: future "Being," if not necessarily one's own being in the future, can seem, in flashes, as immediate as the world one empirically inhabits.

"*Our* destiny, *our* nature, and *our* home," Wordsworth wrote in *The Prelude*, "*is* with infinitude" (emphases mine). Consider again this line that I examined with regard to the Romantic sublime—a sublimity often construed, mistakenly, as egotistical in nature. The corporate nature of the future Wordsworth imagines is unmistakable. He does not speak, as indeed it would be more natural now to speak, of our destinies, our natures, and our homes that *are* with infinitude. Wordsworth's "our" does not partition ("each of us") but rather consolidates ("all of us"). The trio of possessive pronouns found in this line from *The Prelude* becomes in the last, great line of *The River Duddon* a nominative trinity: "We feel that we are greater than we know." I quote the final sonnet of this sequence in its entirety. In it, the speaker addresses the river that has, in the penultimate sonnet, arrived at the sea, "that receptacle vast / Where all his unambitious functions fail":

I thought of Thee, my partner and my guide,
As being past away.—Vain sympathies!
For, *backward*, Duddon! as I cast my eyes,
I see what was, and is, and will abide;
Still glides the Stream, and shall for ever glide;

The Form remains, the Function never dies;

While *we*, the brave, the mighty, and the wise,

We Men, who in our morn of youth defied

The elements, must vanish;—be it so!

Enough, if something from our hands have power

To live, and act, and serve the future hour;

And if, as tow'rd the silent tomb we go,

Thro' love, thro' hope, and faith's transcendent dower,

We feel that we are greater than we know.

The last three lines of this sonnet are more interesting for not making perfect grammatical sense: one must silently add a second "we go" in front of the second-to-last line for this to make sense ("if as we go toward the tomb we go through love, hope, and faith, then we feel that we are greater than we know"). But the absence of that second predicate makes the poem's final affirmation hang a little uncertainly, as though governed by a counterfactual "as if." Wordsworth at his best, and here he is at his best, challenges; he does not reassure.

The artistry of the sonnet's last line is best appreciated by contrasting it to a clunky couplet Wordsworth supplied for his 1836 revision of *Descriptive Sketches*: "We still confide in more than we can know; / Death would be else the favorite friend of woe" (ll. 553–54). *The River Duddon* line does considerably more with ten syllables than its unhappy recasting does with twenty. Its meter places the greatest emphasis on the medial central "we," "we" as an intentional object, while the opening, subjective "we" defers in stress to "feel" and the closing "we" to "know." The relation of these two verbs is richly polyvalent, referring either to an antinomy of feeling and positive or probable knowledge ("we feel we are greater than we know ourselves to be") or to an antinomy of feeling and imperfect knowledge ("we feel we are greater than we can know anything about ourselves, or for that matter about anything"). The effect of the line as a whole is to raise feeling above knowing but at the same time, by ending with a plangent "know," to make feeling seem its own and better kind of knowledge.

In the sonnet as a whole, "our" greatness—the sublime of continuous life—is figured by Aristotle's abiding river: its "Form remains," its "Function never dies," regardless of the changing nature of its material composition. The river is analogous to human community in time: the parts change, but humankind lives on. It advances toward an end that is in one sense always the same (the abyss, death) but in another sense admits a *telos* or transcendent aim: faith, hope, and love, Paul's three theological virtues (1 Corinthians 13:13). Thus we-in-the-present live on in the imagination of future selves and may hope for the future happiness of humanity (aggregate and individual), with faith in the importance of goodness. Advancing Paul's theological virtues, in a manner that allows them to pertain to a detheologized ethics as well as to Christianity, is Wordsworth's ethical achievement here, his service to the future hour.

DUTIES TO THE DEAD AND ABSENT

So far we have been with Wordsworth looking forward, toward a future interest that depends on our present disinterestedness. But Wordsworth looks backward as well, to the dead or absent, including those to whom we have been personally attached and who live on through us. To recur to Wordsworth's 1802 wording about what he sought to accomplish in his poetry, he would "render [our] feelings" toward the dead "more sane, pure, and permanent, in short, more consonant to nature, that is, to eternal nature, and the great moving spirit of things" (letter to John Wilson, quoted earlier, in chapter 8). Seneca had earlier argued that for the Stoic sage *apatheia* is not a lack of feeling but rather "a soul that cannot be harmed" (*invulnerabilem animum*): "our wise man feels (*sentit*) his troubles, but overcomes them" (*Epistles* 9:2–3). Similarly, Wordsworth mourns the dead, but with some degree of invulnerability; he typically does so insofar as such mourning remains serviceable to the present and future hours or, in other words, inasmuch as the dead contribute to a suprapersonal good. For the Stoic sage, the "supreme good" (*summum bonum,* Seneca, *Epistles* 9:15) is the depersonalized life of rational virtue, in which we realize our shared human nature. To this life, death is not an impediment. The good, in which the sage finds his complete happiness, is in no way dependent upon friends and family, although friends and family are valuable as relations to which both nature and the exercise of the virtues attach us. Seneca writes of the sage:

> As long as he is allowed to order his affairs according to his judgment, he is self-sufficient—and marries a wife; he is self-sufficient—and brings up children; he is self-sufficient—and yet could not live if he had to live without the society of man. Natural promptings, and not his own selfish needs, draw him into friendships. . . . Nevertheless, though the sage may love his friends dearly, often comparing them with himself, and putting them ahead of himself, yet all the good will be limited to his own being, and he will speak the words which were spoken by . . . Stilbo. . . . For Stilbo, after his country was captured and his children and his wife lost, as he emerged from the general desolation alone and yet happy [*beatus*], spoke as

follows to Demetrius, called Sacker of Cities because of the destruction he brought upon them, in answer to the question whether he had lost anything: "I have all my goods with me" [*bona mea mecum sunt*]. (*Epistles* 9:17–18)

Without an understanding of Stoic ethics, it is impossible to appreciate what Wordsworth sought to accomplish in his poetry, especially after 1807. And yet Wordsworth stresses, as no Stoic does, the interdependence—even the reciprocal duties—of the living and the dead.

In Seneca, the lost spouse or child simply ceases to be. In Wordsworth, by contrast, the quick are bound to the dead by a duty of judgment. What we owe the dead is the opposite of melancholia, the pained refusal to let go; it is, rather, a judgment on (and to some degree a responsibility toward) their happiness, both in retrospect (as they lived) and in the present (as they lie underground).[8] What the dead owe the living, in turn, is to stay dead: not to recur, to rise up, fixating us in the past. We should be able to build a future upon the firm ground of their graves. This complex interdependence between the living and the dead is suggested in Wordsworth's seminal ballad "We are Seven," where to the uncomprehending narrator's consternation the little girl who lives among her dead siblings does so in "peace, / The central feeling of all happiness" (*Excursion* 3:338–89). Her independence is not compromised by the past, but the dead are, to her mind, made happy by her presence.

The interdependence of the living and the dead finds more explicit formulation in *The Excursion,* at the end of the Pastor's epitaph on a girl who died young. Although her family were at first distraught,

Time wants not power to soften all regrets,
And prayer and thought can bring to worst distress
Due resignation. Therefore, though some tears
Fail not to spring from either Parent's eye
Oft as they hear of sorrow like their own,
Yet this departed Little-one, too long
The innocent troubler of their quiet, sleeps
In what may now be called a peaceful grave. (7:712–19)

It may *now* be so called, or judged, because the parents are at peace, and on their peace their dead child's depends (she is otherwise an agent of trouble). The converse of this principle is that when the parents suffered her loss, the girl, as it were, rose up from a troubled grave. The dead, then, depend on us for (a judgment on) their own peace or happiness, and such a judgment depends on our ability to lay the dead to rest. This claim will, of course, seem absurd unless one refers it to the subrational feeling of responsibility we tend to have toward our dead, routinely expressed in rites of corpse preparation, burial, commemoration, and so on. In the Pastor's tale of the dead girl, that responsibility is simply extended to include the happiness (or what the living may call the happiness) of the dead. Here the dead girl's parents suffer loss, but they overcome their feeling of despondency through prayer (dependency sublime) and "thought" (presumably Stoic therapy), with the added motive that only through their own happiness will their daughter's past and enduring life be judged a happy one.

Looking back from this churchyard vantage to the end of book 1 of *The Excursion*, a similar sense of the living and dead linked by reciprocal duties lies behind the Wanderer's conclusion to the tale he tells of Margaret's decline and fall along with her cottage. Margaret, the long-suffering, is now at peace (rather than extinct) because of the Wanderer's own tranquil happiness, which is the happiness he owes to her, and she to him:

> Be wise and cheerful; and no longer read
> The forms of things with an unworthy eye.
> She sleeps in the calm earth, and peace is here.
> I well remember that those very plumes,
> Those weeds, and the high spear-grass on that wall,
> By mist and silent rain-drops silver'd o'er,
> As once I passed, did to my heart convey
> So still an image of tranquility,
> So calm and still, and looked so beautiful
> Amid the uneasy thoughts which filled my mind,
> That what we feel of sorrow and despair
> From ruin and from change, and all the grief
> The passing shews of Being leave behind,
> Appeared an idle dream, that could not live
> Where meditation was. I turned away
> And walked along my road in happiness. (1:969–84)

The Wanderer can afford to be happy because, although no longer a peddler, he has all his goods with him.

At other times, however, Wordsworth could imagine what is now called "survivor's guilt": guilt felt for being alive, for happiness through luck, when a dead friend, spouse, child, or fellow (or, after Auschwitz, so many fellows) are not alive and have no peaceful graves. He expresses something of this guilt, and enduring sorrow, in his 1815 sonnet to his dead daughter Catherine, "Surprized by joy," a poem of inconsolable grief.[9] But he expresses it more clearly, and complexly, in three consecutive sonnets in *The River Duddon,* a subgroup that is not clearly on death but rather on an absent beloved—"The One for whom my heart shall ever beat / With tenderest love"—who may refer, biographically, to his living wife, Mary, although nothing in the text of the poems precludes us from reading it as his dead daughter, Catherine.[10] *The River Duddon* sonnet sequence (*Sonnet Series* 56–75) recounts a walk alongside its titular river that occupies the course of a summer's day, symbolizing at points the course of mortal life. The walk is undertaken alone, and mostly in happiness, accompanied chiefly by recollections of the past and the absent, including the dead: "Some who had early mandates to depart, / Yet are allowed to steal my path athwart / By Duddon's side" (sonnet 21). Four sonnets, numbers 24 to 27, are set in a leafy bower where the poet takes refuge during the heat of the day. Sonnet 25, the first of the three that concern me here, introduces the poet's unidentified, absent "One," at first with eager desire (would that she were here!) but then, turning to an emotional note unprecedented in Wordsworth's writing, with guilt that he is enjoying what this other cannot, an enjoyment that feels morally wrong:

> . . . here dwells soft ease:
> With sweets which she partakes not some distaste
> Mingles, and lurking consciousness of wrong . . .

In dialectical opposition to this eschewal of *undivided* happiness (one not shared with the absent and/or dead beloved), composed in 1818–19, Wordsworth inserts as the twenty-sixth sonnet of his series a much earlier composition, dating from 1802, that lays claim to a happiness as indifferent to other people as the river's own course. Here he recalls following streams as a boy and, in the sonnet's sestet, the lessons they taught and still teach him:

> Nor have I tracked their course for scanty gains,
> They taught me random cares and truant joys,
> That shield from mischief and preserve from stains
> Vague minds, while men are growing out of boys;
> Maturer Fancy owes to their rough noise
> Impetuous thoughts that brook not servile reins.

Coming after worries about unshared pleasure, these lines read like a declaration of independence: the streams that once taught him innocent but *truant* (idle, undutiful) joys now inspire "impetuous thoughts" opposed to "servile *reins*." This last term literally denotes either a harness (the reins of a horse), or "the kidneys" (from Latin *renes,* Johnson notes), traditionally the seat of the emotions and affections: by metonymy, "servile reins" could stand for emotions, or those who have emotions, too dependent on others. Extending the resonance of the poet's defiance, "reins" is also a homophone for "reigns" and, by close association, the French *reines,* or "queens." The poet of this sonnet abides neither church, nor state, nor the bond of absent love: he is like a wild horse or the river's running waters.

In sonnet 25 the poet expresses guilt for enjoying what the absent cannot; sonnet 26 counters that guilt with a defiant independence. Sonnet 27, another poem from 1818–19, imaginatively reconciles present independence, and the dues owed absent others, in a hymn to the interdependence of all things. The sonnet must be quoted as a whole to appreciate Wordsworth's syntactic entanglement of elements and oppositions:

> I ROSE while yet the cattle, heat-opprest,
> Crowded together under rustling trees,
> Brushed by the current of the water-breeze;
> And for *their* sakes, and love of all that rest,
> On Duddon's margin, in the sheltering nest;
> For all the startled scaly tribes that slink
> Into his coverts, and each fearless link
> Of dancing insects forged upon his breast;
> For these, and hopes and recollections worn
> Close to the vital seat of human clay;
> Glad meetings—tender partings—that upstay
> The drooping mind of absence, by vows sworn
> In his pure presence near the trysting thorn;
> I thanked the Leader of my onward way.

The emphatically other-oriented catalogue beginning in line 4, "And for *their* sakes" (not my sake), seems at first to supply a motive for why "I ROSE," departing from his enclosed, self-pleasing bower to follow the river's course to its end. It is only in the sonnet's last line that we recognize this catalogue not (only) as motives to rising but as things to give thanks for, a thanksgiving addressed to "the Leader," the river (of life) that he follows. Thanks are offered first for links in the river's ecosystem (cattle, trees, breeze, birds, fish, insects) and next for the similarly coordinated element of the poet's mind—hopes and recollections, meetings and partings, presence and absence—all of which are grounded, finally, in dutiful attachment to "The One for whom my heart shall ever beat." The triad of sonnets 25–27 thus ends with independence and spontaneity linked to, though not reined in by, vows and attachments to the absent, departed, or lost. In these sonnets, Wordsworth enacts the reconciliation of independence with interdependence, the self-sufficient living and the unbetrayed dead.

CHAPTER TEN

The Poetics of Life

The later Wordsworth devotes himself to poetry about, and reflecting, continuity, procession, fluid motion, change within stable form, temporal infinity rather than spatial totality. This devotion corresponds to the poet's intensified distrust of static images. From his earliest loco-descriptive poetry, Wordsworth set the environmental attachments of the ear against the despotism of the possessive eye. Yet his later poetry grows increasingly iconoclastic in a religious way: echoing Hebraic and Protestant precursors (including Spenser and Milton), Wordsworth searches for poetic means to tear down idols, pagan and Catholic, even, or especially, when he finds them attractive.[1] Wordsworth expresses anxiety about his own poetic art and its complicity with an idealizing, static, and mendacious visual imagination in *Elegiac Stanzas, Suggested by a Picture of Peele Castle, in a Storm, painted by Sir George Beaumont,* written a little more than a year after his 1805 letter to Beaumont on his brother John's death. The timeless and idyllic scene he *would* have once painted, "if mine had been the Painter's hand," is now rejected as "a dream" and "surely blind," and the poem ends with Wordsworth's new poetic agenda: "Not without hope we suffer and we mourn" (*Poems, in Two Volumes* 266–68).[2]

The line could serve as a motto for two of Wordsworth's romances that I examine in this chapter: *The White Doe of Rylstone; or the Fate of the Nortons* (composed 1807–8, rewritten 1814–15), and *The Egyptian Maid; or, the Romance of the Water Lily* (composed c. 1828, published 1835), a prescient piece of Arthuriana written in advance of Tennyson's popularization of Camelot tales.[3] These romances could as well be called "antiromances," because they defy the narrative expectations built into the verse romance since the success of Walter Scott's *Lay of the Last Minstrel* (1805).[4] To put it bluntly, many things happen in Scott's romances (and a fortiori Byron's later ones)—there are forbidden loves, feuds, outlawry, combat—while Wordsworth's romances austerely focus on loss, suffering, and redemption. Wordsworth's experiments with the romance form of both Scott (in *The White Doe of Rylstone*) and Sir Thomas Malory (in *The Egyptian Maid*) result in poems in which there are no vivid characters, indeed no selves or others, but only death and its echoes in life. Both of Wordsworth's romances/antiromances center on female personages, antiprotagonists who do not act but rather who suffer, and who do so on account of images (the banner bearing the cross and Christ's five wounds Emily of *The White Doe* unwillingly weaves; the goddess emerging from a lily or lotus on the prow of the ship that conveys the Egyptian maid). Taken as allegories, both verse tales (as minimal as their narratives are) represent voice over image, temporal continuity over frozen representation. Moreover, through the mediums of voice and memory, both Emily and the maid variously survive death—Emily, that of her entire family, and the maid, her own—within tales that meditate on the shapes such survival might take.

Of the institutions that endure in time, the mature Wordsworth was particularly interested in two of medieval origin: the church and romance form. Medieval history—a past continuous with, ever replenishing, the future—is engaged by Wordsworth on his own terms: in place of the iconic aesthetics of medieval romance, with its crosses, wounds, and grails, Wordsworth offers a Protestant poetics centered on the ear and its responsiveness to natural environments. Wordsworth's own "grail quest," if we may call it that, was in search of semi- and nonnarrative poetic expressions set apart from the temptation and "death" that lie in visual imagery and narrative absorption. To find a poetic equivalent to natural voice (for example, the "call" of streams or birds)—or, increasingly, angelic voice—became, in a variety of his later poems, both his ambition and humility. It is with a bouquet of these poems, concluding with *The Cuckoo at Laverna* (1837)—a poem that reimagines St. Francis as a devotee of springtime birdsong—that I end this chapter.

These last poems are self-consciously focused on how poetry can call back the dead, preserve life, and serve the future hour. Poetry's service to life, its conquest of death, is the burden of the Orpheus story, which Wordsworth once again revisits in his *On the Power of Sound*: "Hell to the lyre bowed low," he writes of Orpheus's rescue of Eurydice (l. 126). But in this late poem Wordsworth also asks us, strangely though wonderfully, to hear life, demythologized, as an *echo* of death:

> To life, to *life* give back thine Ear:
> Ye who are longing to be rid

Of Fable, though to truth subservient, hear
The little sprinkling of cold earth that fell
Echoed from the coffin lid . . . (153–57)

Life, emphatic life, as death's echo: the image is a striking one of the continuity of life and death, indefinitely suggestive of the manner in which the dead survive, and embodied in verse that calls upon the ear above the other senses.

IDOLS TO FACES, DEATH INTO LIFE:
THE WHITE DOE OF RYLSTONE AND THE EGYPTIAN MAID

In *The Prelude,* Wordsworth evokes the "power in sound / To breathe an elevated mood, by [distinct, visual] form / Or image unprofaned" (2:324–26). The profanity of images, their irreverence, is a judgment Wordsworth imbibed from radical Protestantism; it is one he shares with the English and Scottish reformers who stripped church altars and destroyed church statuary and paintings in the seventeenth century.[5] "Thou shalt not make unto thee any graven image, or any likeness of any thing that is in heaven above, or that is in the earth beneath, or that is in the water under the earth" (Exodus 20:4): these words from God to Moses were recognized by the theologian John Calvin, and subsequently by English Puritanism, as a literal commandment.[6] The threat of images is that they too readily become idols, material objects reverenced for their own sakes, or for the sake of the deities or daemons that are thought to inhabit them, and not for the sake of their transcendent Creator. Devisualizing Christianity, Protestant churches elevated the vocal and aural—pulpit, Bible-reading, hymnody, and sermon—above the visual (statues, icons, paintings, crucifixes, sacerdotal garments) and olfactory (smoke, incense).

Wordsworth also elevates the aural over the visual, as we have amply observed throughout this book, but he steps beyond Protestant reform in elevating natural sound or "music" above Christian liturgy. He does so with remarkable frankness in describing a Sabbath service at the outset of *The White Doe of Rylstone,* a poem set during and after the 1569 Rebellion of the Northern Earls, a Roman Catholic rising against Queen Elizabeth's church and government. The first of the poem's seven cantos situates the reader in a narrative present that is "fully fifty years" (l. 17) after the Henrician dissolution of the monasteries (1536–40)—that is, sometime between 1586 and 1590, roughly twenty years after the unsuccessful rebellion and (in Wordsworth's narration) the execution of the Nortons who took part in it.[7] At this point in time the service being held in the surviving chapel of Bolton Priory is securely Church of England. The poem's narrator approves of the church's hymnody but subordinates its liturgy to the sound of a river:

> ... the prelusive hymn is heard:—
> With one consent the people rejoice,
> Filling the church with a lofty voice!
> They sing a service which they feel:
> For 'tis the sun-rise now of zeal,
> And faith and hope are in their prime,
> In great Eliza's golden time.
>
> A moment ends the fervent din,
> And all is hushed, without and within;
> For, though the priest more tranquilly
> Recites the holy liturgy,
> The only voice which you can hear
> Is the river murmuring near. (ll. 36–48)[8]

The very next sound the poem offers, a further supplanting of doctrine by nature, is the step of the mysterious white doe that enters the churchyard to seek out a grave that lies apart from all the others. Once the service ends, the congregants gather round the doe and speculate on what soul lives on inside her: one surmises it is that of the Priory's founder; another, that it is the fairy or nature spirit that once sang, to a local lord, "A song of Nature's hidden powers; / That whistled like the wind, and rang / Among the rocks and holly bowers" (ll. 274–76).

At the end of *The White Doe*, the reader discovers that the doe is not possessed but simply bears in living memory the lone Norton to survive for some years the Northern Uprising—her companion, Emily. Emily, tied by the doe to nature's powers, is also attached, along with her eldest brother Francis, to the "pure religion" (l. 388) or "purer faith" (l. 574) of Reformed Christianity that they learned from their deceased mother. The obstructive idol of the poem is the banner, with cross and wounds, that Emily weaves at her Catholic father's command, obedient but conscientiously objecting. It is a banner he displays on joining the rebelling forces, joined in arms by all of his eight sons excepting Francis. In canto 2, Francis predicts to Emily that the rebellion will end disastrously; she must prepare for ruin and "Hope nothing" (l. 534), but

> ... be worthy of the grace
> Of God, and fill thy destined place:

A soul, by force of sorrows high,
Uplifted to the purest sky
Of undisturbed humanity! (ll. 588–92)

"The still, sad music of humanity" is here recast as "the purest sky of undisturbed humanity," an index—image is not quite the right word (we cannot *see* a "sky of humanity")—of ascent, expansion, and clarity. Emily, instructed in a pure religion and destined for greater purification, provides a counterpoint to her idolatrous father, who has only a fleeting doubt, as the battle turns against him, of the efficacy of the banner, which the narrator calls derisively, and expansively, "that Imagery" (l. 867). Imagery is what Wordsworth largely eschews in his poem, in favor of "compounded abstract words" (in Burke's phrase),[9] and sounds about sounds.

In Judeo-Christian tradition, idols represent a potential spiritual danger. For semiotics and poststructuralism, they represent the illusion of self-present meaning, a pre-Saussurian (as well as pre-Oedipal) faith in signs inherently bonded to a single signification. It is hardly surprising that Wordsworth's poetry, elusively significant and anti-iconic, tending toward infinity over totality, should have found warm welcome among both religious readers and postmodernists; nor is it surprising that its underlying moral assumptions readily accord, as I hope to have showed in earlier chapters, with the Judaic, Protestant-influenced, and postmodern ethics of Emmanuel Levinas. The crucial significance of face-to-face encounter, in both writers, should now be clear.

What I would clarify, however, is that for Levinas—and, I will suggest, for Wordsworth—the *face* is something distinct from, and opposed to, inert image or representation. Levinas's concept of the face, Samuel Moyn argues, derives from Franz Rosenzweig, who described God's gaze as "not the basic form of his countenance, fixed and immutable. It is not the rigid mask that the sculptor lifts off the face of the dead. Rather, it is the fleeting, indefatigable alteration of mien, the ever youthful radiance that plays on the eternal features. Love hesitates to make a likeness of the lover; the portrait would reduce the living countenance to rigor mortis" (quoted and translated by Moyn, 253). Levinas invokes this passage in his claim that "the face of the Other at each moment destroys and overflows the plastic image it leaves me, the idea existing to my own measure" (50–51). "Representation" is a suspect term for Levinas: it is an operation that tends toward reducing the other to the same, to "my own measure," an inadequate equation. It is also an impious attempt to freeze the continuous flow of being. "To represent is not only to render 'anew'; it is to reduce to the present an actual perception which flows on" (127).

A similar scruple about representation inhibits Wordsworth from ever describing a face (as opposed, say, to Hazlitt, who gives us striking images of faces—including Wordsworth's).[10] Faces are just called faces, without qualification. Their significance as the zone of contact is assumed, and their mobility may be implied, as in Emily's first encounter with the doe after the execution of the rest of her family:

> Even to her feet the Creature came,
> And laid its head upon her knee,
> And looked into the Lady's face,
> A look of pure benignity,
> And fond unclouded memory.
> It is, thought Emily, the same,
> The very Doe of other years!
> The pleading look the Lady viewed,
> And, by her gushing thoughts subdued,
> She melted into tears—
> A flood of tears, that flowed apace
> Upon the happy Creature's face. (ll. 1673–84)

The doe brings the isolated Emily the joy of reintegration—with a familiar creature, with her own past self—in a manner that recalls the ass's gift to Peter Bell, though the seriocomic tone of that earlier poem, and its ironic religiosity, contrast with Wordsworth's new tone of pious simplicity. But the importance of face-to-face encounter in *Peter Bell* persists into *The White Doe*. There is, its narrator continues, "promise in . . . [the doe's] speaking face," and Emily comes to accept "this gift of Heaven with grace" (1697–98).

Over time, and in the presence of the caring doe, Emily's "holy, / Though stern and rigorous, melancholy" (1615–16) becomes a "holy, / Mild, delicious melancholy" (1776–77). She attains, in the narrator's altered echo of Francis's earlier words, "the purest sky / Of undisturbed *mortality*" (1871–72, my emphasis), her natural death now anticipated. Emily is an anti-Margaret, who transcends through suffering her desolation and blasted estate; she is also, in her spiritualization, the antithesis of the sensuous Laodamia (a figure who was also, in the ancient accounts Wordsworth worked from, an idolater).[11] She is partly akin to Wordsworth's Stoic heroes (Protesilaus, the Wanderer, the leech gatherer), although her redemption through suffering has a Christian provenance—Evan Radcliffe traces it to Wordsworth's reading in Quakerism and mystical Quietism (163–73).

The doe serves not only as Emily's natural Paraclete or Comforter but also as her double. Wordsworth, in his introductory verses to *The White Doe*, writes of Spenser's Una being "Meek as that emblem of her lowly heart, / The milk-white Lamb" (13–14); correspondingly, the doe serves as the emblem of Emily's humility. But the doe and Emily share a more fundamental bond in the poem: both are bearers of the dead. The poem opens and closes with the doe upon a grave, revealed at the end as Emily's. The doe is "by adversities unmoved" (1921), like the lady whose memory she preserves, and like the poem that embodies them both. Emily's function in the poem is similarly preservative: she survives death by allowing the dead to live on in her, becoming their vessel, their unmoved mover. She carries within her dead brother's admonishment (canto 2) and her dead mother's religious instruction (canto 4). And when she dies, the doe—her naturalized self—lives on.

A vessel for the continuity of others is not uncommonly what Wordsworth wants sisters and daughters to be. It is how he sees his own sister (and comforter), Dorothy, in the final movement of *Tintern Abbey*; it is also how he came to imagine his daughter Dora, whose "obvious duties" probably involve keeping his own poetic flame alive. Wordsworth's instrumental use of sister and daughter is apt to strike us as indefensible, however natural it may have seemed to most of his Victorian audience—a testament to humanity's moral progress, as Mill imagined it. What interests me as a critic, however, is that Wordsworth's problematic attitude toward his female relations has an aesthetic corollary, equally problematic, in his antiromances: they center on women who, in order to be vehicles by which the dead live on, have no consciousness, character, or significant speech of their own. They are blanks, absences. The reader is allowed to feel little or nothing for them, not even the sympathetic (and/or sadomasochistic) pleasure readers of *Lyrical Ballads* might feel for that volume's sensationally and often vocally suffering women: the Mad Mother, the Forsaken Indian Woman, Martha Ray, Goody Blake, Poor Susan.[12] Emily does not speak in *The White Doe* until canto 4, and then it is only to apostrophize her absent mother; in canto 3, her father recalls her speaking to the doe (ll. 879–81), though her words are not reported. She speaks just one more time, also in canto 4, querying a friend of her father's whose report of the Nortons' capture moves the plot along. The rest is silence.

In *The Egyptian Maid*, the maid of the title does not speak or act at all; she is not even given a name. She is the absent center of an eccentric tale. The Egyptian maid and her story, such as it is, are Wordsworth's inventions, but he inserts them into the world of Arthurian legend, invoking in his poem's headnote the influential 1816 modernized version of Sir Thomas Malory's *Le Morte D'Arthur*.[13] The poem begins with Merlin spying a ship, the *Water Lily,* which, unbeknownst to him, carries a maid, a Christian convert, to Britain; her marriage is to be arranged by King Arthur, who once saved her father's land from invaders. Merlin envies the ship its beauty, and determined to humble it, casts a spell that brings a storm down upon it. The ship is wrecked, and the maid, seemingly dead though possibly asleep (the narrator entertains both possibilities), washes up on an island, along with the alluring female idol of the ship's prow, a goddess emerging from a lily flower that is also called "a carved Lotus" (l. 125). The maid's body is rescued from the island by Nina, the Lady of the Lake, and with Merlin's aid it is brought to King Arthur's court. Arthur tells the knights of his table that the one who is destined to be her husband may revive her by touching her hand. Many knights fail this trial, but Sir Galahad succeeds.

The maid survives death by Galahad's recognition of her face—one he has seen before, through Nina's enchantment, in a "waking dream" (298–306)—and of her (unidentified) name, a name to which he devotes his life:

> "Mine was she—mine she is, though dead,
> And to her name my soul shall cleave in sorrow;"
> Whereat, a tender twilight streak
> Of colour dawned upon the damsel's cheek;
> And her lips, quickening with uncertain red,
> Seemed from each other a faint warmth to borrow. (325–30)

The next stanza elaborates on the maid's coming to life, as "relenting Death / Allowed a soft and flower-like breath" (333–34).

But this life, ironically, passes quickly into life-in-death. The maid awakes, and nuptials are quickly arranged, but before a wedding takes place a choir of angels sing a song that concludes the poem: the maid's ship, it is revealed, was punished through Merlin but by Heaven, for the "Idol at her Prow" (l. 361). The maid had to die because of the idol she sailed under—an allegory for the danger of visual art, or why the "ship of the church" (a common medieval trope) needs to be purified of images—and her life with Galahad is collapsed into anticipating the "call" of God "to bowers of endless love." In the poem's last lines, the angelic choir entreats the maid and Galahad:

Blest Pair! whate'er befall you
Your faith in Him approve
Who from frail earth can call you,
To bowers of endless love! (383–86)

What kind of love? The poem seems, in retrospect, to allegorize the triumph of *agapē* over *erōs*, *caritas* over concupiscence. This reading comes into better focus once we see another implication of the poem: the idol under whom the Egyptian Maid earlier sailed was Isis, the Egyptian Venus. Wordsworth writes in his headnote to the poem: "the Lotus, with the bust of the goddess appearing to rise out of the full-blown flower, was suggested by the beautiful work of ancient art, once included among the Townley Marbles, and now in the British museum." Charles Townley (1737–1805) was London's most famous collector of Greek, Roman, and Egyptian antiquities, a collection that became public with its acquisition by the British Museum shortly after his death. The marble bust that Wordsworth mentions, now thought to be a portrait of a Roman lady, was identified by Townley in his catalogue description of his holdings as the Egyptian goddess Isis—the fecund nature goddess who, as Lemprière remarked in his entry on her in his *Classical Dictionary*, refigures in later pagan religions as Venus, Cybele, Proserpine, et al.[14] Wordsworth, transforming this bust into his ship's idol, emphasizes the deity's erotic allure on the isle where it and the maid have washed ashore:

Sad relique, but how fair the while!
For gently each from each retreating
With backward curve, the leaves revealed
The bosom half, and half concealed,
Of a Divinity, that seemed to smile
On Nina as she passed, with hopeful greeting. (126–31)

Nina remains impervious to Isis's charm, rescuing the maiden but not the idol, thus allowing spiritual to win out over carnal love—and, correspondingly, the aural (Galahad's vivifying oath, the angels' song of endless love) over the visual.

The plot of *The Egyptian Maid* is an inversion of, and yet a complement to, that of Tennyson's *The Lady of Shalott* (1832). There the towered lady dies upon leaving the world of visual representation (her tapestry); here it is the idol the maid sails under, along with the physical beauty of her ship itself, which brings vengeance upon her, although she is ultimately redeemed. Yet in both poems the realm of nature, the terrestrial, is that of death: life lies elsewhere. The male protagonist in Tennyson is Lancelot, Malory's knight of adulterous love, whose physical allure entices the lady of Shalott to her fatal entry into the world. Galahad, Lancelot's out-of-wedlock son, is, by contrast, "a clean virgin above all knights" (*The History of the Renowned Prince Arthur* 2:322). Of all the Round Table knights, he has the most complete vision of the holy grail, and seeing in it the face or presence of the Lord, is prepared to be freed from this life by death, so as to enjoy forever the beatific vision of the trinity (2:326–31).

In the structure of *The Egyptian Maid*, the maid assumes the place occupied in Malory's romance by the grail: she is the object that Galahad looks upon and, proleptically, dies. Her substitution for a literal vessel may explain her silence and passivity, while her substitution for the vessel that serves God explains Galahad's devotion to a name not divulged in the poem: it is God's name in pious circumlocution, the Jews' *ha shem* ("the name"), and the Christian's miraculous metaname of Jesus, "the Prince of life . . . [whose] name through faith in his name hath made this [formerly lame] man strong" (Acts 3:15–16). Galahad's union with the maid is not a worldly marriage but rather a recursion to a world without sin, at once eschatological and, in the image of swans who rejoice at Galahad's touching the maiden's hand, prelapsarian:

> The Swans, in triumph clap their wings;
> And their necks play, involved in rings,
> Like sinless snakes in Eden's happy land . . . (321–23)

With *The Egyptian Maid*, surviving death may no longer be a useful rubric; surviving mortal life, and birth into eternal life, has become Wordsworth's Christian theme. Yet on another level he is still the historian of institutions, the maid representing, like Una, the spirit of the church on earth, freshly liberated from its idolatrous lodging and newly attuned to an impersonal choir of voices.

THE ROMANCE OF LIFE AS SHE IS

The Egyptian Maid was first published in *Yarrow Revisited, and Other Poems* (1835), an unexpected success that outsold any of Wordsworth's previous volumes. It is unclear what role, if any, *The Egyptian Maid* played in the volume's success; with its foretaste of a beatific vision (or audition) that can only be sustained in heaven, it stands apart from the bulk of the volume's other poems, which are very much rooted in human time and place—with life as it is. The volume opens with a sequence of poems, headed by "Yarrow Revisited," described as "Composed . . . during a Tour in Scotland, and on the English Border, in the Autumn of 1831."[15] Accompanied by Dora, Wordsworth had set out to visit Sir Walter Scott, seriously ill, at his Abbotsford home, before Scott's physician-recommended trip to Naples (Scott would die the following year). "Yarrow Revisited" begins with a headnote describing the poem as "a memorial of a day passed with Sir Walter Scott . . . visiting the Banks of the Yarrow under his guidance." The poem develops into a defense of poetry's memorial power ("And what, for this frail world, were all / That mortals do or suffer, / Did no responsive harp, no pen, / Memorial tribute offer?"), and, more specifically, of "localised Romance" (like *Lay of the Last Minstrel*—or *The White Doe of Rylstone*) to "sustain the heart in feeling / Life as she is." The enjambment in these last lines is particularly effective: we syntactically expect romance to sustain *feelings* (for example, of pity, excitement, or delight); it comes as a surprise, however, that *romance,* often taken as a mere fiction of what never was, should sustain feelings of "life as she is"—that its artistry should be wholly at the service of nature.

Perhaps we shouldn't be surprised. From his earliest poems Wordsworth has romanced the ordinary. As Coleridge explains in his well-known account of the aims of *Lyrical Ballads:* "Mr. Wordsworth . . . was . . . to give the charm of novelty to things of every day, and to excite a feeling analogous to the supernatural, by awakening the mind's attention from the lethargy of custom, and directing it to the loveliness and wonders of the world before us" (*Biographia Literaria* 2:6–7). But keeping this agenda in mind, there is still something stark and factual about "life as she is"—particularly if we recall Wordsworth's Stoic commitment to life as it actually is (the life of things), and to bringing human desires into accord with it. As we've seen, he eschews "murmuring" or harboring sullen discontent with fortune. Murmuring is beneath the dignity of the African woman expelled from France, the discharged soldier, the old leech gatherer, Francis and Emily Norton. However, by according the *romance* of place ("localized Romance") the power to attach us to life as "she is"—that *she* providing a certain romance or figural distance from bare life—Wordsworth reveals the degree to which being and desire, actuality and possibility, are intertwined in his poetry. Whatever is—for example, Yarrow Water, the ruins of Bolton Abbey, the displacement of the rural poor—is, after being touched by poetry, no longer a brute fact but rather a face that calls to us. We care, and are in some vicarious way responsible for, the river, the Abbey, the soldier. Something in us seeks their preservation or flourishing, and that of whatever their counterparts might be in the worlds within each of us dwells.

Resolving the apparent antinomy of romance and fact—or, broadening the terms, of art and nature—is an ongoing concern of the "Poems Composed . . . during a Tour in Scotland." Sonnet 4, "Composed in Roslin Chapel, During a Storm," concludes with an image of herbs growing alongside the abandoned chapel's sculpted leaves, themselves grown green with age and mold:

> . . . in the Temple they a friendly niche
> Share with their sculptured fellows, that, green-grown,
> Copy their beauty more and more, and preach,
> Though mute, of all things blending into one.

Here image or artifice, by "growing" green, becomes part of the nature that covers and subsumes it—and this process, in an oral/aural metaphor, "preaches" the oneness of things, specifically of art and nature. These concepts may appear to be mutually exclusive, however, in Wordsworth's next sonnet, "The Trosachs" (a narrow Highlands valley between Loch Achray and Loch Katrine), in which an October landscape bespeaks the actuality of death, and art the illusion of immortality:

> There's not a nook within this solemn Pass,
> But were an apt confessional for One
> Taught by his summer spent, his autumn gone,
> That Life is but a tale of morning grass,
> Withered at eve. From scenes of art that chase
> That thought away, turn, and with watchful eyes
> Feed it 'mid Nature's old felicities,
> Rocks, rivers, and smooth lakes more clear than glass
> Untouched, unbreathed upon. Thrice happy quest,
> If from a golden perch of aspen spray
> (October's workmanship to rival May)
> The pensive warbler of the ruddy breast
> This moral sweeten by a heaven-taught lay,
> Lulling the year, with all its cares, to rest.

Nature teaches transience, and (some) art distracts from it: but the antinomy is not as clear as it might at first seem. First, the Trosachs is a place to which many readers of Wordsworth and many of his original readers would have been preattached by the romance Scott set there, *The Lady of the Lake* (1810)—the lake in question being Loch Katrine. Second, nature itself, as Wordsworth's poem presents it, is infused with art, that of the psalmist, who teaches all flesh is grass (see, for example, Psalm 90:5–6), and that of the bird whose "lay" sweetens death, doing what birds have always done and will always do in Wordsworth's verse. The bird's song reconciles us to life as it is but only because poetry—Biblical, Roman ("thrice happy"), and Wordsworthian—has already derealized it.

In 1833 Wordsworth made a fifth and final tour of Scotland, commemorating it in another sonnet sequence. Its most interesting poem, "On the Frith of Clyde. (In a Steam-Boat)," is another meditation on the interdependence of romance and nature, here correlated, respectively, with ambition (the desire to transcend what is) and humility (submission to it). The poem begins with an apostrophe to the island of Arran, its mountains, outlined in the distance, bringing to mind other islands (Teneriffe, St. Helena) with storied mountains:

> Arran! a single-crested Teneriffe,
> A St. Helena next—in shape and hue,
> Varying her crowded peaks and ridges blue;
> Who must but covet a cloud-seat or skiff
> Built for the air, or winged Hippogriff,
> That he might fly, where no one could pursue,
> From this dull Monster and her sooty crew;
> And, like a God, light on thy topmost cliff.
> Impotent wish! which reason would despise
> If the mind knew no union of extremes,
> No natural bond between the boldest schemes
> Ambition frames, and heart-humilities.
> Beneath stern mountains many a soft vale lies,
> And lofty springs give birth to lowly streams.

The poem is rich and difficult. There is no easy explanation for why the speaker deems compatible with "heart-humilities" his romance ambition to rise above a "sooty" actuality—to soar like an Olympian, or hero in Ariosto (the poet who invents the hippogriff), to the top of Arran's mountains. How can a fantasy of escape and superior vantage, with its contempt for the steamship and distaste for those who operate it, be at the same time a self-effacement? How can *this* romance be squared with life as it is?

The answer, I think, is that romance ambition accords with humility when set against the vaunting, antinatural ambitions of modernity. This is a central paradox not only of Wordsworth but also of the modern environmental movement. Setting oneself apart from common practices (cruising in steamships; driving monstrous, gas-guzzling vehicles; inhabiting large, difficult-to-heat houses) is not (just) pride but (also) humility insofar as it is done not to raise oneself above others but rather to submit oneself to an ethical imperative: the environment, the world-as-it-is, ought to be preserved. This humility looks in the face not of the present but of the future, and the future selves in whom humanity will continue onward, in an environment of which we are the temporary stewards. Recalling lines from Wordsworth's *Processions* that I quoted earlier (chapter 3), environmental humility opposes "that licentious craving in the mind / To act the God among external things." Yet this craving comes to the fore, poetically, in the metaphoric substitutions with which "On the Frith of Clyde" begins (Arran as Teneriffe as St. Helena), and emphatically in the desire "like a God, [to] light on . . . [Arran's] topmost cliff." In this we find a "union of extremes," the thinking of things and their opposites that gives Wordsworth's poetry its special life.

Wordsworth's ultimate figure of humility and ambition, nature and romance, is St. Francis of Assisi (1181–1226), founder of the Franciscan order. Wordsworth, touring Italy with Henry Crabb Robinson in the spring of 1837, visited the friary of La Verna, in the isolated mountains north of Arezzo, which had been founded in St. Francis's honor. La Verna (or, in Latin, Alverna) is famous in Franciscan lore as the mountain hermitage where St. Francis, having retreated for private meditation and fasting in 1224, received the stigmata, Christ's wounds becoming his own. Edith Batho has argued that Wordsworth "seems to be the first Englishman . . . to understand St. Francis, and he got his understanding not from books but from less than a full day's visit."[16]

By Wordsworth's account, his understanding came from a bird's song, the bird that begins and ends *The Cuckoo at Laverna,* a poem begun shortly after the poet's visit on May 25th. Of course he gleaned from other sources basic elements of Francis's life and legend: the reality of poverty and strict self-discipline he imposed upon himself and his followers (ll. 29–47); the romance of his companionship "with beast and bird . . . so free / So pure, so fraught with knowledge and delight, / As to be likened in his Followers' minds / To that which our first Parents, ere the fall / . . . . Held with all Kinds in Eden's blissful bowers" (53–65). This ideal eco-Eden, so near to Wordsworth's own heart, leads him to admire Francis's "loving spirit" and "the power, the faith, / Of a baptized imagination" (68–71). But his spiritual link to both Francis and La Verna's present-day friars is found rather in nature than in dogma—in the voice of the springtime cuckoo that Wordsworth hears, the voice that they have heard. In a startling revision of the gospels, the cuckoo assumes the role of John the Baptist, "the voice of one crying in the wilderness" (Matthew 3:3), announcing spring's rebirth in inarticulate voice:

If they received into a conscious ear
The notes whose first faint greeting startled me,
Whose sedulous iteration thrilled with joy
My heart—may have been moved like me to think. . . .
On the great Prophet, styled the Voice of One
Crying amid the wilderness, and given,
Now that their snow must melt, their herbs and flowers
Revive, their obstinate winter pass away,
That awful name to Thee, thee, simple Cuckoo,
Wandering in solitude, and evermore
Foretelling and proclaiming . . . (88–99)

The cuckoo lives on, recurrent prophet of life as it is, in a poem that conse-
crates for English readers a new locale, a wilderness mountaintop and the seat
of heart-humility.

The Cuckoo at Laverna is one of the best poems of Wordsworth's late period,
a fresh revisiting of elements of Wordsworth's ethics and style traced in this
book: anti-iconic sublimity of description—we are left, finally, in the unspeci-
fied "wilderness" of Hebrew prophecy—mixes with the moral sublime of Fran-
ciscan self-overcoming. Ambition unites with humility, romance with things as
they are. Song, natural and poetic, attaches its auditors to life. As long as nature
is preserved, there will be new life, in humanity as in nonhuman nature, and the
disinterested person can partake of it up to, and perhaps beyond, the moment
of her death.

We have come both a long way, and not so far at all, from Wordsworth's earli-
est loco-descriptive poems. One significant change is that other people, of a
nonhistorical or otherwise proximate variety, rarely enter the older Words-
worth's verse: his poetry of interpersonal encounter vanishes after 1807. In the
terms of this book, Wordsworth abandons first the Other (and thus, in Levi-
nas's peculiar sense, "ethics") and then the ego (or "enjoyment"), his poetry
exploring instead the parameters of "we," what we know or do together, and
growing ever more impersonal, Stoic, and Quietist. But the poet's romance en-
dures with locales where mankind is not, or not many: it extends from *An Eve-
ning Walk* and "Poems on the Naming of Places," through the dozens of un- or
depopulated sites commemorated in his late itinerary poems, and on to La
Verna, the site of St. Francis's vision, passed over in silence, and of the lone
springtime cuckoo, a type of the poet's own voice.

Envoy
Wordsworth's Afterlives

On June 6, 1851, Theodore Parker wrote of Christopher Wordsworth's *Memoirs of William Wordsworth* in a familiar letter to Miss Hannah Stevenson, who usually lived in Parker's Boston household and whom he addressed in correspondence as "dear old ladye":

> I have just finished the Life of Wordsworth . . . Wordsworth was a dear old granny, with a most hearty love of mankind, especially of the least attractive portions of it,—*beggars* and *fools,* and Bishop Doane, who he thinks was a great and good man. . . . If Wordsworth had lived a little in London, and felt the presence of some one who was manly and differed from him, it would have done him service. He runs in a narrow round of objects, ideas, and sentiments; is humane (and means to be so in his penal sonnets), devout, self-denying, and genial; but he lived too much in solitude, was too much with his worshippers, and limited himself in his reading. . . . But I love the dear old poetical Betty more after reading his Life than before. You will rejoice in the book, which will wait for you when you return.[1]

That Parker here banters affectionately with a forty-four-year-old woman in his care takes some of the sting out of his references to the older Wordsworth as a "dear old granny" and a "dear old poetical *Betty*"—a name, as the OED tells us, "given in contempt to a man who occupies himself with a woman's household duties" (the related "to betty about" is illustrated by a quotation from Parker). Parker's complaint that this feminized Wordsworth was too fond of "the least attractive portions" of mankind is not in itself remarkable—the vulgarity of Wordsworth's subjects was bemoaned since Southey's review of *Lyrical Ballads* and his "namby-pamby" manner since Jeffrey's review of the 1807 *Poems, in Two Volumes.*[2]

But Parker's letter also treats Wordsworth as one who declined into dotage: behind his words is the now-familiar assumption of Wordsworth's anticlimax. Wordsworth's poetic decline is tied to his political apostasy in Edwin Percy Whipple's thirty-two-page *North American Review* essay on Wordsworth's career, framed as a review essay of Henry Reed's 1837 Philadelphia edition of Wordsworth's poems. Whipple writes: "When Wordsworth deals with virtue, freedom, justice, and truth in the abstract . . . no poet can be more grand and impressive [thus, we are later told, Wordsworth's best work marks him with Shelley as a utopian "poet of the future"]; but when he connects these [virtues] with the acts and policy of English Tory politicians, or with the state and church of England, we are conscious that the analogy is false, if not ludicrous" (381).

Whipple's judgment would become standard Romanticist fare in the twentieth century. Yet athwart the critical genealogy that connects Whipple to Nicholas Roe's *Wordsworth and Coleridge: The Radical Years* (1988) we find a vector from Henry Reed's own critical writings to James Chandler's *Wordsworth's Second Nature* (1984), highlighting Wordsworth's abiding commitments to custom and place, church and state. As though anticipating charges of anticlimax and apostasy, Reed proclaims in his 1839 *New York Review* essay on Wordsworth, "there is a symmetry in the productions of Wordsworth's youth, his manhood, and more advanced years . . . his imagination strengthening with his years" (25). In his *Lectures on the British Poets,* Reed explained to his University of Pennsylvania students that Wordsworth's brief sympathies with the French Revolution "were only with the pure elements of the cause," namely, "the miseries of the peasantry." But the Revolution was soon "stricken with the worst of Egypt's plagues; benighted in moral darkness, it was visited with the pestilence of blood throughout the land"; Wordsworth rightly sought "the homeward road to England" (2:211).[3] Annealed in the fires of the French inferno, Wordsworth's poetry has the power to shed "benignant light . . . on your domestic hearth, upon all your intercourse with your fellow-men, upon your civic responsibilities to your country, and the sublimer relations in which man is placed" (2:219).

A sentence such as the last reminds us that in his lectures Reed was attempting to educate an audience of students and that the educational aims of the age were for the most part unabashedly moral and political. Reed's broad-ranging *Lectures on English Literature* begin with an 1850 lecture on literature's place in higher education, "which is akin to religion, for it is a ministry of the soul, and deals not so much with what we know as with what we are, what we can do and what we can suffer, and what we may become here and hereafter" (39). Very many, perhaps most, literature professors today will smile or cringe at this unabashed statement of literature's place in a religion of humanity. I do not unqualifiedly endorse it myself, but I do find in it a useful corrective or counterweight to the antihumanist excesses that have come to characterize many literary studies and that have made them largely irrelevant to any but the most rarefied academic audiences.

We need more than ever what Wordsworth has to offer: his hope in continuity amidst change, survival within death—perhaps too, in a selfish age, in his vexed belief in an "equipoise of love" "unvexed" by partial interest—and finally, in an age more dominated than his by visual media and multiple-screen distraction, a faith in the ethical power of attuning ourselves to sounds, environments, words, music, as well as the form in which these all converge, audible poetry.

A concern voiced in several recent monographs, including one on Wordsworth,[4] is how to make Romantic authors relevant to contemporary students. I would humbly suggest the answer lies in making it of more than historical interest. Without turning our backs on the valuable insights offered by historicist and political criticism of the past thirty years, we need to move beyond it—back to the poems, as poems, that make the Romantic era so special, but also toward a fuller engagement with the explicit and important ethical concerns of the Romantics and modern poetry more generally. We went too far in making Romantic literature the handmaiden to history, especially social history; we need boldly to present literature as crucial in its own right, both for the pleasures of its form and the ethical engagements it encourages.

Over the past thirty years strong scholarly work has been done on Romantic-era authors' intricate relations to particular historical events, institutions, and contexts: the promise and specter of the French Revolution; the debates leading to the abolition of the slave trade; the history of sexuality and gender; the Napoleonic wars; empire and colonialism; popular agitation and the Reform bill; print capitalism and the professionalization of authorship; credit economy and double-entry bookkeeping; copyright laws; the politics of canon formation; the institutionalization of knowledge. All these contexts have enriched our understanding of the Romantic era. But historical concerns should not eclipse our view of the fundamental reason readers turn to imaginative literature: that is, to enjoy through verbal style other human beings thinking and feeling; choosing, acting, and suffering; interacting with one another and with "us" as both implied and actual auditors. Recall the question that Wordsworth's speaker poses to the leech gatherer: *how is it that you live, and what is it that you do?* The question is, and ought to be, of more than academic interest. Wordsworth is ready for a new afterlife.

Notes

INTRODUCTION

Epigraph. From the Cornell edition of *The Ruined Cottage*, ms. B Transcriptions, 263, and *The Letters of William and Dorothy Wordsworth* 2:148.

1. *Autobiography and Literary Essays* 137–55 (recto pages only, from Mill's holograph manuscript in the Columbia University Library).

2. "Musings Near Aquapendente," l. 348 (*Sonnet Series* 756).

3. Arnold, *English Literature and Irish Politics* 51. Arnold quotes from Wordsworth's Preface to *The Excursion* (also known as the Prospectus to *The Recluse*), line 18.

4. Arnold, however, was not without a sense of Wordsworth's antithetical attraction to tragedy, solitary anguish, and (to quote the "Intimations" *Ode*) "all that is at enmity with joy." On Arnold's tacit appreciation of the fragility of joy in Wordsworth's oeuvre, see Seamus Perry, "Joy Perplexed." For an assessment of Wordsworth's sometimes ill-fitting role in the Victorian culture of aesthetic therapy, see Noel Jackson, 132–62.

5. Keats coined the phrase "egotistical sublime" and defended his own poetic practice in contradistinction to Wordsworth's in a letter of October 1818: "As to the poetical Character itself, (I mean that sort of which, if I am any thing, I am a Member; that sort distinguished from the wordsworthian or egotistical sublime; which is a thing per se and stands alone) it is not itself—it has no self—it is every thing and nothing.... It has as much delight in conceiving [the villainous] Iago as an Imogen [a virtuous heroine]. What shocks the virtuous philosopher, delights the camelion [*sic*] Poet" (*Letters* 157). Keats was familiar with Hazlitt's *Lectures on the English Poets* (1818), which concludes of Wordsworth: "His poetry is not external, but internal . . . he furnishes it from his own mind, and is his own subject" ("On the Living Poets" 302); "His egotism is in some respects a madness" (316). Of more contemporary critics, Geoffrey Hartman has the most interesting analysis of Wordsworth's "engulfing solipsism of Imagination" (*Wordsworth's Poetry* 242), which the poet sustains in creative tension with his attachment to external nature. Opposing the solipsistic school of Wordsworth studies, Emma Mason excavates a Wordsworth of "tact and fellow feeling" (18), "a watcher and a listener of his world" (ix).

6. Here I paraphrase a main argument of Clifford Siskin, *The Historicity of Romantic Discourse;* quoted at 12, 77. Richard Gravil, by contrast, stresses "the public dimension of Wordsworth's personal poetry" (6), his emphasis shaped, as is mine, by an attention to Wordsworth's nineteenth-century reception.

7. Wordsworth, *Sonnet Series and Itinerary Poems* 75.

8. Quoted in Stephen Gill, "The Philosophical Poet" 148–49.

9. Thomas Weiskel, *The Romantic Sublime* 37.

10. The New Historicist tendency to subordinate ethics to politics (a tendency rooted, as I suggest in chapter 7, in Fredric Jameson's *The Political Unconscious*), and its converse, the tendency in postmodern ethics (stemming from Levinas and late-period Derrida) to condescend to politics as merely administrative and delimiting, are both answered in Terry Eagleton's eloquent, Aristotelian discussion of ethics and politics as "different viewpoints on the same reality": "The ethical is a matter of how we may live with each other most rewardingly, while the political is a question of what institutions best promote this end" (325).

11. Pater, "Wordsworth" 137. I develop Pater's insight into Wordsworth in chapter 4.

12. See particularly Abrams's *Natural Supernaturalism* (1971), a Wordsworth-centric work of high humanism that derives from Thomas Carlyle's *Sartor Resartus* (1833–34) its title as well as it central thesis: the Romantics endeavored "to naturalize the supernatural and humanize the divine" (68). From the 1940s onward Abrams spearheaded a mid-twentieth-century Romantics revival that was advanced in no small part by fellow Jewish-American academics (Geoffrey Hartman, Harold Bloom) who found in the Romantics, and particularly in Wordsworth, an alternative to a Renaissance and modernist canon, formulated by T. S. Eliot and advanced by F. R. Leavis among others, that was populated largely by explicitly Christian authors—including, of course, Eliot himself.

13. Aristotle states at the opening of book 2 of *Nichomachean Ethics* (1103a): "Moral virtue . . . is formed by habit, *ethos,* and its name, *ethike,* is therefore derived, by a slight variation, from *ethos*" (Martin Ostwald trans., 33).

14. Wordsworth opposes active benevolence to "the pestilential calm / Of negative morality" (*"Lyrical Ballads," and Other Poems* 310).

15. Within Wordsworth's poetic corpus the turn toward accepting the orthodox Christian doctrine of the atonement begins with the sonnet, written c. 1828, "A Grave-Stone upon the Floor in the Cloisters of Worcester Cathedral," which concludes, "To save the contrite, Jesus bled" (*Last Poems* 96).

16. On the more general program of the major Romantic poets to impart (moral) wisdom without precepts or direct instruction, see David Duff, 96, 102, 117–18.

17. I am indebted to Simon Jarvis's argument that "a different kind of thinking happens in verse" than in philosophy (4), one that—at least in Wordsworth's verse—entangles apparent oppositions, including those of duty and desire, norm and fact, meter and rhythm, system and singularity (1–32). On Wordsworth's poetic thinking, see also Gill, "The Philosophic Poet," and Andrew Bennett, *Wordsworth Writing* 119–39.

18. "The Foregoing Subject Resumed" (companion piece to "Lines suggested by a Portrait from the Pencil of I. F. Stone"), *Last Poems* 275. Wordsworth's focus on awe and wonder as valuable emotions spans his poetic career, originating in his 1793 poem *An Evening Walk:* "Now with religious awe the farewell light / Blends with the solemn coloring of the night" (ll. 329–30).

19. Wordsworth, *Essays upon Epitaphs* 1, *Prose Works* 2:53.

20. Beyond the purview of this study is the "poetics of epiphany" that extends into modern poetry from Wordsworth's imaginative transformation of ordinary into extraordinary moments; on this tradition in English-language literature, see Ashton Nichols.

21. See Clare Cavanagh, 19–21, 261–65.

22. Bennett, in a work that does not index Wordsworth, argues in a way highly consonant with Wordsworth's poetic program that "enchantment" within (an allegedly disenchanted) modernity derives from being "struck and shaken by the extraordinary that lives amid the familiar and the everyday"; encounters with, for example, communicative nonhumans (birds, ants, plants) "provoke joyful attachment" to the world (4).

23. Harpham, 18–19, 25.

24. Among the more successful forays of philosophers into literary criticism are Alasdair MacIntyre on Jane Austen, 181–87, 239–43, and Colin McGinn on *The Picture of Dorian Gray* 123–43.

25. Adorno's dictum, along with his later finessing of it (including limiting "poetry" to "lyric poetry"), are quoted and contextualized in Nouri Gana, 33–40, an article that proceeds to situate contemporary Arabic poetry, particularly its elegies, in relation to Adorno: "it is a poetry that emerges from the full consciousness of its impossibility or, worse, its futility and discomfiting complicity in Arab suffering" (41). Other recent works written against the backdrop of Adorno's dictum are those by Sara Guyer, Ryan Cull, and Rachel Cole. Charging lyric form with a- or antisociality is a largely Western European and American phenomenon: by contrast, as Clare Cavanagh argues, in Central and Eastern Europe, lyric form served in the mid- to late twentieth century to protest the anti-individualistic values of the totalitarian state (6–22).

26. Thus, Leith Davis (127–33) and Evan Gottlieb (143–56) read Wordsworth's "The Solitary Reaper" as an English colonization of a woman singing in Gaelic, while James O'Rourke sees the fallen women of *The Prelude* book 7 as figures born of Wordsworth's culpable suppression of his own sexual irregularities with Annette Vallon (63–94).

27. On this poem, see Cavanagh 229–33.

28. The argument, made concisely by Robert Miles, is that the Victorians invent Romanticism as the corpus of a limited number of male poets who subscribe to certain "counter-Enlightenment" values including a preference for the local and particular over the universal and systematic and a hostility to theory, particularly political economy (11–13). On the Victorian institutionalization of Wordsworth in particular, see Miles, 92–97.

29. The freshman blooper recorded by Anders Henriksson is "The renascence bolted in from the blue" (169), but "Romanticism," according to most college syllabi, has a very similar way of bolting in.

30. David Fairer has also recently sought to stress the "creative dialogues" the poets of the 1790s had "with the poets of the previous decades" (2).

31. On Wordsworth's nineteenth-century reception, see Gill, *Wordsworth and the Victorians*. Recent critics who have shed sympathetic light on *The Excursion* and Wordsworth's later poetry include, in order of their appearance, Peter Manning, William Galperin (*Revision and Authority*), Mark Canuel, Sally Bushell, and Kevis Goodman—to these scholars I am most grateful.

32. My three quotations are, respectively, from "Yarrow Revisited," ll. 84 and 94–95, and from the "Conclusion" (sonnet 33) to *The River Duddon*.

33. On the general shift in the Romantic-era critical theory from seeing poetry as akin to painting to seeing it as akin to music, see Abrams, *The Mirror and the Lamp* 78–99; on the

concurrent rise of a notion of "pure" (i.e., nonvocal or programmatic) music, see John Neubauer, *The Emancipation of Music from Language.*

34. Jarman, *Blue* (New York: Overlook, 1994), 15, quoted in Jacques Khalip, "The Archaeology of Sound," 87. Khalip's basic argument about *Blue,* which I discovered after my first chapter was drafted, parallels its argument about Wordsworth: the film, like Wordsworth's poetry, provides "a groundwork for a mode of audition that poses a moving counterweight to ocularcentric and logocentric assumptions" (77).

CHAPTER 1: AUDITION AND ATTACHMENT

1. "To recognize the Other is to give. But it is to give to the master, to the lord, to him whom one approaches as 'You' (*Vous*) in a dimension of height" (*Totality and Infinity* 75).

2. Bruns here elaborates on a passage from Heidegger's essay "Logos (Heraklit, Fragment 50)": "We have heard [*gehört*] when we belong to [*gehören*] the matter addressed" (Bruns 127).

3. For a recent theoretical formulation of such an aesthetic, see Timothy Morton.

4. See my essay "Ear and Eye: Counteracting Senses in Loco-Descriptive Poetry." The phenomenological ethics of sound that I staked out there, and develop in this chapter, is buttressed by Stuart Allen's recent essay "Wordsworth's Ear and the Place of Aesthetic Autonomy" (*Wordsworth and the Passions of Critical Poetics* 72–96). Allen argues, as I do, that Wordsworth's "poetics of the ear" is "an opening of the self to otherness" (93), but he adds as a counterpoint that such openness threatens the loss or death of self, as in the Winander Boy episode of *The Prelude* book 5: "the recollection of the Boy's early death . . . insinuates a distance between Wordsworth and his poetics of listening" (92).

5. Although Wordsworth lent his authority to the phrase, it goes back further: Robert Aubin adduces the title of Daniel Walters's "Landough: A Loco-descriptive Poem," published 1780 (vii, 339). The popularity of a genre with at least titular interest in actual locales is staggering: Aubin's bibliography of, as he calls it, "topographical" poetry lists roughly 3,500 items, all but a few of them from the period 1700–1840 (297–394).

6. In addition to *The Idea of Landscape,* see his *English Literature in History, 1730–80.* Building on Barrell's work, Jacqueline Labbe (1998) stresses the gendered aspect of this prospect gaze.

7. Thomson's "the landscape laughs around" is a Virgilianism (*omnia nunc rident, Eclogues* 7:55).

8. This episode of Amelia, struck by lightning on her walk with her lover Celadon, was among the most popular set pieces of *The Seasons,* a poem which, as Sandro Jung notes, reached its height of popularity in the 1790s; the episode, according to Jung, was set to music, imitated by other poets, and frequently illustrated in a variety of media including book-illustrations, paintings, and furniture prints (498–99).

9. Looking back in *The Prelude* on his youthful "willfulness of fancy," Wordsworth writes: "Then common death was none, common mishap, / But . . . / The tragic [was rendered] super-tragic" (8:521, 530–32).

10. Wordsworth's unpublished 1794 revision of *An Evening Walk* appears in the Cornell edition of that poem, 131–56; my quotation is from p. 135, emphasis mine.

11. Wordsworth defines "sugh" (l. 437) in a footnote: "a Scotch word expressive of the sound of the wind through the trees."

12. Cf. Marshall Brown's assessment: "*Descriptive Sketches* reverses what in Wordsworth's time was still, if precariously, the traditional hierarchy of the creation"; "Here the poetry of man is stifled, but the poetic life of an inhuman nature takes its place" (326, 324).

13. Part 2 of Burke's *A Philosophical Enquiry into the Origin of our Ideas of the Sublime and Beautiful* (1757) enumerates the various attributes of the sublime, starting with terror, obscurity, and power, and illustrating these with quotations from sources including Milton, Job, and Psalms.

14. In "Wordsworth's 'Illustrated Books and Newspapers,'" Peter Manning observes that Wordsworth did not in practice oppose all textual illustrations (e.g., the *Poems* of 1815 included engravings by Sir George Beaumont) and argues that in context the particular illustrations that Wordsworth opposed were those of the *Illustrated London News,* published from 1842 and containing a sensationalistic hodgepodge of stories and images (including a bad representation of Wordsworth upon his acceptance of the Laureateship). A useful corrective to oversimplifying accounts of Wordsworth's *practical* iconoclasm, Manning's argument does not, however, register the theoretical comprehensiveness of Wordsworth's satire here on "a dumb Art," encompassing "illustrated books" (not apparently excepting his own) as well as newspapers.

15. In a footnote to *Descriptive Sketches* (1793 version), l. 332f., Wordsworth criticizes the picturesque as "cold rules of painting" divorced from the emotions communicated by place. On Wordsworth's transformation of picturesque canons in his *Guide through the District of the Lakes,* see Tim Costelloe (chap. 5, ms.): for Wordsworth the picturesque is a naturally occurring phenomenon rather than, as it is for William Gilpin and Uvedale Price, an artificial standard that can inform the pictorial representation, or technological "improvement," of landscape.

16. My analysis of Wordsworth's counteracting senses builds upon Geoffrey Hartman's sketch of "the dialectic of the senses" in *The Unremarkable Wordsworth* 18–30 (24).

17. Cf. Noel Jackson: "Wordsworth's poetry describes and models a form of inwardness firmly grounded in a regime of the bodily senses; this mindset does not represent a condition of hermetic isolation from the world, but a state of consciousness in continual interaction with it" (7).

18. According to Lane Cooper's *Concordance,* Wordsworth employs these terms roughly four hundred times in his verse.

19. Denise Gigante (69) quotes Robert Southey: "Wordsworth has no sense of smell. . . . He has often expressed to me his regret for this privation."

20. "Emma" was a codename of Wordsworth's for his sister Dorothy. The poem first appeared in 1800 in the second volume of *Lyrical Ballads.*

21. The music of and in the poem is passed over as well in Michael Wiley's reading of the poem, one that nonetheless has the merit of responding in advance to the anticipated charge of moral impropriety in any act of naming a place that isn't one's own: "Wordsworth's . . . naming of a utopian space involves the gentlest of usurpations" (88).

CHAPTER 2: CLOSE ENCOUNTERS I

1. The category, revived by David Simpson, *Wordsworth's Historical Imagination* 162, originates in Frederick Garber, *Wordsworth and the Poetry of Encounter.* Garber, using "The

Solitary Reaper" as his test case, analyzes the Wordsworthian encounter in terms of episte-
mology, not ethics: "it is an event in which the self may break through to a fleeting, incom-
plete, but definite understanding of something about the world of the other, an understand-
ing which can result in a permanent increase of self and its knowledge" (14).

2. On the generic interplay between poetry and the novel in period, see G. Gabrielle
Starr, who specifically addresses several of Wordsworth's poems of encounter, 187–98.

3. I thank Seamus Perry for his help in putting together this list.

4. I return to *De Officiis* in chapter 8.

5. *Enquiry concerning Political Justice* 1:xxv ("Summary of Principles"), 1:447 (4.11).

6. Wordsworth worried over gratitude throughout his career: cf. the late poem "Human-
ity. (Written in the Year 1829)," in which the gratitude of a slave isn't virtuous but "pitiable"
(l. 69), in *Last Poems* 212.

7. J. M. S. Tompkins quotes this tale as an example of the literature of sensibility
"brood[ing] gratefully over the alms-deeds of the poor" (106).

8. Wordsworth, "Essay, Supplementary to the Preface," in *Prose Works* 2:72. See Duncan
Wu, *Wordsworth's Reading, 1770–1799* (36–37), on the date of Wordsworth's reading of Shaft-
esbury and the Rydal Mount copy of *Characteristicks*. On Wordsworth's debt to Shaftesbury
(as well as to Edmund Burke), see also Stuart Allen, 1–30.

9. For a fuller treatment of "ethical joy" in the Stoics and Shaftesbury, see Potkay, *The
Story of Joy* 95–118. Earlier versions of my Godwin discussion and my reading of *The Old Cum-
berland Beggar* appear on pp. 118–28.

10. "Statesmen" is a word that in Wordsworth's usage carries a variety of possible refer-
ents: Pitt and his ministry; "the political economists whose campaign against 'mendicity'
would later result in the Poor Law of 1834" (James Chandler, *Wordsworth's Second Nature* 85);
and, as a Westmorland regionalism, the small landowners of the Lake District. David Simp-
son notes that the "statesman" of Westmorland owns his land in true freehold, as distinct
from those who hold property through customary tenure; this class of owner-occupier
statesmen, in whose civic virtue Wordsworth generally trusted, was in decline during
Wordsworth's lifetime (*Wordsworth's Historical Imagination* 82–89).

11. Wordsworth's use of the word "habit" in *The Old Cumberland Beggar* sparked a critical
controversy among political-minded critics in the 1980s, with James Chandler arguing that it
evoked the conservative social philosophy of Edmund Burke (*Wordsworth's Second Nature* 81–
92) and Alan Grob responding, less persuasively, that it conjures Godwin's "radical ideas . . . of
rational benevolence" (347–50). Yet trying to tie "habit" to any one philosopher is akin to tying
"love" to any one poet. Wordsworth's ethical trust in habit, I would add, contrasts with his
complaints, in his "Intimations" *Ode* and *Prelude,* against the deadening *perceptual* effect of
"custom" or "habit": e.g., "the tendency . . . / Of habit to enslave the mind" (1805 *Prelude* 13:138–
39); cf. Coleridge's account of Wordsworth's poetic aims in *Biographia Literaria,* chapter 14 (2:6).

12. For examples of the eighteenth-century charge of hedonism against "the Scottish
Shaftesburians" (including Hutcheson and Fordyce), see Isabel Rivers, 2:306–8. Leveled
against the "man of feeling," the charge persists through J. M. S. Tompkins, 100–103, and
R. S. Crane, "Suggestions towards a Genealogy of the 'Man of Feeling.'"

13. Hutcheson, *On the Nature and Conduct of the Passions* 18. Cf. Aristotle's discussion of
pleasure in *Nichomachean Ethics* book 10 (1174b): "Pleasure completes the activity not as a

characteristic completes an activity by being already inherent in it, but as a completeness that superimposes itself upon it, like the bloom of youth in those who are in their prime" (281–82); Seneca's *De Beata Vita*, pt. 15, sec. 2: "Even the joy [*gaudium*] which is born of virtue, although it is a good, is not part of the greatest good any more than gladness [*laetitia*] and tranquillity" (*Moral Essays* 2:136).

14. My quotations are from the Parallel Reading Texts of mss. B and D found in the Cornell edition of *Home at Grasmere*.

15. Quoted by Gary Harrison in *Wordsworth's Vagrant Muse* 141.

16. Levinas writes of ethics as "an orientation toward the Other" (50, cf. 215). On "postmodern ethics," see Bauman; for a synopsis of Levinas's ethics as well as of challenges to it, see Buell, 14–16.

17. See Moyn, 13, 256–57.

18. In 1843, Wordsworth published the play with a note on its origin in the French Revolutionary period, but as Melynda Nuss observes, "the root source of cruelty in *The Borderers* is not (or not necessarily) revolutionary violence, but the failure to see" (608). Alan Richardson, commenting on the complex repetitions that shape character in the play (e.g., Mortimer repeats Rivers's earlier crime, Rivers repeats Satan's original seduction as well as Iago's villainy), ventures a claim that equally applies to Wordsworth's ethics: "self-consciousness must be fundamentally redefined as including consciousness of the other" (34).

19. My calculations are from the Lane Cooper *Concordance,* based on the 1842 text of the play. The visual keywords of *The Borderers* are nowhere else so concentrated in Wordsworth's other poems (*The White Doe of Rylstone* comes closest): for example, "see," occurring thirty-eight times in the 2,321 lines of the 1842 *Borderers,* occurs very slightly more, forty-two times, in the nearly 8,000-line 1850 *Prelude.* "Look" appears twenty-seven times in *The Borderers* and thirty-five times in *The Prelude.*

20. My quotations are from the early version of *The Borderers* (1797–99), printed with the late version (1842) on facing pages in the Cornell edition of the play. The late version changes the names of several lead characters: Mortimer becomes Marmaduke, Rivers becomes Oswald, and Matilda becomes Idonea.

21. The themes of deception and self-deception in the play are emphasized by Reeve Parker, who argues the untenability of Matilda's "abiding faith in the face as a transparent sign of the heart" (97). But from Mortimer's point of view the play dramatizes the face, through its very opacity, as a deterrent to murder or "just" retaliation.

22. Wordsworth earlier drafted similar lines for the female vagrant of his *Salisbury Plain* poems, though this vagrant closes on a more defiant note: "such reproach of heavenly ordonnance / As shall *not need forgiveness*" (*Salisbury Plain Poems* 289, emphasis mine). Cf. Wordsworth's vehement protest against inequities in England's systems of distributive and retributive justice in the oratorical conclusion of *Salisbury Plain* (1793–94), ll. 415–549; this protest is greatly truncated in Wordsworth's succeeding draft of the poem, *Adventures on Salisbury Plain* (1795–c. 1799), ll. 802–28.

23. The tension between benevolence and justice is a problem for moral philosophy, especially in the eighteenth century: as Joseph Butler and David Hume respectively argued, the demands of strict justice can go against our sympathy for the criminal and show that benevolence alone cannot be the basis for ethics (see Potkay, *The Passion for Happiness* 97–98).

Wordsworth adopted the Humean position in old age, in his *Sonnets on the Punishment of Death* (1842), where he argues that the artificial virtue of justice demands that we restrain our "compassion" for offenders with reference to the sympathy we feel for victims and the bereaved (see sonnet no. 2 in *Sonnet Series and Itinerary Poems* 870). Hume's position has recently been challenged, philosophically, by Michael L. Frazer, who observes that although Hume (and, I would add, the older Wordsworth) treats justice as obedience to the rules that allow for social cooperation—and especially for the preservation of property—he never describes these rules themselves as just or unjust. Frazer suggests that Hume's sentimental ethics might serve as a useful counterforce to his or to any strict model of justice (65–88).

24. The uncertainty of Rivers's motives occasioned Wordsworth's prefatory essay of 1797, in which the author seeks with ingenuity and variety, but no clear success, to account for why Rivers acts as he does (*The Borderers* 61–68).

25. Kant ends his *Critique of Practical Reason*: "Two things fill the mind with ever new and increasing admiration and reverence, the more often and more steadily one reflects on them: *the starry heavens above me and the moral law within me*" (133).

26. Levinas's translator Alphonso Lingis notes: "with the author's permission, we are translating '*autrui*' (the personal Other, the you) by 'Other,' and '*autre*' by 'other'" (24, note). Levinas maintains, "*The other qua other is the Other*," for which Lingis provides the original French: "*L'Autre en tant qu'autre est Autrui*" (71).

27. Geoffrey Jackson sees this verse as informing Wordsworth's "Afflictions of England," the thirty-sixth sonnet of *Ecclesiastical Sketches*, pt. 2: see Jackson's editorial note in *Sonnet Series and Itinerary Poems* 267.

28. Moyn expertly traces Levinas's conception of the Other or "wholly other" back to three related sources: Søren Kierkegaard's assertion, against Hegelian immanence, of a radically transcendent God; the French interwar discovery of Kierkegaard's thought; and the interwar Protestant theology of Rudolf Otto and Karl Barth (113–94).

29. Judith Butler stresses that the Levinasian face "communicates both the precariousness of life and the interdiction on violence. He gives us a way of understanding how aggression is *not* eradicated in an ethics of non-violence; aggression forms the incessant matter for ethical struggles" (xviii, cf. 128–51).

30. David Simpson remarks of this passage (*Wordsworth, Commodification and Social Concern* 7–22) that Wordsworth does not imagine (even in his period of Revolutionary sympathy) the extirpation of extreme poverty per se but only of extreme poverty among the industrious poor, implying an opposing category of the idle and irremediable poor that is indeed assumed in social welfare schemes from the 1790s to Jeffrey Sachs's *The End of Poverty* (2005).

31. This cogent point about Rivers and the Revolutionaries is made by David Bromwich, 62–65.

32. My quotation, and examples from *The Prelude*, are from Evan Radcliffe, 162.

33. Vivasvan Soni finds Wordsworth's turn from utopianism in *The Female Vagrant*, a poem included in the 1798 *Lyrical Ballads* but extracted from Wordsworth's earlier *Salisbury Plain* poems (1793–95). This poem, as Soni reads it, involves a trajectory through a series of utopian spaces, each of which proves untenable, from the shattered pastoral utopia in which the female speaker begins, to an American republic (and, by association, the French one) scarred by constant warfare, to the band of (*Borderer*-like) bandits with whom she

briefly takes up with back in England. Soni sees in the vagrant's final, hopeless vagrancy an image of a *directionless* modernity ("Modernity and the Fate of Utopian Representation in Wordsworth's 'Female Vagrant'").

34. Among those English radicals who read the French Revolution through the Book of Revelation, we need to include the Wordsworth of the 1793 *Descriptive Sketches*—"Lo, from th' innocuous flames, a lovely birth!"; no more "On his pale Horse shall fell Consumption go" (ll. 782–91)—and the Coleridge of the 1797 *Religious Musings* (ll. 296–322).

35. At the end of *The Robbers*, the chieftain Charles de Moor evidences his freedom—"I—am free!"—in killing the woman who loves him and declaring to his men that her death frees him from his oath of loyalty to them, the (literal) sacrifice of her life making up for the (figurative) sacrifice of their lives to him. He then sacrifices his own criminal life for the sake of a poor man, who might benefit from the reward that has been offered for de Moor's capture (118–20).

36. Quoted in Moyn, 226. Utopian Marxist intellectuals still active as I write prominently include Fredric Jameson, Michael Hardt and Antonio Negri, Slavoj Žižek, and Alain Badiou.

37. My thinking here is indebted to William Galperin's "'Describing What Never Happened': Jane Austen and the History of Missed Opportunities."

CHAPTER 3: CLOSE ENCOUNTERS II

1. On Wordsworth's "border poetry," see Jonathan Wordsworth, *William Wordsworth: The Borders of Vision* 1–35.

2. David Simpson, *Wordsworth, Commodification and Social Concern* 26–27.

3. Alan Bewell discusses *The Discharged Soldier* in *Romanticism and Colonial Disease* 116–19; Simpson cites Bewell on p. 95. More germane to my own concerns is Bewell's earlier analysis of the poem, in *Wordsworth and the Enlightenment* (71–93), in which it is compared to Rousseau's quasi-anthropological narrative of "the primitive encounter" (73) between solitary, presocial men.

4. The encounter on which the poem is based took place, according to Wordsworth's placement of it in *The Prelude,* in the summer of 1788, during the poet's return to the Lakes after his first year at Cambridge.

5. Cf. Daniel Carey's critique of the new historicist/postcolonial protocol of drawing out historical truths that are silent or marginal in a literary text: "it runs the risk of appropriating literature as a mere allegory of history while assigning to criticism the task of determining the ways in which such texts represent historical truths outside themselves" (109).

6. Leviticus 19:18, Romans 13:9. When Jesus reiterates the commandment in Luke's gospel, a lawyer asks him, "And who is my neighbor?" (10:27–29). Jesus's reply, the parable of the Good Samaritan, teaches that the neighbor is "the one who shows mercy" (v. 37).

7. "Processions. Suggested on a Sabbath Morning in the Vale of Chamouny" (ll. 48–69) in *Sonnet Series and Itinerary Poems* 391.

8. See especially Wordsworth's Prospectus to *The Recluse* and M. H. Abrams's commentary on it in *Natural Supernaturalism* 19–29.

9. These lines were originally composed for ms. B of *The Ruined Cottage*, January–March 1798 (see the Cornell edition of *The Ruined Cottage* 46)—the same period in which Wordsworth wrote *The Discharged Soldier.*

10. Akenside attributes "th' eternal joy" to the mind that can trace the Platonic idea of beauty in the physical beauties of the cosmos (*The Pleasures of the Imagination* 1:108); Warton places "the deep-felt joys, by Contemplation taught" above the pleasures of sense (*The Pleasures of Melancholy*, l. 299). Wordsworth's coordinated concern with depth in the unfathomable space of the heavens and in the mind of man, especially as it appears in "A Fragment [A Night Piece]" (*"Lyrical Ballads," and Other Poems* 276–77), derives in part from an important precursor poem, Barbauld's *A Summer Evening's Meditation* (1773), in which the "self-collected soul / Turns inward, and beholds a stranger there / Of high descent, and more than mortal rank; / An embryo GOD, a spark of fire divine" (ll. 53–56). The lineage of Barbauld's "stranger"—itself a spark of Neoplatonic divinity and also the inner genius that shines forth in solitude—is shrewdly traced by Robert Miles, 190–97; I am not persuaded, however, by Miles's accompanying claim that a belated Romantic emphasis on depth, particularly in Wordsworth and Coleridge, occurs in response to an increasingly impersonal and crowded print marketplace: see 92–97 (on Wordsworth) and 203–7 (on Coleridge).

11. I here paraphrase *Totality and Infinity* 110–14.

12. *Poems, in Two Volumes* 185.

13. Langan, 197–99.

14. This concession may be indebted to Thomas Gray's lines in *Elegy Written in a Country Church-yard* in which the solitary poet appears incomprehensible to the elderly shepherd who beholds him: "Hard by yon wood, now smiling *as in* scorn, / Mutt'ring his wayward fancies he wou'd rove, / Now dropping, woeful wan, *like one* forlorn . . ." (ll. 105–7, my emphases).

15. Wordsworth reused the locution in an 1850 revision to *The Prelude* 3:12: the Cambridge student he regards "till he was left a hundred yards behind" (1805) becomes the student regarded "till he was left an arrow's flight behind."

16. On Wordsworth's thematic and structural contributions to *The Ancyent Marinere,* see J. C. C. Mays's editorial introduction to the poem in Coleridge, *Poetical Works I*, pt. 1, p. 366.

17. On the dialogic or interrogative mode in Wordsworth, see Susan Wolfson, *The Questioning Presence* 17–21, 42–70; Don Bialostosky, 55–78.

18. As John B. Stewart explains, sympathy as Hume and other eighteenth-century philosophers understood it "is part of a process of perception, a process by which feelings are shared; it is not a particular feeling, and, of course, is not to be confused with either compassion (pity) or benevolence" (116). On Wordsworth's criticism of sympathy, see also Joshua King. Terry Eagleton offers an incisive critique of eighteenth-century moral philosophy as narcissistic or, in Jacques Lacan's sense, "imaginary" (*Trouble with Strangers* 1–82).

19. *Cato's Letters* no. 104 (November 24, 1722), in John Trenchard and Thomas Gordon, *Cato's Letters* 2:738.

20. Wordsworth's sonnet on Williams appears in *Early Poems and Fragments* 396; *Lines on the Bicentenary of Hawkshead School* 356–61 (Wordsworth's list of moral virtues occupies ll. 77–98). Of the Williams sonnet, Adela Pinch astutely remarks, "If . . . the blurring of the boundaries between Williams's body and Wordsworth's makes sense, it is because this is a body that is not proper to anyone; it is rather a body of shared [literary] convention, which only becomes animate in affective exchange" (81).

21. See especially the poems under the headings *The Orchard Pathway* in vol. 1, and *Moods of my Own Mind* in vol. 2.

22. To which we might add, any more knowable than those whom Lynn Festa calls "sentimental figures of empire" (the dying Indian, grateful Negro, noble savage): colonized and enslaved others whose alterity is erased by facile sympathetic responses. Yet, as Festa concludes, "The fact that eighteenth-century writers [Festa refers, among others, to Laurence Sterne—and I would add Wordsworth] are as interested in the failure of sympathy as they are in its ostensible successes suggests that they recognize the existence of these irreducible differences, the inadequacy of sentimental knowledge to its object" (240).

23. Cf. the speaker of *The Old Cumberland Beggar:* "Then let him pass, a blessing on his head!" (l. 155); Armytage on the widow in *The Ruined Cottage:* "I blessed her in the impotence of grief" (500); and, in Coleridge's *Rime of the Ancyent Marinere,* the Mariner on the water snakes: "I bless'd them unaware" (277).

24. *Home at Grasmere,* ms. D, ll. 149-51, p. 49.

25. My Pope allusion ("whatever is, is right") derives from *An Essay on Man* 1:294. My thinking about the normativity of facts to authors of the Romantic era—and about Romantic /post-Romantic dissatisfaction with or resistance to this perceptual normativity—is indebted to Rei Terada, 1-34; however, I trace the normative force of "the world as it is" not to Kant, as does Terada, but further back, to ancient Stoicism. Wordsworth's introduction to Stoic thought came, as part of his classical education, through Seneca and parts of Cicero and Virgil: see Duncan Wu, *Wordsworth's Reading, 1770-1799* 165-66. I discuss Wordsworth's Stoicism further in chapters 4 and 8.

26. Quoted from White's introduction to his translation of *The Handbook of Epictetus* 3-4.

27. "Murmuring" and "murmurers" are insistently denounced in *A Homily against Disobedience and Wilful Rebellion* preached under Elizabeth in the wake of the 1569 Rebellion of the Northern Earls (Charles Percy of Northumberland and Charles Neville of Westmorland), which Wordsworth may have come to know through his antiquarian research for *The White Doe of Rylstone,* a poem set during the Northern Uprising. See *Homily against Disobedience,* pt. 4, in *The Two Books of Homilies,* ed. John Griffiths (Oxford, 1859), 576-77.

28. *Poems, in Two Volumes* 161-62.

29. Unless otherwise noted, my quotations are from the 1799 ms. version reproduced, on pages facing the 1819 first edition, in the Cornell edition of *Peter Bell.*

30. Hazlitt's recollection of the 1798 recitation is quoted in *Peter Bell,* introduction, 4-5.

31. The notion of nature as moral instructor comes from the Stoics, as Irving Babbitt noted, disapprovingly, in an indictment of Romanticism that remains valuable for its erudition. "No one," Babbitt writes, "would question that Wordsworth has passages of great ethical elevation. But in some of these passages he simply renews the errors of the Stoics who also display at times great ethical elevation; he ascribes to the natural order virtues that the natural order does not give" (221).

32. "But he is too fond of the ass" comes from an unsigned review of August 1819, reproduced in *William Wordsworth: The Critical Heritage, 1793-1820,* ed. Robert Woof, 705-7. Woof also includes a July 1819 review that satirizes Wordsworth's "heroic donkey" (696-97). Hunt's May 1819 *Examiner* review appears on 651-54. Richard Cronin, *The Politics of Romantic Poetry,* observes that in the year Wordsworth chose to publish his poem England's Methodist leadership opposed the popular movement of Parliamentary reform, and so Wordsworth

might be seen as opposing it, too (149–50); according to my reading, however, the poem's Methodism is tangential or parodic.

33. The ass is "othered" for Wordsworth's reader in literary terms as well: this is not the ass of the literature of sensibility, fit for easy communion and even (half-comic) converse with the man of feeling. In Laurence Sterne's *Tristram Shandy* (vol. 7, chap. 32), Tristram professes both pity and conversational affection for the long-suffering ass: "'tis an animal (be what hurry I may) that I cannot bear to strike. . . . I have ever something to say to him on my part; and as one word begets another (if he has as little to do as I)—I generally fall into conversation with him" (431–32). Ignatius Sancho, an Afro-British man of letters acquainted with Sterne, lamented cruelty to jackasses in his published correspondence: "I am convinced we feel instinctively the injuries of our *fellow creatures*. . . . Before Sterne had wrote . . . [jackasses] into respect, I had a friendship for them—and many a civil greeting have I given them at casual meetings—" (*Letters of the Late Ignatius Sancho, An African* 92). Sancho's "our fellow creatures" implicitly refers to enslaved Africans, whose treatment was more scandalous than that of British pack animals. This sentimental tradition of social protest leads to Coleridge's Pantisocratic "To a Young Ass" (1794).

34. *The Story of Joy* vii.

35. Betty Foy's reunion with her idiot boy is the fullest representation I know of the corporeality of joy: "'Tis he whom you so long have lost,/He whom you love, your idiot boy./She looks again—her arms are up—/She screams—she cannot move for joy;/She darts as with a torrent's force,/She almost had o'erturned the horse,/And fast she holds her idiot boy . . . She kisses o'er and o'er again,/Him whom she loves, her idiot boy,/She's happy here, she's happy there,/She is uneasy every where;/Her limbs are all alive with joy." The scene ends with a tongue-in-cheek reference to the joy of Johnny's pony, and thus a comic counterpoint to the ass of *Peter Bell*: "She pats the pony, where or when/She knows not, happy Betty Foy!/The little pony glad may be,/But he is milder far than she,/You hardly can perceive his joy" (ll. 380–406). He is, in short, either a pony of moderate or moderated passion—we are earlier told, "he is a horse that thinks!" (122)—or one who feels no more than Betty, or the reader, attributes to him. *The Idiot Boy* appears in *Lyrical Ballads* 91–104.

36. Donne, *Sermons* 3:342 (sermon no. 16). See my *Story of Joy* (5–7) on the Stoic and early modern European distinction between *laetitia* and *gaudium*.

37. The comparison of human and animal reasoning goes back to Epicurus and Lucretius; in the seventeenth and eighteenth centuries it is developed by, among others, Hobbes, Pierre Bayle, Bolingbroke, Hume, and Diderot. Before Wordsworth, joy and sorrow were occasionally attributed to animals: e.g., in 1607 Gervase Markham proposed that horses feel love and hatred, joy and sorrow; in the 1650s and '60s Margaret Cavendish, Duchess of Newcastle, maintained that beasts possessed not only the full range of human passions but reason and language as well. See Keith Thomas, 101, 128–29. However, before Wordsworth the joys of animals were never, as far as I know, portrayed in realistic detail. Onno Oerlemans adduces *Peter Bell* in surveying the English Romantic representation of animal consciousness (94) but does not observe Wordsworth's focus on animal joy.

38. In a particularly garrulous passage, the narrator teases the audience internal to the poem—a cottage full of auditors to whom he recites the poem—with images of what the submerged face Peter sees *may* belong to, before it is revealed to be the face of an ordinary man,

and it is here that the narrator includes the faces of the damned that offended early readers (including Percy Shelley, who responded in *Peter Bell the Third*): "Is it some party in a parlour,/ Crammed just as they on earth were cramm'd—/ Some sipping punch, some sipping tea,/ But as you by their faces see/ All silent, and all damn'd?" (ll. 541–45). Wordsworth omitted this passage from 1820 onward.

39. Peter's moral enlightenment, as Alan Bewell suggests, parallels the Enlightenment's main narrative of the progress of religion from its psychological origin in fear, its first embodiment in superstition, and its final, Protestant turn toward love and sociality (*Wordsworth and the Enlightenment* 120–41).

CHAPTER 4: THE ETHICS OF THINGS

1. Quotations from "Lines Written in early spring," *Tintern Abbey*, and *The Old Cumberland Beggar* are from *"Lyrical Ballads," and Other Poems, 1797–1800.*

2. Benso writes of the expression "ethics *of* things": "*Of* things means . . . the directionality of a double movement: that which moves out from the things to reach the I and the other, and that which, in response to the first, moves from the I and the other to reach the things and to be concerned by them. The first movement is that of the demand or the appeal that things place on human beings by their mere impenetrable presencing there. It is the thingly side of the ethics of things. The second movement is that of tenderness, as the [human] response to the demand . . ." (142). Benso's "ethics of things" accords in principle, though not in its philosophical elaboration, with positions held by literary ecocritics: compare Patrick Murphy's "ecofeminist" call for a "heterarchical" relation to the "anotherness" of nature or the nonhuman (3–8, 22–23).

3. Quoted in John Beer, "Wordsworth and the Face of Things" 110. On Rawnsley, see Stephen Gill, *Wordsworth and the Victorians* 243–44, 256–60.

4. Jonathan Bate, in his seminal work of green Romanticism, *Romantic Ecology* (1991), enlists the Victorians John Ruskin and William Morris as allies in his conservationist, or "green," understanding of Romanticism, offered against the political critique of Wordsworth regnant in the 1980s. Subsequent responses to the New Historicist critique of Wordsworth include those by Frances Ferguson (146–52), Thomas McFarland (1–33), Mark Edmundson (120–40), Seamus Perry ("Coleridge, Wordsworth, and Other Things"), and Simon Jarvis (56–83). Supplementing a "green" Romanticism, Wordsworth's complementary insight into the "gray" of nature—into our ontological unity with mineral being, rocks, and stones—has been provocatively explored by Marshall Brown (301–61) and Paul Fry (60–74).

5. Karl Kroeber suggests a similarly paradoxical connection in Malthus and in pieces of English Romantic writing between viewing nature as a deterministic (if evolving) system and yet seeing the individual within it as free (13–15, 88–89).

6. "Thing" appears 125 times and "things" 314 in Lane Cooper's 1911 concordance to the works of Wordsworth (based on the poet's final revised texts).

7. "Mē wearð Grendles þing on mīnre ēþeltyrf undyrne cūð," *Beowulf*, ll. 409–10. For her aid with Old English, I thank Monica Brzezinski Potkay.

8. Before adducing Blackstone the OED offers two citations of *things* that do not clearly refer to a material object as distinct from person, times, places, or events: "things . . . of general

use or pleasure to mankind" (William Temple, 1689-90); "things . . . are all to be used according to the Will of God" (William Law, 1732).

9. On the cinematic effects of *The Prelude* book 7, and Wordsworth's reluctant kinship to the mass culture he ostensibly criticizes, see Galperin, *The Return of the Visible* 112-28.

10. Cf. Shaftesbury's private notebook: "'The Deity is present with all things, knows all things, and is provident over all" (*Life* 20).

11. Hamlet plays with the paradox that a "thing" can be a "nothing"—that is, a word, designation, role, affair, etc., can be illusory, grounded on no more than language, or a usurpation, erected upon an absence (here the dead body of the king his father). Hamlet exclaims, "The King is a thing— / *Guildenstern:* A thing, my lord? / *Ham.*: Of nothing" (4.2.29-31).

12. See Yahweh's contradictory statement in Exodus 33:20: "Thou canst not see my face: for there shall no man see me, and live."

13. Lucretius opens book 3 of *De Rerum Natura* with praise of Epicurus's illumination of, in Creech's 1682 translation, "the rise of things" (l. 19). In the eighteenth century, another impediment to seeing clearly the status of things is their constant change or becoming: thus Defoe remarks in his preface to *A Tour thro' the Whole Island of Great Britain* (1724) that "the Face of Things so often alters . . . that there is Matter of new Observation every Day presented to the Traveller's Eye" (quoted in Turner 189).

14. Pope, *The Odyssey of Homer,* books 9:195-96, 10:210-11, 14:510-11. Cf. Genesis 1:2, "and darkness was upon the face of the deep."

15. The "face of things" that include us is also formulated, in the period, as "the face of nature"; instead of being veiled, however, the face of nature is what we are more clearly allowed to see, by power of philosophy or revelation. See, for example, Young, *Night Thoughts* (1742-45), *Night the Fourth,* ll. 474-504; Beattie, *The Minstrel* (1774), book 2, stanza 47; and Hume, *Dialogues concerning Natural Religion* (1779), pt. 12 (the skeptic Philo's partial and perhaps ironic concession to natural religion that we find God discoverable "on the whole face of Nature").

16. On "face" as the figure of figuration itself in book 5 of *The Prelude*, see Cynthia Chase, 13-31.

17. The best introduction to Wordsworth and Roman Stoicism remains Jane Worthington, 43-74; see also John Cole's 2008 PhD thesis for Wordsworth's debts to Cicero and Quintilian. James Averill (153-54) finds in Wordsworth the Stoic concept of a world soul as expressed in *Aeneid* 6.724-27—"the heaven and earth . . . a spirit within sustains, and mind, pervading its members, sways the whole mass and mingles with its mighty frame"—a passage Erasmus Darwin used as the epigraph to his 1794-96 medical and naturalist treatise, *Zoonomia.*

18. As A. A. Long argues, Spinoza's debts to the Stoics are extensive: both are often thought of as "materialists" but are better termed "vitalists" (154); the Stoic *logos,* like Spinoza's God, is the "indwelling cause of all things" (165); Spinoza's notion of freedom and necessity is comparable to the Stoics' (168); Spinoza's ethics are fundamentally Stoic, deduced in both cases from premises "describing the all-inclusive attributes of a Nature which is perfect" (185). Spinoza's main difference from the Stoics, for Long as for other commentators, is his rejection of the Aristotelian-Stoic doctrine of "final causes": the idea that all things, including humans, are made by or within nature for a particular goal or end (208-9).

19. Levinson, in "A Motion and a Spirit: Romancing Spinoza," offers an introduction to Spinoza's philosophy for students of Romanticism (378–88) and an incisive Spinozist reading of "A Slumber did my Spirit Seal" (391–93). For a general overview of *The Ethics*, see Nadler 224–44. Jonathan Israel evidences Spinoza's centrality to a pan-European, "radical Enlightenment" that, unlike the "moderate Enlightenment" rooted in Bacon, Newton, and Locke, broaches materialism and atheism, challenging alike revealed religion and divinely constituted political authority: see especially 159–74, 515–27.

20. *The Prelude*, p. 496 ("Fragments from *Peter Bell* Ms. 2," ll. 16–20, c. February 1799). "Christian pantheism" was first imputed to Wordsworth in the Victorian era by George Mac-Donald, "Wordsworth's Poetry," collected in *The Imagination and Other Essays* (245–63). Jane Worthington (48–52) and E. D. Hirsch (29–31) were among the first to maintain that Wordsworth was not a pantheist but rather a "panentheist," a term coined by K. C. F. Krause (1781–1832) to designate the belief that god is *in* all things but that all things are not God. Hirsch also identifies Wordsworth as a "panvitalist," defining that term with a 1762 quotation from F. C. Oetinger: "He who rightly sees God's presence in the life of all things . . . will at length discern in animals, plants, and stones, a single uniform life" (Hirsch, 38–39). Critics who trace Wordsworth's sense of the one life to eighteenth-century Unitarianism (particularly in Priestley and Barbauld) include Mary Jacobus (59–80) and Martin Priestman (123–28, 147–49).

21. Spinoza's conception of "joyful understanding" is summarized by Susan James: "the clear, adequate ideas with which we reason demonstratively belong to a totality identical with God's thoughts or God's mind. So when we infer one adequate idea from another, we think some of God's thoughts, and in this way begin to merge with God or nature by partaking of his (or its) perfection and power. The knowledge that this is what reasoning is gives rise to a joy, stemming this time from the capacity to blur the boundaries of the self, and become a part of the greatest totality of all" (195).

22. Seneca characterizes Stoic joy (*gaudium*), as distinct from vulgar pleasure, through metaphors of depth: "The yield of poor mines is on the surface; those are really rich whose veins lurk deep, and they will make more bountiful returns to him who delves unceasingly. So too those baubles which delight the common crowd afford but a thin pleasure, laid on as a coating, and every joy that is only plated lacks a real basis. But the joy of which I speak . . . is something solid, disclosing itself the more fully as you penetrate into it" (*Epistles* 1:161–63).

23. For example, the phrase appears eight times, with Wordsworthian resonance, in Ellison's *Madmoments* (1839). The only notable use of "the life of things" before Wordsworth comes in Edmund Spenser's *Amoretti* sonnet "The glorious portrait of that Angels face," a poem on female beauty that cannot be captured by visual art: "A greater craftsman's hand thereto doth neede, / That can express the life of things indeed." Spenser uses the phrase to evoke the spark of thinking things that eludes manual or mechanical reproduction; Wordsworth, by contrast, conjures the quasi- or nonvisual ("with an eye made quiet") apprehension of all things in their united or respective existence(s).

24. The rhetorical concept of *energeia* derives from Aristotle (*Rhetoric* 1411b), who associates it with *kinēsis* ("motion") and "speaking of lifeless or soulless things [*apsycha*] as living things [*empyscha*]" (my translation). *Energeia* is variously translated into English: e.g., it

appears as "actuality" in Freese's Loeb translation of Aristotle, and "animation" (my preferred term) in Hobbes's abridgment and translation (173).

25. Bruce Graver, working with the same Stoic lexicon I employ in this chapter, reads *Tintern Abbey* as a progress from *effrenata laetitia*, "unbridled gladness"—Wordsworth's "aching joys" and "dizzy raptures" (ll. 85–86)—to the *gaudium* or rational joy of seeing into the life of things ("Disturbed with Joy," 51–52).

26. "Thinking thing" is a redundancy or minimal differentiation according to an (erroneous) etymology that Wordsworth may have known about—that of the London radical John Horne Tooke. Tooke's derivation of "think" from "thing" (as *reor* from *res*) is a cornerstone of his noun-derived and materialist basis for all verbs and abstractions (2:405–6). Wordsworth's deconstruction of the human/thing opposition is echoed in his subsequent lyric "A Slumber did my Spirit Seal"—"She seemed a thing that could not feel / The touch of earthly years"—in a manner that renders problematic the aporetic logic J. Hillis Miller finds in "the unbridgeable gap between one meaning of the word 'thing' ["person," or more particularly, "young woman"] and the other ["object"]" (107).

27. Wordsworth's note to *The Thorn*, *Lyrical Ballads* 351. William Keach places this note in the context of a wider Romantic concern with "words as things" (23–45). Cf. Coleridge's rejection of the word/thing opposition in a letter, also of 1800, to Godwin, urging him "to destroy the old antithesis of *Words* & *Things*, elevating, as it were, words into Things, & living Things too" (*Collected Letters* 1:626).

CHAPTER 5: MUSIC VERSUS CONSCIENCE

1. Entry for "Conscience," *The Oxford Dictionary of the Christian Church*, ed. F. L. Cross and E. A. Livingstone, 335.

2. See Robert Javelet's monumental study of commentary on Genesis 1:26, *Image et Resemblance au douziéme siècle de Saint Anselm à Alain de Lille.*

3. "The Children in the Wood" appears in Thomas Percy, *Reliques of Ancient English Poetry* 3:170–77 (I quote lines 129–32). Wordsworth quotes another stanza from this poem, in defense of ballad art, in the 1800 Preface to *Lyrical Ballads.* On the hell of conscience, see also Fanny Holcroft's ballad "Conscience the Worst of Tortures" (*Monthly Magazine*, April 1798), reprinted in Wordsworth and Coleridge, *"Lyrical Ballads" and Related Writings*, ed. William Richey and Daniel Robinson, 270–71.

4. Joseph Butler, *Fifteen Sermons preached at the Rolls Chapel* (1726), sermon 3, "Upon Human Nature"; in Butler, *The Analogy of Religion . . . and Fifteen Sermons* 410–11.

5. Vicesimus Knox, essay 146 ("On the Weight and Efficacy which Morality may derive from the Influence and Example of Those Who are Called the Great"), in *Essays Moral and Literary* 2:259.

6. William Crowe, *Lewesdon Hill: A Poem* 4–5. Wordsworth read *Lewesdon Hill* in 1795, according to Duncan Wu, *Wordsworth's Reading, 1770–1799* 42.

7. On Wordsworth as a poet of guilt and mourning, see Duncan Wu, *Wordsworth: An Inner Life*, p. x and passim.

8. In *Jane Eyre* Mr. Rochester attributes to the title character this credo of conscience: "Strong wind, earth-quake-shock, and fire may pass by: but I shall follow the guiding of that

still small voice which interprets the dictates of conscience" (177 [Chap. 19]). On *Mary Barton,* see the end of this chapter.

9. Fragment, "There is an active principle alive in all things," l. 73, in *"Lyrical Ballads," and Other Poems, 1797–1800* 310.

10. Peter Kivy, *Sound Sentiment* 2–15, 46–52. Kivy establishes his crucial distinction between expression and looks/sounds that are "expressive of" through a critical reading of Johann Mattheson's 1739 treatise *Der Vollkommene Capellmeister,* concluding, "what we see as, and say is, *expressive* of φ is parasitic on what we see as, and say is, *expressing* φ"; "Mattheson's legacy . . . is the notion that *music, in many respects, resembles our expressive behavior"* (50–52). I would suggest that this legacy may ultimately derive from Aristotle's *Poetics,* which holds that the "motions" of music (its rhythms and arrangements of sound) resemble human actions and manners: Thomas Twining grapples with this aspect of Aristotle's musical theory in *Aristotle's Treatise of Poetry* 55–61. Aaron Ridley's recent survey, *The Philosophy of Music: Themes and Variations,* notes that Kivy's linkage between music and expressive human behavior now has "widespread acceptance" (73), arguing that Kivy's only weak spot is that he does not show that, or how, music is or should be *valued* for its expressive properties.

11. Quoted in James Butler's editorial introduction to *The Ruined Cottage* 15.

12. Wordsworth, "O Nightingale!" in *Poems, in Two Volumes* 205, emphasis mine.

13. This phrase, offered as an insight into Wordsworth's style, is originally from John Jones, 206; Christopher Ricks more thoroughly analyzes Wordsworth's "busy prepositions," 110–34.

14. Most critics of Wordsworth assume that the music emanates *from* humanity: for example, Thomas McFarland writes: "the phrase is a subliming of the real distresses of real people, a distillation and mourning of countless such distresses" (17).

15. *Georgics Translations* in *Early Poems and Fragments, 1785–1797* 642. Dryden renders Virgil's lines more faithfully: "Trees bent their heads to hear him sing his Wrongs, / Fierce Tygers couch'd around, and loll'd their fawning Tongues" (4:740–41). Landon and Curtis (*Early Poems and Fragments* 508–9) note that behind Wordsworth's rendition of Virgil's lines lie Milton's from *Paradise Lost* 7:34–36: "that wild Rout that tore the *Thracian* Bard / In *Rhodope,* where Woods and Rocks had Ears / To rapture"; however, in Milton the rapture of the woods and rocks is not, as it is in Wordsworth, specifically a response to a song of sorrow.

16. Kurt Fosso writes engagingly of Wordsworth himself as an Orpheus figure, the pastoral-elegist who mourns incessantly (31–32, 164–69). My only qualification is to note that in Wordsworth, Orphic-mourning has or ought to produce joy in its auditors. Cf. Emily Dickinson poem no. 1545: "The Bible is an antique volume, / Written by faded Men . . . / Had the Tale a warbling Teller / All the Boys would come / Orpheus's sermon captivated / It did not condemn."

17. 1800 endnote to *Lyrical Ballads,* quoted in *"Lyrical Ballads," and Other Poems* 357. On the ode as the representative Romantic genre and on enhanced genre consciousness in the Romantic era, see David Duff, 201–11.

18. Walter Pater, "The School of Giorgione," from *The Renaissance: Studies in Art and Poetry,* in *Selected Writings* 55.

19. Wordsworth claimed that each of his poems had "a worthy *purpose"* in the 1800 Preface to *Lyrical Ballads* (*Prose Works* 1:124).

20. Cf. Jonathan Wordsworth, *The Music of Humanity* 146–47.

21. Relating *The Ruined Cottage* to the georgic mode, David Fairer writes: "Life goes on. . . . As things break down and crumble, new possibilities arise. . . . The distinctive character of . . . [*The Ruined Cottage*] can be found in the way in which pastoral tragedy is embraced by a kind of georgic stoicism" (284).

22. Critics tend to see in this "Waiting for the Horses" episode Wordsworth's guilt-ridden hostility toward his father, John: see, for example, Eugene Stelzig, "Wordsworth's Bleeding Spots: Traumatic Memories of the Absent Father in *The Prelude*." On John Wordsworth's neglect of his children after his wife's early death, see Kenneth R. Johnston, 33–41.

23. *Guilt and Sorrow* quoted from *The Salisbury Plain Poems* 281.

24. James Chandler reads *On the Power of Sound* in relation to Wordsworth's earlier *Ode* ("The 'Power of Sound' and the Great Scheme of Things: Wordsworth Listens to Wordsworth"). On the ascendancy of the aural over the visual in the later ode, see also David P. Haney.

25. On Gaskell's debt to Wordsworth, see Gill, *Wordsworth and the Victorians* 117–44.

CHAPTER 6: CAPTIVATION AND LIBERTY IN POEMS ON MUSIC

1. In 1769, Johann Gottfried Herder similarly called poetry "the music of the soul" (quoted in Abrams, *The Mirror and the Lamp* 93). The trope derives, ultimately, from Plato on lyric poetry as the means of introducing harmony into the soul (*Protagoras* 326a, *Republic* 400c–403c).

2. The essayist is not identified in Jackson, *Contributors and Contributions to "The Southern Literary Messenger."* The essay appears eleven months after Edgar Allan Poe had been sacked as editor of the journal on account of heavy drinking.

3. Henry Reed's first American edition of Wordsworth's poems (Philadelphia, 1837) contains two headings of "Sonnets dedicated to Liberty" ("Part First" and "Part Second"), 211–23.

4. A phrase from the 1800 Preface to *Lyrical Ballads* (*Prose Works* 3:150).

5. Cf. Caesar on the subversive potential of Cassius: "he hears no music" (*Julius Caesar* 1.2.204).

6. See, e.g., Prior, "Down-Hall: A Ballad" and "For his own Epitaph"; Montagu, "The Lover: A Ballad" (a poem much admired by Byron); John Cunningham, "Newcastle Beer"; Blake, "Chimney Sweeper" in *Songs of Innocence*.

7. The iambic-anapestic stanza, chiefly used for comedic verse in the eighteenth century, was applied to moralistic or didactic subjects in two poems that Wordsworth most likely read *after* completing "The Power of Music" and the 1807 *Poems, in Two Volumes*: Scott's "Helvellyn," published in William Whyte's miscellany *A Collection of Scottish Airs* (1806–7)—a stanza from which Wordsworth singled out for praise in the Fenwick note to his own poem on the same topic, "Fidelity"—and Cowper's "Poplar Field," published in Southey's fifteen-volume *Works of William Cowper* (1835–37), but not in any eighteenth-century collection of Cowper's poems I have been able to find. Thus Adela Pinch may be mistaken in attributing the meter of "Poor Susan" to the moralizing model of "Poplar Field" (101).

8. Wordsworth used a strict ballad stanza for two pieces in the original *Lyrical Ballads* ("We are Seven" and "The Tables Turned"); four out of his five Lucy poems ("Strange Fits of

Passion," "She dwelt among the untrodden ways," "I traveled among unknown men," "A slumber did my spirit seal"); three other poems in the enlarged 1800 *Lyrical Ballads* ("Lucy Gray," "The Two April Mornings," "The Fountain"); one poem in the 1807 *Poems, in Two Volumes* ("To the Cuckoo"); and in a few later, minor works (e.g., "George and Sarah Green").

9. In the 1798 *Lyrical Ballads,* see also "Goody Blake and Harry Gill," "It is the first mild day of March," "Simon Lee," "Anecdote for Fathers," *The Thorn,* and "Expostulation and Reply."

10. The poem's speaker meditates on a Scottish woman's greeting, "What you are stepping westward?": "I liked the greeting; 'twas a sound / Of something without place or bound."

11. Peter Manning observes the importance of sequencing in *Poems, in Two Volumes* and in particular in the section "Poems written during a Tour in Scotland" (*Reading Romantics* 258-68). I would question only Manning's claim that in "Rob Roy's Grave" Wordsworth defuses the radical charge of "liberty" by associating it with "traditional society" (264). Wordsworth's *Beau Monde* reviewer, by contrast, is clearly made nervous by the poem's "Jacobin" implication that the poor would be justified in violently seizing their rights, or having rights seized on their behalf.

12. Of course, "The Solitary Reaper" speaks of the lost thing not explicitly as freedom but, conjecturally, as "some natural sorrow, loss, or pain"; yet the loss or pain-of-loss could involve liberty lost in battle: "old, unhappy, far-off things, / And battles long ago."

13. The Pantheon was built in 1770, designed by James Wyatt after the Hagia Sophia in Constantinople. It burned in 1792 but was rebuilt. Later converted to a theater, and still later to a bazaar and warehouse, it was demolished in 1937.

14. This charge is still more applicable to Wordsworth's late poem, *On the Power of Sound,* in which music mitigates the sufferings of slavery and forced labor—and thus, by extension, helps to preserve these institutions (stanza 4, ll. 49–64). Even here, however, music as possible opiate is counterbalanced by music as the engine of "civic renovation" and "of Freedom" (ll. 65–71).

15. Cf. Coleridge's 1819 *Philosophical Lectures*: "Music . . . produces infinite [or "infantine"] Joy—while the overbusy worldlings are buzzed round by night-flies in a sultry climate" (168).

16. Wu suggests that Wordsworth read *The Life of Samuel Johnson* in August 1800 (*Wordsworth's Reading, 1800–1815* 27).

CHAPTER 7: THE MORAL SUBLIME

1. Samuel Holt Monk calls this passage the "apotheosis" of the eighteenth-century sublime (231).

2. In Longinus we find the germ of everything the Romantics have to say about the sublime, including the inability of the physical universe to satisfy the yearnings of men, into whose heart nature [*phusis*] has implanted "an unconquerable passion [*erōta*, the accusative case of *erōs*] for whatever is great and more divine than ourselves. Thus the whole universe is not enough to satisfy the speculative intelligence of human thought; our ideas often pass beyond the limits that confine us" (section 35). Unless otherwise noted, quotations from Longinus *On the Sublime* (cited by section number) are from the W. H. Fyfe translation, revised by

Donald Russell, found in the Loeb Classical Library collection of ancient literary criticism alongside Aristotle's *Poetics* and Demetrius's *On Style*.

3. Nicholas Boileau-Despréux offered this much-quoted assessment in the preface to his 1674 French translation of Longinus (see *The Continental Model: Selected French Critical Essays of the Seventeenth Century, in English Translation,* ed. Scott Elledge and Donald Schier, 270). Compare Alexander Pope's *An Essay on Criticism* (1711) on Longinus, "Whose own Example strengthens all his Laws, / And Is himself the great Sublime he draws" (ll. 679–80).

4. See Nicholas Roe, 91–98.

5. The first two definitions of *partial* in Samuel Johnson's 1755 *Dictionary* are "inclined antecedently to favor one party in a cause, or one side of the question more than the other," and "Inclined to favour without reason."

6. David Vallins (102–40, 191) assesses the influence of Akenside (as well as Priestley and Schelling) on Coleridge's association of spiritual ascent and moral improvement.

7. On this tension, see David Collings, 126–27.

8. Perry, "Wordsworth and Coleridge" 174.

9. The distinction between incident and constitutive luck is made by Bernard Williams, *Moral Luck* 20–39.

10. On Wordsworth's redemption of the accidental, see Ross Hamilton, 189–216.

11. Kant, *Critique of Judgment,* book 2, "Analytic of the Sublime," section 29, p. 127. On the aesthetic and the conditions for morality, see also Robert R. Clewis, 9–12.

12. I quote from the King James Bible, which uses "charity" (from the Latin *caritas,* "love") in place of the "love" found in both earlier and later English translations of this Pauline passage. The term for love in Paul's original Greek is *agapē.*

13. Compare Paul's Epistle to the Colossians 3:12–14, where love (*agapē*) is the acme and perfection of all the virtues (including kindness, compassion, and longsuffering): "and over all these things [put on] love, which is the bond of completeness (*teleiotētos*)." I translate from *The Greek New Testament,* eds. Aland and Aland.

14. Wordsworth's commendation of the poem is noted by Coleridge's editor, J. C. C. Mays, in *Poetical Works I,* 189.

15. Susan Wolfson similarly blurs the hierarchical relation at poem's end in arguing that William's identification with Dorothy, as with a feminine-gender nature, involves an inverse identification of Wordsworth as feminine: "a female alter ego, far from being simply or automatically recruitable to a masculine egotistical sublime, may entail alienation in the alterity" (*Romantic Interactions* 155).

16. See, as a further step toward this revision, my essay "Rethinking the British Romantic Sublime."

17. Walter Savage Landor "Southey and Porson," *Imaginary Conversations* 3:210. Hazlitt, in "Mr. Wordsworth" (1818), singles out *Laodamia* as an instance of Wordsworth's classical, moral sublime: "It is a poem that could be read aloud in Elysium . . . it bends a calmer and keener eye on morality" (*Selected Writings* 224).

18. On the dangers of such uncritical acceptance, see Peter De Bolla, who claims that there is a radical break between the Romantic sublime (based wholly on Weiskel's view of what this is) and earlier eighteenth-century discourses on the sublime. The relation between

the two seems to me far more fluid. Weiskel's synopsis of the Kantian sublime (38-44), upon which many literary critics have relied for their knowledge of Kant, does not address the broader ethical concerns of Kant's third *Critique*.

19. I here employ my own translation of the opening of Sappho's poem.

20. Cf. Addison in *Spectator* no. 229 (2:390-93).

21. Hugh Blair, lecture 4, "The Sublime in Writing," 1:59; Henry Home, Lord Kames, *Elements of Criticism*, chapter 4, "Grandeur and Sublimity," 1:159.

22. On the "Sapphic sublime" in eighteenth-century and Romantic literature, see also Margaret Reynolds, 147-64; Ian Baucom, 252-58; Richard C. Sha, 154-63.

23. *Laodamia* is quoted from Wordsworth, *Shorter Poems, 1807-1820* 147-52.

24. Haydon's diary account is quoted in a note to the Cornell edition of the poem, p. 530.

25. On the ethics of care, or relational ethics, see Carol Gilligan, *In a Different Voice,* and Nel Noddings, *Caring.*

26. One exception is Laurence Lockridge, *The Ethics of Romanticism,* which argues against a Marxist dismissal of ethics (22-33), touching upon the ethical function of the sublime in Wordsworth and in the "anti-sublime" in Shelley (232-34, 291-96). On *the Sublime,* as we currently have it, ends with a dialogue on whether political or ethical conditions are most important for sublime eloquence (section 44). Longinus (as we call the shadowy author of this text) argues for ethics, and his interlocutor for politics, but the debate is hardly conclusive; the lack of resolution may point to the fruitlessness of any attempt to extricate political from ethical conditions.

27. Compare Barbara Claire Freeman: "Unlike the masculinist sublime that seeks to master, appropriate, or colonize the other, I propose that the politics of the feminine sublime involves taking up a position of respect in response to an incalculable otherness" (11).

28. The instability of the opposition masculine/feminine sublime is addressed by Markus Poetzsch (6-16), whose study of the "quotidian sublime"—i.e., the Romantic sensitivity to the wonders of everyday life—cuts across the boundaries of gender, in reading, for example, Dorothy alongside William Wordsworth and Joanna Baillie alongside Robert Burns.

29. I quote the sonnet "I griev'd for Buonaparte" from Wordsworth's *"Poems, in Two Volumes," and Other Poems, 1800-1807.*

30. Burke, 110-17 (pt. 3, sections 9-17), 149-60 (pt. 4, sections 19-25).

31. Both poems appear in the 1800 *Lyrical Ballads.*

32. Galperin, "Wordsworth's Double-Take" 127.

CHAPTER 8: INDEPENDENCE AND INTERDEPENDENCE

1. *The Prelude* did not appear in print until after the poet's death in 1850, and it attained its current critical estimate only in the twentieth century.

2. Mary Shelley's verdict was based in good part on Wordsworth's dedication of *The Excursion* to the Tory Earl of Lonsdale, who in 1813 secured Wordsworth a tax collector post in Westmorland and part of Cumberland.

3. In 1923, H. W. Garrod deemed the last four decades of Wordsworth's career "the most dismal anti-climax of which the history of literature holds record" (quoted in Galperin, *Revision and Authority* 15). *Wordsworth's Anti-Climax* next appears as the title of a 1935 monograph

by Willard Sperry, which, Galperin notes, "ponders the problem but does not contest the issue" (15).

4. Yousef also shrewdly detects in the poem a "counterplot" of familial and social dependency that spans from the infant babe passage of book 2 to the acknowledgments of the sustaining help of Coleridge and Dorothy at the end of book 13 (*Isolated Cases* 122, 140–48).

5. Quoted by Noel Jackson, 2, from the first of Hegel's *Lectures on the Fine Arts* (1835). The term *aesthetic* derives from the Greek verb stem *aisthe*, "feel, apprehend by the senses," and was first applied to the philosophical study of art by Alexander Baumgarten in *Aesthetica*, published 1750–58.

6. The phrase goes back to the Greek Stoic Cleanthes: *homologoumenōs zēn tē phusei*, "living conformably with nature" (Cicero, *De Finibus*, ed. note to 3:21, p. 239).

7. Cicero translated the Greek Stoic term for irrational emotion or passion, *pathē*, as the Latin *perturbationes animi*, "perturbations [or disorders] of the soul" (*Tusculan Disputations* 3.7). Among the affects or *eupatheia* ("good emotion" or "proper feeling") the Stoics approved are rational joy (*gaudium*—on which, see chapter 4), prudent caution (*cautio*), and rational wishing (*voluntatem*, which I address below, in this chapter): see *Tusculan Disputations* 4:12–14.

8. My attention was drawn to this phrase by Ralph Pite (181), who also prefigures a key element of my thesis: "Avoiding 'dependence' is . . . essential to Wordsworth's idea of 'kindred' and hence to his concept of our proper relationship to the natural world" (188–89).

9. Carroll's poem begins: "I met an aged, aged man / Upon the lonely moor: / I knew I was a gentleman, / And he was but a boor. / So I stopped and roughly questioned him, / 'Come, tell me how you live!' / But his words impressed my ear no more / Than if it were a sieve." Later stanzas find the Wordsworthian speaker kicking, pinching, and boxing the ear of the old man.

10. This point is made by Simon Jarvis, 13, in the midst of his provocative reading of the poem (8–21).

11. I quote here from Rousseau's Sixth Promenade in his *Reveries of a Solitary Walker* (my translation).

12. Quoted by Ann Jessie Van Sant, 5. Van Sant proceeds to give Sir John Hawkins's counterargument against sentimentalists and Rousseuvians (from his *Life of Samuel Johnson*): "Their generous notions supersede all obligation: they are a law to themselves, and having *good hearts* and abounding in the *milk of human kindness* are above those considerations that bind men to that rule of conduct which is founded on a sense of duty" (6).

13. In "Gipsies," a later poem that would also appear in the 1807 *Poems, in Two Volumes*, Wordsworth contrasts the duty or "tasks" of the stars with the idleness of a gypsy caravan: "The silent Heavens have goings on; / The stars have tasks—but these have none" (*Poems* 212). Wordsworth's 1827 revisions make the stars moral agents in their own right: "Life which the very stars reprove / As on their silent tasks they move!" Wordsworth's basic conceit is a Stoic one, via Seneca, who wrote of the starry sky overhead "conducting its mighty task in silence" (*silentio tantum opus ducens*), *Moral Epistles* 90: 42.

14. Cicero maintains that "as to who ought most to receive our dutiful services, our country and our parents" are foremost, "for we are obliged to them for the greatest kindnesses" (1:58, *On Duties* 24).

15. Seneca, *Moral Epistles* 28:2; cf. *Epistles* 2, 104. Compare also Horace, *Epistles* book 1, poems 11 and 14.

16. I am thinking in particular of Herbert's poems "Arion," "Marcus Aurelius," and "Maturity" (on Seneca). On Herbert's "heroes of harmony for whom history has no place," see Peter Dale Scott's introduction to his 1963 *Hudson Review* translation (68).

17. Richard Gravil writes: "The Solitary struck [Francis] Jeffrey [who reviewed the poem in 1815] as the liveliest character in the poem. He will strike most readers as guilty only of a rational scepticism, a welcome tendency to interrupt the Wanderer's longer flights, an understandable tendency to fidget while the Pastor is speaking, and as being the only character in the poem who is at any point shown to be, rather than said to be, an engaged member of a community" (209).

18. Hartman sees *The Excursion* as a Book of Job-like drama, with the Solitary as a Job figure who is not in the end bowled over by the belittling voice of God (*Wordsworth's Poetry, 1787-1814* 300).

19. Graver distinguishes the Ciceronian philosophical dialogue from Plato's Socratic dialogue with its "analytical give-and-take" (95). As in Cicero's dialogues, all of Wordsworth's interlocutors speak in the same elevated voice; the poem is not, in Mikhail Bakhtin's phrase, "heteroglossic." Still, *The Excursion* is no more *monologic* than any other philosophical dialogue, which is as a genre susceptible to Hazlitt's critique of Wordsworth's poem: "the dialogues introduced in the present volume are soliloquies of the same character, taking different views of the subject" ("On Mr. Wordsworth's 'The Excursion'" 346).

20. On *conscientia* as "knowledge shared with someone else" in Seneca, see Molenaar, 173: "Knowledge shared with someone else is contrasted ... with knowledge just shared with oneself." Compare, as a kind of knowing together, the central Stoic therapy of seeing oneself as another sees one, the mirror or impartial spectator motif that runs from Seneca to Shaftesbury: I discuss this in "Philosophic and Discursive Prose," forthcoming.

21. The lack of consensus at the end of the poem—with the Solitary not converted to an Arminian natural religion by the Wanderer, and none of the characters converted by the Pastor's Calvinist-tinged final sermon—might be compared to the understanding of dialogue as open-ended process that Michael Prince attributes to Shaftesbury's character Philocles in *The Moralists*, as well as to the deliberate disruption of consensus Hume enacts at the end of his *Dialogues concerning Natural Religion* (Prince 49–51, 136–54).

22. In the King James Bible, "glory" is used to translate a Hebrew term for God's weight (power), visible authority, or splendor (*kavod*). On "glory" in Wordsworth's "Immortality Ode," see Jarvis, 201–3.

23. The Stoic distinctions between *voluntas* and *libido*, rational and irrational joy (*gaudium* and *laetitia gestiens*), and prudent caution and irrational fear (*cautio* and *metus*), appear in Cicero, *Tusculan Disputations* 4:12–14.

24. Compare, among the Pastor's "authentic epitaphs," the fate of Wilfred Armathwaite, adulterer, who "against his Conscience rose in arms" (an 1827 revision of 6:1106–33, *Excursion* 225) and "through remorse and grief ... died" (6:1151).

25. On the evangelical resonance of the Dalesman's "perfection," see Richard Brantley 120, 127–28.

26. In Virgil's fourth *Georgic*, as Goodman notes (115), Eurydice vanishes from the backward-looking Orpheus "like smoke commingling with thin air" (*fumus in auras / commixtus tenuis*, ll. 499–500); Goodman then marks Wordsworth's "fairly pointed allusions" to

this scene in the Solitary's account of his successive losses, first of his wife ("so consumed, she melted from my arms"), and next of his Revolutionary ardor ("Liberty, I worshipped thee, and find thee but a Shade!").

27. Hazlitt here recalls the effect of hearing Wordsworth recite *Peter Bell* ("My First Acquaintance with Poets" in *Selected Writings* 59–60).

CHAPTER 9: SURVIVING DEATH

1. R. D. Archer-Hind sees Wordsworth's poem as inverting Plato's theory of knowledge: "According to Wordsworth we are born with the antenatal radiance clinging about us and spend our lives gradually losing it; according to Plato we lose the vision at birth and spend our lives in gradually recovering it" (quoted in A. W. Price, 221). For an incisive reading of the poem in relation to its classical sources, including Virgil's *Georgics*, see Peter Manning, "Wordsworth's Intimations Ode and Its Epigraphs."

2. The religion of humanity, arguably inferable from Wordsworth's poems, derives immediately from Auguste Comte (1798–1857), with whom Mill corresponded. Mark Johnston, in *Surviving Death*, provides sustained analytic content for "Mill's metaphor of the unselfish living on in the lives of those who are to follow them" (305). Johnston's analysis of *agapē*—"the command to love the arbitrary other as oneself" which is also "the command to treat oneself as if one were an arbitrary other, albeit one whose life one is called to live" (236)—might be fortified by an engagement with Paul Ricoeur's *Oneself as Another*, a rich work of Continental philosophy.

3. For a careful analysis of Hazlitt's essay in relation to contemporary personal identity theory, see Raymond Martin and John Barresi. Jacques Khalip offers a broader inquiry into "Disinterested Agency in Hazlitt and Keats" in chapter 1 of *Anonymous Life* (25–65).

4. On "the problem of evil" in Wordsworth, and his shift from a hermeneutic register in *The Ruined Cottage* ("no longer *read* / The forms of things with an unworthy eye," ll. 510–11, my emphasis) to a typological one in the final revision of *The Excursion*, see Colin Jager, 188–200.

5. Plato writes in the *Cratylus*: "Heracleitus says somewhere that everything passes away and nothing remains, and in likening beings to the flow of a river says that you could not step into the same river twice." Terence Irwin quotes Plato (25) and explains this quip on rivers: "their water is always flowing away and being replaced, and since [for Heracleitus] loss of constituents means destruction, they are always being destroyed and replaced by other rivers." Aristotle, by contrast, "rejects the compositional principle [of identity]; he argues that if the form remains stable, even though the composition changes, the same thing remains in existence, so that we can, contrary to Heracleitus, step into the same river twice" (125–26).

6. On Wordsworth and the Oxford Movement, see Gill, *William Wordsworth* 396–99, 414–19; Manning, "Wordsworth at St. Bees"; and my "Wordsworth, Henry Reed, and Bishop Doane." George Washington Doane (1799–1859), the second Episcopalian Bishop of New Jersey, was the chief American proponent of the Oxford Movement and a personal friend of Wordsworth's from 1841 onward.

7. Galperin, *Revision and Authority* 225–35; Canuel, 161–204. Galperin also observes "the anti-narrative or paratactic" arrangement of *Ecclesiastical Sketches*, which he argues is cor-

relative to "the gradualism . . . that Wordsworth privileges over more willful efforts to alter the disposition of things" (229).

8. I here build on Vivasvan Soni's provocative thesis in *Mourning Happiness* that for some ancient (pre-Socratic) Greek thinkers the question of whether or not to count a person happy was to be determined, at his death, by a public judgment on the narrative of his life, and that this judgment implies some degree of communal responsibility *for* that life. See also Hannah Arendt on retrospective characterization in the Greek *polis*: "the essence of who somebody is . . . can come into being only when life departs, leaving behind nothing but a story" (193).

9. On this poem, which appears in *Shorter Poems* 112–13, see my *Story of Joy* 137–38.

10. Eric C. Walker, in a challenging study of Austen's novels and a selection of Wordsworth's later poems, treats marriage's transformation, in the wake of the Napoleonic wars, into the preeminent site of ethics (the locus of fidelity, trust, and love). Wordsworth, he argues, was widely perceived after 1815 to have retreated into "the inscrutability of marriage" (61), though it is an institution the poet depicts in terms of risk rather than retreat (179–202). Walker classifies *The River Duddon* sequence as a marriage poem, one that revisits a site where William and Mary walked on an 1811 summer vacation, before the traumatic deaths of Catherine and Thomas in 1812 (185–89)—though this biographical context suggests to me the fine line between the absent living and absent dead.

CHAPTER 10: THE POETICS OF LIFE

1. Ernest B. Gilman explains the vexed iconoclasm of Wordsworth's Protestant precursors, including Spenser and Milton: "By nearly every precept of Renaissance aesthetic theory, the poet was encouraged to assume the deep affiliation of literary and pictorial art. Poetry, he knew, was a 'speaking picture,' its figures and structures designed by creative acts as fully visual as verbal. Yet he also knew, on the authority of the Reformation's attack on idolatry, that not only devotional images in churches but the very imaging power of the mind was tainted by the pride and sensuality of fallen humanity and open to the perils of worship misdirected from the Creator to the creation. From the one point of view, *pictura* and *poesis* were companionable sisters in the service of the poet's art; from the other, the word was the bulwark of the spirit against the carnal enticements of the image" (1). The classic study of Wordsworth's vexed iconoclasm—his desire to transcend images, including natural ones, dialectically opposed to his bond to them—remains Geoffrey Hartman's *Wordsworth's Poetry, 1787–1814*.

2. On *Elegiac Stanzas* as a movement from "the iconophilic desire to gaze" to "the iconoclastic urge to violate," see James A. W. Heffernan, 94–107.

3. *The Egyptian Maid* is quoted below from Wordsworth, *Last Poems* 124–47.

4. On the literary context and critical reception of *The White Doe*, see W. J. B. Owen; on Wordsworth's complicated attitude toward Scott, see Peter Manning, "The Other Scene of Travel."

5. Though he does not share it consistently or wholeheartedly: see, for example, his claim in *The Prelude* that in Revolutionary France souvenirs from the fallen Bastille were less moving to him than Charles Le Brun's painting of Mary Magdalene (9:63–80).

6. The debate on images in Protestant theology is summarized in Gilman 31–49.

7. In historical actuality, as Scott informed Wordsworth in 1808, all but one of the Nortons escaped to Flanders; Wordsworth responded, more or less jocularly, "a plague upon your industrious Antiquarianism that has put my fine story to confusion" (editorial introduction to *The White Doe* 7).

8. Compare *Ecclesiastical Sketches*, pt. 1, sonnet 17, on early Christian proselytizing in Britain: Wordsworth depicts a pagan priest overturning his idols (Woden and Thor) and harkening to "the inviting voice / Heard near fresh streams."

9. A *Philosophical Enquiry* 164: "Of these I am convinced, that whatever power they may have on the passions, they do not derive it from any representation raised in the mind of the things for which they stand. As compositions, they are not real essences, and hardly cause, I think, any real ideas. No body, I believe, immediately on hearing the sounds virtue, liberty, or honour [or, I would add, sky of humanity], conceives any precise notion of the particular modes of action and thinking . . . for which these words are substituted."

10. See "My First Acquaintance with Poets," *Selected Writings* 58–59.

11. In most accounts (Apollodorus, Ovid, et al.), Laodamia is an idolater: she sleeps with a wax image of the deceased Protesilaus and finally throws herself into the fire along with it. See Lemprière's *Classical Dictionary*, entry for "Laodamia," and also Timothy Gantz, 593.

12. See Adela Pinch, 72–110, on the relationship between male writers/readers and female suffering, and Wordsworth's use of female characters in *Lyrical Ballads* to explore the crucial relationship of feeling and language.

13. The book, copies of which were owned by Keats and by Tennyson, is *The History of the Renowned Prince Arthur, King of Great Britain; with his Life and Death, and All his Glorious Battles; Likewise, the Noble Acts, and Heroic Deeds of his Valiant Knights of the Round Table,* 2 vols. (London, 1816).

14. On the bust, also known as "Clytie" (the nymph who loved Helios and was transformed into a sunflower), and Townley's catalogue description of it, see B. F. Cook, 15, 55. Eric Gidal remarks of Wordsworth's use of this bust and its Egyptian resonance: "The challenge for Arthurian Britain is to simultaneously subdue . . . [Egypt's] power and incorporate it as a rejuvenating presence within the imperial body. . . . The allure of the Roman bust is repudiated as idolatrous in favor of the maiden it signifies, a maiden who may be re-inscribed within the confines of Anglican piety" (198).

15. The sequence appears in *Sonnet Series and Itinerary Poems* 480–550.

16. Edith Batho, *The Later Wordsworth* (Cambridge UP, 1933), 296–97, quoted in the Cornell edition of *Sonnet Series and Itinerary Poems* 803.

ENVOY: WORDSWORTH'S AFTERLIVES

1. Quoted in Frothingham, 297–98. Parker read the American edition of the *Memoirs* (Boston, 1851), edited by Henry Reed, to which Reed appends his correspondence with Wordsworth; it is here that Parker found Wordsworth's references to Reed's friend, Bishop George Washington Doane.

2. The early responses to Wordsworth's poems are conveniently summarized in John L. Mahoney, 1–30. Francis Jeffrey's *Edinburgh Review* attack on Wordsworth's *Poems, in Two Vol-*

umes (1807) inaugurated the complaint that Wordsworth descended to still more vulgar topics—daisies and daffodils—in a feminine, "namby-pamby" manner: see Judith W. Page, 38.

3. When he addresses *Tintern Abbey,* Reed's confusion about where Wordsworth spent his five years' absence from the banks of the Wye leads to this thrillingly Burkean account of the Revolution: "the beauteous forms of the external world revisited his memory and his feelings even in unpropitious circumstances—doubtless amid the tumultuous agitations of the Parisian mobs, the frenzy of the factions, the waves of a ruthless multitude beating against the ancient palace of their kings, the convulsion of every resting-place of society, the unnatural ferocity of revolutionary women, and the boundless vengeance of the metropolis, with the sympathetic restlessness of the provinces" (*Lectures on the British Poets* 2:214).

4. Simpson, *Wordsworth, Commodification and Social Concern* 15–16.

Works Cited

Abrams, M. H. *The Mirror and the Lamp: Romantic Theory and the Critical Tradition*. Oxford: Oxford UP, 1953.

———. *Natural Supernaturalism: Tradition and Revolution in Romantic Literature*. New York: Norton, 1971.

———. "Structure and Style in the Greater Romantic Lyric." In *From Sensibility to Romanticism: Essays Presented to Frederick A. Pottle*. Ed. F. W. Hilles and Harold Bloom. New York: Oxford UP, 1965. 527–60.

Addison, Joseph, and Richard Steele. *The Spectator*. 5 vols. Ed. Donald F. Bond. Oxford: Clarendon, 1965.

Akenside, Mark. *Poetical Works*. Ed. Robin Dix. Teaneck, NJ: Fairleigh Dickinson UP, 1996.

Aland, Barbara, Kurt Aland, et al., eds. *The Greek New Testament*. 4th rev. ed. Stuttgart: Deutsche Bibelgesellschaft, 1993.

Allen, Stuart. *Wordsworth and the Passions of Critical Poetics*. Houndmills: Palgrave Macmillan, 2010.

Alter, Robert. *The Book of Psalms: A Translation with Commentary*. New York: Norton, 2007.

[Anon.] "William Wordsworth." *Southern Literary Messenger* 3:12 (Dec. 1837): 705–11.

Arendt, Hannah. *The Human Condition*. Chicago: U of Chicago P, 1958.

Aristotle. *The Art of Rhetoric*. Trans. John Henry Freese. Loeb Classical Library. Cambridge: Harvard UP, 1926.

———. *Nichomachean Ethics*. Trans. Martin Ostwald. Indianapolis: Bobbs-Merrill, 1962.

Arnold, Matthew. *English Literature and Irish Politics*. Ed. R. H. Super. Ann Arbor: U of Michigan P, 1973.

Atterbury, Francis. *Sermons and Discourses on Several Subjects and Occasions*. 4 vols. 8th ed. London: 1766.

Aubin, Robert Arnold. *Topographical Poetry in XVIII-Century England*. New York: Modern Language Association of America, 1936.

Averill, James. *Wordsworth and the Poetry of Human Suffering*. Ithaca: Cornell UP, 1980.

Babbitt, Irving. *Rousseau and Romanticism*. Boston: Houghton & Mifflin, 1919.

Barrell, John. *English Literature in History, 1730–80: An Equal, Wide Survey*. London: Hutchinson, 1983.

———. *The Idea of Landscape and the Sense of Place, 1730–1840: An Approach to the Poetry of John Clare*. Cambridge: Cambridge UP, 1972.

———. *Poetry, Language and Politics*. Manchester: Manchester UP, 1988.

Bate, Jonathan. *Romantic Ecology: Wordsworth and the Environmental Tradition*. London: Routledge, 1991.

Baucom, Ian. *Specters of the Atlantic: Finance Capital, Slavery, and the Philosophy of History*. Durham: Duke UP, 2005.

Bauman, Zygmunt. *Postmodern Ethics*. Oxford: Blackwell, 1993.

Beattie, James. *The Poetical Works of Beattie, Blair, and Falconer*. Ed. George Gilfillan. Edinburgh: James Nichol, 1854.

Beer, John. "Wordsworth and the Face of Things" (originally pub. in *The Wordsworth Circle* 10 [1979]: 17–29). Rpt. *The Wordsworth Circle* 37 (2006): 104–11.

Bennett, Andrew. *Wordsworth Writing*. Cambridge: Cambridge UP, 2007.

Bennett, Jane. *The Enchantment of Modern Life: Attachments, Crossings, and Ethics*. Princeton: Princeton UP, 2001.

Benso, Silvia. *The Face of Things: A Different Side of Ethics*. Albany: SUNY P, 2000.

Beowulf. Ed. F. Klaeber. 3rd ed. Lexington, MA: D. C. Heath, 1958.

Bewell, Alan. *Romanticism and Colonial Disease*. Baltimore: Johns Hopkins UP, 1999.

———. *Wordsworth and the Enlightenment: Nature, Man, and Society in the Experimental Poetry*. New Haven: Yale UP, 1989.

Bialostosky, Don. *Wordsworth, Dialogics, and the Practice of Criticism*. Cambridge: Cambridge UP, 1992.

Blackstone, William. *Commentaries on the Laws of England*. 4 vols. 13th ed. London, 1800.

Blair, Hugh. *Lectures on Rhetoric and Belles Lettres*. 2 vols. Ed. Harold F. Harding. Carbondale: Southern Illinois UP, 1965.

———. *Sermons*. Edinburgh, 1772.

Blake, William. *Poetry and Designs*. Ed. Mary Lynn Johnson and John E. Grant. New York: Norton, 1979.

Boswell, James. *The Life of Samuel Johnson, LL.D.* 6 vols. 2nd ed. Ed. G. B. Hill, rev. L. H. Powell. Oxford: Clarendon, 1934–64.

Bowie, Andrew. *Music, Philosophy, and Modernity*. Cambridge: Cambridge UP, 2007.

Brantley, Richard. *Wordsworth's "Natural Methodism."* New Haven: Yale UP, 1975.

Brimble, Willam. *Poems, attempted on various Occasions*. Bath, 1765.

Broglio, Ron. *Technologies of the Picturesque: British Art, Poetry, and Instruments, 1750–1830*. Lewisburg: Bucknell UP, 2008.

Bromwich, David. *Disowned by Memory: Wordsworth's Poetry of the 1790s*. Chicago: U of Chicago P, 1998.

Brontë, Charlotte. *Jane Eyre*. Ed. Richard J. Dunn. 2nd ed. New York: Norton, 1987.

Brooks, Cleanth. "Wordsworth and Human Suffering: Notes on Two Early Poems." In *From Sensibility to Romanticism*. Ed. F. W. Hilles and Harold Bloom. New York: Oxford UP, 1965. 373–87.

Brown, Bill. *A Sense of Things: The Object Matter of American Literature*. Chicago: U of Chicago P, 2003.

———. "Thing Theory." In *Things*. Ed. Bill Brown. Chicago: U of Chicago P, 2004. 1–22.

Brown, Marshall. *Preromanticism*. Stanford: Stanford UP, 1991.

Bruns, Gerald L. "Disappeared: Heidegger and the Emancipation of Language." In *Languages of the Unsayable: The Play of Negativity in Literature and Literary Theory*. Ed. Sanford Budick and Wolfgang Iser. New York: Columbia UP, 1989. 117–39.

Buell, Lawrence. "In Pursuit of Ethics." *PMLA* 114 (1999): 7–19.

Burke, Edmund. *A Philosophical Enquiry into the Origin of our Ideas of the Sublime and Beautiful*. Ed. James T. Boulton. London: Routledge and Kegan Paul, 1958.

Bushell, Sally. *Re-Reading "The Excursion": Narrative, Response and the Wordsworthian Dramatic Voice*. Aldershot, Hampshire: Ashgate, 2002.

Butler, Joseph. *The Analogy of Religion . . . to which are added, Two Brief Dissertations . . . and Fifteen Sermons*. London: George Bell and Sons, 1878.

Butler, Judith. *Precarious Life: The Powers of Mourning and Violence*. London: Verso, 2004.

Canuel, Mark. *Religion, Toleration, and British Writing, 1790–1830*. Cambridge: Cambridge UP, 2002.

Carey, Daniel. "Reading Contrapuntally: *Robinson Crusoe,* Slavery, and Postcolonial Theory." In *Postcolonial Enlightenment*. Ed. Daniel Carey and Lynn Festa. Oxford: Oxford UP, 2009. 105–36.

Carroll, Lewis. "Upon the Lonely Moor." In *The Longman Anthology of British Literature,* vol. 2A: *The Romantics and Their Contemporaries*. Ed. Susan Wolfson and Peter Manning. New York: Pearson Longman, 2006. 524–26.

Cavanagh, Clare. *Lyric Poetry and Modern Politics: Russia, Poland, and the West*. New Haven: Yale UP, 2009.

Chandler, James. "The 'Power of Sound' and the Great Scheme of Things: Wordsworth Listens to Wordsworth." In *"Soundings of Things Done": The Poetry and Poetics of Sound in the Romantic Ear and Era*. Ed. Susan Wolfson. *Romantic Circles: Praxis Series,* internet publication, 2008.

———. *Wordsworth's Second Nature: A Study of the Poetry and Politics*. Chicago: U of Chicago P, 1984.

Chase, Cynthia. *Decomposing Figures: Rhetorical Readings in the Romantic Tradition*. Baltimore: Johns Hopkins UP, 1986.

Chatterton, Thomas. "An Excelente Balade of Charitie: As wroten by the gode Prieste Thomas Rowley, 1464." In *Eighteenth-Century Poetry: An Annotated Anthology*. Ed. David Fairer and Christine Gerrard. Oxford: Blackwell, 1999. 415–18.

Cicero. *De Finibus Bonorum et Malorum*. Trans. H. Rackham. Loeb Classical Library. Cambridge: Harvard UP, 1931.

———. *On Duties*. Ed. and trans. [from *De Officiis*], M. T. Griffin and E. M. Atkins. Cambridge: Cambridge UP, 1991.

———. *The Treatise of Cicero, "De Officiis"; or, His Essay on Moral Duty*. Trans. William McCartney. Edinburgh and London, 1798.

———. *Tusculan Disputations*. Trans. J. E. King. Loeb Classical Library. Cambridge: Harvard UP, 1945.

Clewis, Robert R. *The Kantian Sublime and the Revelation of Freedom*. Cambridge: Cambridge UP, 2009.

Cohen, Abraham. *The Psalms: Hebrew Text & English Translation with an Introduction and Commentary*. London: Socino Press, 1945.

Cole, John J. "'*Radical* Difference': Wordsworth's Classical Imagination and Roman Ethos." PhD thesis, University of Auckland, NZ, 2008.

Cole, Rachel. "Rethinking the Value of Lyric Closure: Giorgio Agamben, Wallace Stevens, and the Ethics of Satisfaction." *PMLA* 126 (2011): 383–97.

Coleridge, Samuel Taylor. *Biographia Literaria*. 2 vols. in 1. Ed. James Engell and W. Jackson Bate. Princeton: Princeton UP, 1983.

——. *Collected Letters*. 6 vols. Ed. Earl Leslie Griggs. Oxford: Clarendon, 1956–71.

——. *Philosophical Lectures*. Ed. Kathleen Coburn. London: Pilot Press, 1949.

——. *Poetical Works I: Poems (Reading Text)*. Ed. J. C. C. Mays. Princeton: Princeton UP, 2001.

Collings David. *Wordsworth's Errancies: The Poetics of Cultural Dismemberment*. Baltimore: Johns Hopkins UP, 1994.

Cook, B. F. *The Townley Marbles*. London: British Museum Publications, 1981.

Cooper, Lane. *A Concordance to the Poems of William Wordsworth*. London: Smith, Elder & Co., 1911.

Costelloe, Timothy. *A History of British Aesthetics*. Cambridge: Cambridge UP, forthcoming.

Cowper, William. *"The Task" and Selected Other Poems,* ed. J. Sambrook. London: Longman, 1994.

Crane, R. S. "Suggestions towards a Genealogy of the 'Man of Feeling.'" *ELH* 1 (1934): 205–30.

Cronin, Richard. *The Politics of Romantic Poetry*. New York: St. Martin's, 2000.

Cross, F. L., and E. A. Livingstone, eds. *The Oxford Dictionary of the Christian Church*. 2nd ed. Oxford: Oxford UP, 1983.

Crowe, William. *Lewesdon Hill, A Poem*. Oxford: Clarendon, 1788.

Cull, Ryan. "Beyond the Cheated Eye: Dickinson's Lyric Sociality." *Nineteenth-Century Literature* 65 (2010): 38–64.

Daniel, Samuel. *Poems and a Defence of Rhyme*. Ed. Arthur Colby Sprague. Cambridge: Harvard UP, 1930.

Davis, Leith. *Acts of Union: Scotland and the Literary Negotiation of the British Nation, 1707–1830*. Stanford: Stanford UP, 1998.

De Bolla, Peter. *The Discourse of the Sublime: Readings in History, Aesthetics, and the Subject*. Oxford: Blackwell, 1989.

Dick, Alex J. "Poverty, Charity, Poetry: The Unproductive Labors of 'The Old Cumberland Beggar.'" *Studies in Romanticism* 39 (2000): 365–96.

Dickinson, Emily. *Complete Poems*. Ed. Thomas H. Johnson. Boston: Little, Brown, 1960.

Donne, John. *Sermons*. 10 vols. Ed. George R. Potter and Evelyn M. Simpson. Berkeley: U of California P, 1953–62.

Dryden, John. *Works*, vol. 5: *The Works of Virgil in English*. Ed. William Frost and Vinton Dearing. Berkeley: U of California P, 1987.

Duff, David. *Romanticism and the Uses of Genre*. Oxford: Oxford UP, 2009.

Dyer, John. *The Poetical Works of Armstrong, Dyer, and Green*. Ed. G. Gilfillan. Edinburgh: James Nichol, 1858.

Eagleton, Terry. *Trouble with Strangers: A Study of Ethics.* Chichester: Wiley-Blackwell, 2009.

Edmundson, Mark. *Literature against Philosophy, Plato to Derrida: A Defence of Poetry.* Cambridge: Cambridge UP, 1995.

Elledge, Scott, and Donald Schier, eds. *The Continental Model: Selected French Critical Essays of the Seventeenth Century, in English Translation.* Ithaca: Cornell UP, 1970.

Ellison, Henry. *Madmoments: or, First Verseattempts.* 2 vols. London, 1839.

Epictetus. *Handbook.* Trans. Nicholas P. White. Indianapolis: Hackett, 1983.

Fairer, David. *Organising Poetry: The Coleridge Circle, 1790–1798.* Oxford: Oxford UP, 2009.

Ferguson, Frances. *Solitude and the Sublime: Romanticism and the Aesthetics of Individuation.* New York: Routledge, 1992.

Festa, Lynn. *Sentimental Figures of Empire in Eighteenth-Century Britain and France.* Baltimore: Johns Hopkins UP, 2006.

Fosso, Kurt. *Buried Communities: Wordsworth and the Bonds of Mourning.* Albany: SUNY P, 2004.

Frazer, Michael L. *The Enlightenment of Sympathy: Justice and the Moral Sentiments in the Eighteenth Century and Today.* New York: Oxford UP, 2010.

Freeman, Barbara Claire. *The Feminine Sublime: Gender and Excess in Women's Fiction.* Berkeley: U of California P, 1995.

Frothingham, Octavius Brooks. *Theodore Parker: A Biography.* Boston: James R. Osgood & Co., 1874.

Fry, Paul. *Wordsworth and the Poetry of What We Are.* New Haven: Yale UP, 2008.

Galperin, William. "'Describing What Never Happened': Jane Austen and the History of Missed Opportunities." *ELH* 73 (2006): 355–82.

———. *The Return of the Visible in British Romanticism.* Baltimore: Johns Hopkins UP, 1993.

———. *Revision and Authority in Wordsworth: The Interpretation of a Career.* Philadelphia: U of Pennsylvania P, 1989.

———. "Wordsworth's Double-Take." *The Wordsworth Circle* 41 (2010): 123–27.

Gana, Nouri. "War, Poetry, Mourning: Darwish, Adonis, Iraq." *Public Culture* 22 (2010): 33–65.

Gantz, Timothy. *Early Greek Myth: A Guide to Literary and Artistic Sources.* Baltimore: Johns Hopkins UP, 1993.

Garber, Frederick. *Wordsworth and the Poetry of Encounter.* Urbana: U of Illinois P, 1971.

Garrard, Greg. "Radical Pastoral?" *Studies in Romanticism* 36 (1996): 449–65.

Gaskell, Elizabeth. *Mary Barton, A Tale of Manchester Life.* Ed. Stephen Gill. Harmondsworth: Penguin, 1970.

Gerard, Alexander. *An Essay on Taste.* London, 1759.

Gidal, Eric. *Poetic Exhibitions: Romantic Aesthetics and the Pleasures of the British Museum.* Lewisburg: Bucknell UP, 2001.

Gigante, Denise. *Taste: A Literary History.* New Haven: Yale UP, 2005.

Gill, Stephen, ed. *The Cambridge Companion to Wordsworth.* Cambridge: Cambridge UP, 2003.

———. "The Philosophic Poet." In *The Cambridge Companion to Wordsworth* 142–60.

———. *William Wordsworth: A Life.* Oxford: Oxford UP, 1990.

————. *Wordsworth and the Victorians*. Oxford: Clarendon, 1998.

Gilligan, Carol. *In a Different Voice*. Cambridge: Harvard UP, 1982.

Gilman, Ernest B. *Iconoclasm and Poetry in the English Reformation: Down Went Dagon*. Chicago: U of Chicago P, 1986.

Godwin, William. *Enquiry concerning Political Justice and its Influence on Morals and Happiness*. 3 vols. Ed. F. E. L. Priestley. Toronto: U of Toronto P, 1946.

Goodman, Kevis. *Georgic Modernity and British Romanticism: Poetry and the Mediation of History*. Cambridge: Cambridge UP, 2004.

Gottlieb, Evan. *Feeling British: Sympathy and National Identity in Scottish and English Writing, 1707–1832*. Lewisburg: Bucknell UP, 2007.

Graver, Bruce E. "Disturbed with Joy." *The Charles Lamb Bulletin* n.s. 134 (April 2006): 50–55.

————. "The Oratorical Pedlar." In *Rhetorical Traditions and British Romantic Literature*. Ed. Don H. Bialostosky and Lawrence D. Needham. Bloomington: Indiana UP, 1995. 94–107.

Gravil, Richard. *Wordsworth's Bardic Vocation, 1787–1842*. Houndmills: Palgrave Macmillan, 2003.

Gray, Thomas, and William Collins. *Poetical Works*. Ed. Roger Lonsdale. Oxford: Oxford UP, 1977.

Grob, Alan. "Afterword: Wordsworth and the Politics of Consciousness." In *Critical Essays on William Wordsworth*. Ed. George H. Gilpin. Boston: G. K. Hall, 1990. 347–50.

Grossman, Allen. *True Love: Essays on Poetry and Valuing*. Chicago: U of Chicago P, 2009.

Guyer, Sara. *Romanticism after Auschwitz*. Stanford: Stanford UP, 2007.

Hall, J. R. Clark. *A Concise Anglo-Saxon Dictionary*. 4th ed. Toronto: U of Toronto P, 1984.

Hamilton, John. *Music, Madness, and the Unworking of Language*. New York: Columbia UP, 2008.

Hamilton, Ross. *Accident: A Philosophical and Literary History*. Chicago: U of Chicago P, 2007.

Haney, David P. "'Rents and Openings in the Ideal World': Eye and Ear in Wordsworth." *Studies in Romanticism* 36 (1997): 173–99.

Harpham, Geoffrey Galt. *Shadows of Ethics: Criticism and the Just Society*. Durham: Duke UP, 1999.

Harrison, Gary. *Wordsworth's Vagrant Muse: Poetry, Poverty, and Power*. Columbus: Ohio State UP, 1994.

Hartman, Geoffrey H. *The Unremarkable Wordsworth*. Minneapolis: U of Minnesota P, 1987.

————. *Wordsworth's Poetry, 1787–1814*. 2nd ed. New Haven: Yale UP, 1971.

Hawkins, John. *A General History of the Science and Practice of Music*. 2 vols. London: 1853; rpt. New York: Dover, 1964.

Hazlitt, William. *An Essay on the Principles of Human Action* (London, 1805). Intro. John R. Nabholtz. Gainesville: Scholars' Facsimiles and Reprints, 1969.

————. "On Mr. Wordsworth's 'The Excursion.'" In *Lectures on the English Poets*. 3rd ed. London, 1841. 343–67.

————. "On Poetry in General." *Lectures on the English Poets*. 1–37.

————. "On the Living Poets." *Lectures on the English Poets*. 276–34.

————. *Selected Writings*. Ed. Ronald Blythe. Harmondsworth: Penguin, 1970.

Heffernan, James A. W. *Museum of Words: The Poetics of Ekphrasis from Homer to Ashbery*. Chicago: U of Chicago P, 1993.

Heidegger, Martin. *Poetry, Language, Thought*. Trans. Albert Hofstadter. New York: Harper & Row, 1971.

Henriksson, Anders. "A History of the Past: 'Life Reeked with Joy.'" *Wilson Quarterly* (1983): 168–71.

Hirsch, E. D., Jr. *Wordsworth and Schelling: A Tropological Study of Romanticism*. New Haven: Yale UP, 1960.

[Hobbes, Thomas.] *A Briefe of the Art of Rhetorique, containing in substance all that Aristotle hath written in his three bookes of that subject*. London, 1637.

Horace. *Odes and Epodes*. Loeb Classical Library. Trans. C. E. Bennett. Cambridge: Harvard UP, 1968.

——. *Satires, Epistles, Ars Poetica*. Loeb Classical Library. Trans. H. R. Fairclough. Cambridge: Harvard UP, 1929.

Horne, George. *A Commentary on the Book of Psalms*. 2 vols. 3rd ed. Oxford: Clarendon, 1784.

Hume, David. *Dialogues concerning Natural Religion*. Ed. Norman Kemp Smith. London: Thomas Nelson & Sons, 1947.

Hutcheson, Francis. *On the Nature and Conduct of the Passions*. Ed. Andrew Ward. Manchester: Clinamen, 1999.

Irwin, Terence. *Classical Thought*. Oxford: Oxford UP, 1989.

Israel, Jonathan I. *Radical Enlightenment: Philosophy and the Making of Modernity, 1650–1750*. Oxford: Oxford UP, 2001.

Jackson, David. *Contributors and Contributions to "The Southern Literary Messenger."* Charlottesville, VA: Historical Publishing Co., 1936.

Jackson, Noel. *Science and Sensation in Romantic Poetry*. Cambridge: Cambridge UP, 2008.

Jacobus, Mary. *Tradition and Experiment in Wordsworth's Lyrical Ballads*. Oxford: Clarendon, 1976.

Jager, Colin. *The Book of God: Secularization and Design in the Romantic Era*. Philadelphia: U of Pennsylvania P, 2007.

James, Susan. *Passion and Action: The Emotions in Seventeenth-Century Philosophy*. Oxford: Clarendon, 1997.

Jameson, Fredric. *The Political Unconscious: Narrative as a Socially Symbolic Act*. Ithaca: Cornell UP, 1981.

Jarvis, Simon. *Wordsworth's Philosophic Song*. Cambridge: Cambridge UP, 2007.

Javelet, Robert. *Image et Resemblance au douziéme siècle de Saint Anselm à Alain de Lille*. 2 vols. Paris: Letouzey & Ané, 1967.

Johnston, Kenneth R. *The Hidden Wordsworth: Poet, Lover, Rebel, Spy*. New York: Norton, 1998.

Johnston, Mark. *Surviving Death*. Princeton: Princeton UP, 2010.

Jones, John. *The Egotistical Sublime: A History of Wordsworth's Imagination*. London: Chatto and Windus, 1954.

Jung, Sandro. "Print Culture, High-Cultural Consumption, and Thomson's *The Seasons*, 1780–1797." *Eighteenth-Century Studies* 44 (2011): 495–514.

Jupp, W. J. "Neglected Sources of Joy." *Hibbert Journal* 19 (Oct. 1920–July 1921): 679–89.

Kames, Henry Home, Lord. *Elements of Criticism*. 2 vols. Ed. Peter Jones. Indianapolis: Liberty Fund, 2005.

Kant, Immanuel. *Critique of Judgment.* Trans. Werner S. Pluhar. Indianapolis: Hackett, 1987.

———. *Critique of Practical Reason.* Trans. Mary Gregor. Cambridge: Cambridge UP, 1997.

———. *Groundwork for the Metaphysics of Morals.* Trans. Allen W. Wood. New Haven: Yale UP, 2002.

———. *Observations on the Feeling of the Beautiful and Sublime.* Trans. John T. Goldthwait. Berkeley: U of California P, 1965.

Keach, William. *Arbitrary Power: Romanticism, Language, Politics.* Princeton: Princeton UP, 2004.

Keats, John. *Complete Poems,* ed. Jack Stillinger. Cambridge: Harvard UP, 1978.

———. *Letters.* Ed. Robert Gittings. Oxford: Oxford UP, 1970.

Khalip, Jacques. *Anonymous Life: Romanticism and Dispossession.* Stanford: Stanford UP, 2009.

———. "'The Archaeology of Sound': Derek Jarman's *Blue* and Queer Audiovisuality in the Time of AIDS." *Differences: A Journal of Feminist Cultural Studies* 21:2 (2010): 73–108.

King, Joshua. "'The Old Cumberland Beggar': Form and Frustrated Sympathy." *The Wordsworth Circle* 41 (2010): 45–52.

Kivy, Peter. *Introduction to a Philosophy of Music.* Oxford: Oxford UP, 2002.

———. *Sound Sentiment: An Essay on the Musical Emotions.* Philadelphia: Temple UP, 1989.

Knox, Vicesimus. *Essays Moral and Literary.* 2 vols. London, 1795.

Kroeber, Karl. *Ecological Literary Criticism: Romantic Imagining and the Biology of Mind.* New York: Columbia UP, 1994.

Labbe, Jacqueline M. *Romantic Visualities: Landscape, Gender, and Romanticism.* New York: St. Martin's, 1998.

Landor, Walter Savage. "Southey and Porson." In *Imaginary Conversations.* 6 vols. Ed. Charles G. Crump. London: J. M. Dent, 1891. 3:185–214.

Langan, Celeste. *Romantic Vagrancy: Wordsworth and the Simulation of Freedom.* Cambridge: Cambridge UP, 1995.

Lemprière, John. *Classical Dictionary* [1788]. 3rd ed. London: Routledge and Kegan Paul, 1984.

Levinas, Emmanuel. *Totality and Infinity: An Essay on Exteriority.* Trans. Alphonso Lingis. Pittsburgh: Duquesne UP, 1969.

Levinson, Marjorie. "A Motion and a Spirit: Romancing Spinoza." *Studies in Romanticism* 46 (2007): 367–408.

———. *Wordsworth's Great Period Poems.* Cambridge: Cambridge UP, 1986.

Liu, Alan. "Wordsworth: The History in 'Imagination.'" *ELH* 51 (1984): 505–48.

Lockridge, Laurence. *The Ethics of Romanticism.* Cambridge: Cambridge UP, 1989.

Long, A. A. *Hellenistic Philosophy: Stoics, Epicureans, Sceptics.* 2nd ed. Berkeley: U of California P, 1986.

Longinus. *On the Sublime.* Trans. W. H. Fyfe, rev. Donald Russell. Loeb Classical Library. Cambridge: Harvard UP, 1995.

Lucretius. *De Rerum Natura.* Trans. Thomas Creech. Oxford, 1682.

MacDonald, George. *The Imagination and Other Essays.* Boston: D. Lothrop, 1883.

MacIntyre, Alasdair. *After Virtue: A Study of Moral Virtue.* 2nd ed. Notre Dame: U of Notre Dame P, 1984.

Magnuson, Paul. *Coleridge and Wordsworth: A Lyrical Dialogue*. Princeton: Princeton UP, 1988.

Mahoney, Charles. "Poetic Pains in Formal Pleasures Bound." *The Wordsworth Circle* 33:1 (2002): 27–32.

Mahoney, John L. *Wordsworth and the Critics: The Development of a Critical Reputation*. Rochester, NY: Camden House, 2001.

[Malory, Thomas.] *The History of the Renowned Prince Arthur, King of Great Britain; with his Life and Death, and All his Glorious Battles; Likewise, the Noble Acts, and Heroic Deeds of his Valiant Knights of the Round Table*. 2 vols. London, 1816.

Manning, Peter J. "Cleansing the Images: Wordsworth, Rome, and the Rise of Historicism." *Texas Studies in Language and Literature* 33 (1991): 271–326.

———. "The Other Scene of Travel: Wordsworth's 'Musings Near Aquapendente.'" In *The Wordsworthian Enlightenment: Romantic Poetry and the Ecology of Reading*. Ed. Helen Regueiro Elam and Frances Ferguson. Baltimore: Johns Hopkins UP, 2005. 191–211.

———. *Reading Romantics: Texts and Contexts*. New York: Oxford UP, 1990.

———. "Wordsworth at St. Bees: Scandals, Sisterhoods, and Wordsworth's Later Poetry." *ELH* 52 (1985): 33–58.

———. "Wordsworth's 'Illustrated Books and Newspapers' and Media of the City." In *Romanticism and the City*. Ed. Larry H. Peer. Houndmills: Palgrave Macmillan, 2011. 223–40.

———. "Wordsworth's Intimations Ode and Its Epigraphs." *Journal of English and Germanic Philology* 82 (1983): 526–40.

Marcuse, Herbert. *One-Dimensional Man: Studies in the Ideology of Advanced Industrial Society*. Boston: Beacon, 1964.

Martin, Raymond, and John Barresi. "Hazlitt on the Future of the Self." *Journal of the History of Ideas* 56 (1995): 463–81.

Mason, Emma. *The Cambridge Introduction to William Wordsworth*. Cambridge: Cambridge UP, 2010.

McFarland, Thomas. *William Wordsworth: Intensity and Achievement*. Oxford: Clarendon, 1992.

McGann, Jerome J. *The Romantic Ideology: A Critical Investigation*. Chicago: U of Chicago P, 1983.

McGinn, Colin. *Ethics, Evil, and Fiction*. Oxford: Clarendon, 1997.

McKelvy, William R. *The English Cult of Literature: Devoted Readers, 1774–1880*. Charlottesville: U of Virginia P, 2007.

McKusick, James. *Green Writing: Romanticism and Ecology*. New York: St. Martin's, 2000.

Mellor, Anne K. *Romanticism and Gender*. New York: Routledge, 1993.

Miles, Robert. *Romantic Misfits*. New York: Palgrave Macmillan, 2008.

Mill, John Stuart. *Autobiography and Literary Essays*. Ed. John M. Robson and Jack Stillinger. Toronto: U of Toronto P, 1981.

———. *"Nature," "The Utility of Religion," and "Theism."* London, 1874.

Miller, J. Hillis. "On Edge: The Crossways of Contemporary Criticism." In *Romanticism and Contemporary Criticism*. Ed. Morris Eaves and Michael Fischer. Ithaca: Cornell UP, 1986. 96–118.

Milton, John. *Complete Poems and Major Prose*. Ed. Merritt Y. Hughes. New York: Odyssey, 1957.

Modiano, Raimonda. "The Kantian Seduction: Wordsworth on the Sublime." In *Deutsche Romantik and English Romanticism*. Ed. Theodore G. Gish and Sandra G. Frieden. Munich: Fink, 1984. 17–26.

Molenaar, G. "Seneca's Use of the Term *Conscientia*." *Mnemosyne*, 4th ser., vol. 22 (1969): 170–80.

Monk, Samuel Holt. *The Sublime: A Study of Critical Theories in Eighteenth-Century England*. New York: MLA, 1935.

Montaigne, Michel de. *The Essays of Michael Seigneur de Montaigne, Translated into English*. 3 vols. 7th ed. London, 1759.

Morse, David. *The Age of Virtue: British Culture from the Reformation to Romanticism*. London: Palgrave, 2000.

Morton, Timothy. *Ecology without Nature: Rethinking Environmental Aesthetics*. Cambridge: Harvard UP, 2007.

Moyn, Samuel. *Origins of the Other: Emmanuel Levinas between Revelation and Ethics*. Ithaca: Cornell UP, 2005.

Mulvey, Laura. "Visual Pleasure and Narrative Cinema." *Screen* 16:3 (1975): 6–18.

Murphy, Patrick D. *Literature, Nature and Other: Ecofeminist Critiques*. Albany: State University of New York P, 1995.

Nadler, Steven. *Spinoza: A Life*. Cambridge: Cambridge UP, 1999.

Nancy, Jean-Luc. *Listening*. Trans. Catherine Mandell. New York: Fordham UP, 2007.

Neubauer, John. *The Emancipation of Music from Language: Departure from Mimesis in Eighteenth-Century Aesthetics*. New Haven: Yale UP, 1980.

Newman, Steve. *Ballad Collection, Lyric, and the Canon: The Call of the Popular from the Restoration to the New Criticism*. Philadelphia: U of Pennsylvania P, 2007.

Nichols, Ashton. *The Poetics of Epiphany: Nineteenth-Century Origins of the Modern Literary Moment*. Tuscaloosa: U of Alabama P, 1987.

Nietzsche, Friedrich. *"The Birth of Tragedy" and "The Case of Wagner,"* trans. Walter Kaufman. New York: Vintage, 1967.

Noddings, Nel. *Caring: A Feminine Approach to Ethics and Moral Education*. Berkeley: U of California P, 1984.

Nuss, Melynda. "'Look in my Face': The Dramatic Ethics of *The Borderers*." *Studies in Romanticism* 43 (2004): 599–621.

Nussbaum, Martha C. *Upheavals of Thought: The Intelligence of Emotions*. Cambridge: Cambridge UP, 2001.

Oerlemans, Onno. *Romanticism and the Materiality of Nature*. Toronto: U of Toronto P, 2002.

O'Rourke, James. *Sex, Lies, and Autobiography: The Ethics of Confession*. Charlottesville: U of Virginia P, 2006.

Owen, W. J. B. "*The White Doe of Rylstone* and Its Time." *The Wordsworth Circle* 29 (1998): 20–25.

Page, Judith W. *Wordsworth and the Cultivation of Women*. Berkeley: U of California P, 1994.

Parker, Blanford. *The Triumph of Augustan Poetics: English Literary Culture from Butler to Johnson*. Cambridge: Cambridge UP, 1998.

Parker, Reeve. *Romantic Tragedies: The Dark Emplotments of Wordsworth, Coleridge, and Shelley.* Cambridge: Cambridge UP, 2011.

Pater, Walter. "The School of Giorgione." In *Selected Writings.* Ed. Harold Bloom. New York: New American Library, 1974; rpt. New York: Columbia UP, 1982. 52–58.

———. "Wordsworth." In *Selected Writings.* 125–42.

Paulson, Ronald. *Representations of Revolution, 1789–1820.* New Haven: Yale UP, 1983.

Percy, Thomas. *Reliques of Ancient English Poetry.* 3 vols. London, 1765.

Perry, Seamus. "Coleridge, Wordsworth, and Other Things." *The Wordsworth Circle* 29 (1998): 31–41.

———. "Joy Perplexed: Optimism and Complication in Wordsworth, T. H. Green and A.C. Bradley." *TLS* July 14, 2006: 13–15.

———. "Wordsworth and Coleridge." In Gill, *The Cambridge Companion to Wordsworth* 161–79.

Pfau, Thomas. *Wordsworth's Profession: Form, Class, and the Logic of Early Romantic Cultural Production.* Stanford: Stanford UP, 1997.

Pinch, Adela. *Strange Fits of Passion: Epistemologies of Emotion, Hume to Austen.* Stanford: Stanford UP, 1996.

Pite, Ralph. "Wordsworth and the Natural World." In Gill, *The Cambridge Companion to Wordsworth* 180–95.

Poetzsch, Markus. *"Visionary Dreariness": Readings in Romanticism's Quotidian Sublime.* New York: Routledge, 2006.

Pope, Alexander. *The Iliad of Homer.* Ed. Steven Shankman. London: Penguin, 1996.

———. *The Odyssey of Homer.* 6 vols. London: 1725–26.

———. *Poetry and Prose.* Ed. Aubrey Williams. Boston: Houghton Mifflin, 1969.

Potkay, Adam. "Ear and Eye: Counteracting Senses in Loco-Descriptive Poetry." In *A Companion to Romantic Poetry.* Ed. Charles Mahoney. Oxford: Wiley-Blackwell, 2010. 176–94.

———. *The Passion for Happiness: Samuel Johnson and David Hume.* Ithaca: Cornell UP, 2000.

———. "Philosophic and Discursive Prose: The Transformation of the Ancient Schools in Eighteenth-Century Philosophy." Forthcoming in *The Oxford History of Classical Reception in English Literature,* vol. 3: *1660–1790.* Ed. David Hopkins and Charles Martindale. Oxford: Oxford UP, 2012.

———. "Rethinking the British Romantic Sublime." Forthcoming in *The Sublime: From Antiquity to the Present.* Ed. Tim Costelloe. Cambridge: Cambridge UP, 2012.

———. *The Story of Joy: From the Bible to Late Romanticism.* Cambridge: Cambridge UP, 2007.

———. "Wordsworth, Henry Reed, and Bishop Doane: High-Church Romanticism on the Delaware." In *Wordsworth in American Literary Culture.* Ed. Joel Pace and Matthew Scott. Houndmills: Palgrave Macmillan, 2005. 101–20.

Pound, Ezra. *Selected Poems.* New York: New Directions, 1957.

Price, A. W. "Wordsworth's *Ode on the Intimations of Immortality.*" In *Platonism and the English Imagination.* Ed. Anna Baldwin and Sarah Hutton. Cambridge: Cambridge UP, 1994. 217–28.

Priestley, Joseph. *A Course of Lectures on Oratory and Criticism.* Ed. Vincent M. Bevilacqua and Richard Murphy. Carbondale: Southern Illinois UP, 1965.

Priestman, Martin. *Romantic Atheism: Poetry and Freethought, 1780–1830*. Cambridge: Cambridge UP, 1999.

Prince, Michael. *Philosophical Dialogue in the British Enlightenment: Theology, Aesthetics, and the Novel*. Cambridge: Cambridge UP, 1996.

Radcliffe, Evan. "Wordsworth and the Problem of Action: *The White Doe of Rylstone*." *Nineteenth-Century Literature* 46 (1991): 157–80.

Reed, Henry. *Lectures on English Literature from Chaucer to Tennyson*. Philadelphia, 1855.

———. *Lectures on the British Poets*. 2 vols. Philadelphia, 1857.

———. "Wordsworth's Poetry." *New York Review* 4:7 (January 1839): 1–70.

Reiman, Donald H., ed. *The Romantics Reviewed: Contemporary Reviews of British Romantic Writing. Part A, The Lake Poets*. 2 vols. New York: Garland, 1972.

Reynolds, Margaret. *The Sappho Companion*. New York: Palgrave, 2002.

Richardson, Alan. *A Mental Theater: Poetic Drama and Consciousness in the Romantic Age*. University Park: Pennsylvania State UP, 1988.

Ricks, Christopher. *The Force of Poetry*. Oxford: Clarendon, 1984.

Ricoeur, Paul. *Oneself as Another*. Trans. Kathleen Blamey. Chicago: U of Chicago P, 1992.

Ridley, Aaron. *The Philosophy of Music: Themes and Variations*. Edinburgh: Edinburgh UP, 2004.

Rivers, Isabel. *Reason, Grace, and Sentiment: A Study of the Language of Religion and Ethics in England, 1660–1780*; vol. 2: *Shaftesbury to Hume*. Cambridge: Cambridge UP, 2000.

Roe, Nicholas. *Wordsworth and Coleridge: The Radical Years*. Oxford: Clarendon, 1988.

Rousseau, Jean-Jacques. *Les Rêveries du Promeneur Solitaire*. Ed. Jacques Voisine. Paris: Garnier-Flammarion, 1964.

Rzepka, Charles. "Pictures of the Mind: Iron and Charcoal, 'Ouzy Tides' and 'Vagrant Dwellers' at Tintern, 1798." *Studies in Romanticism* 42:2 (2003): 155–85.

Sancho, Ignatius. *Letters of the Late Ignatius Sancho, An African*. Ed. Vincent Carretta. New York: Penguin Putnam, 1998.

Schiller, Friedrich von. *On the Sublime*. In *"Naïve and Sentimental Poetry" and "On the Sublime": Two Essays*. Trans. Julius A. Elias. New York: Frederick Ungar, 1966. 193–212.

———. *The Robbers: A Tragedy*. Trans. Alexander Fraser Tytler. New York, 1793.

Schmitt, Carl. *Political Theology: Four Chapters on the Concept of Sovereignty* (1922), trans. George Schwab. Cambridge: Massachusetts Institute of Technology P, 1985.

Schneewind, J. B. *The Invention of Autonomy: A History of Modern Moral Philosophy*. Cambridge: Cambridge UP, 1998.

Schneider, Ben Ross. *Wordsworth's Cambridge Education*. Cambridge: Cambridge UP, 1957.

Scott, Peter Dale. "Translations from Zbigniew Herbert." *Hudson Review* 16:1 (1963): 68–73.

Seneca. *Epistles (Epistulae Morales)*. 3 vols. Trans. Richard M. Gummere. Loeb Classical Library. Cambridge: Harvard UP, 1917.

———. *Moral Essays*. 2 vols. Trans. John W. Basore. Loeb Classical Library. Cambridge: Harvard UP, 1928.

Sha, Richard C. *Perverse Romanticism: Aesthetics and Sexuality in Britain, 1750–1832*. Baltimore: Johns Hopkins UP, 2009.

Shaftesbury, 3rd Earl of. *Characteristicks of Men, Manners, Opinions, Times*. 2 vols. Ed. Philip Ayres. Oxford: Clarendon, 1999.

————. *Life, Unpublished Letters, and Philosophical Regimen*. Ed. Benjamin Rand. New York: Macmillan, 1900.

Shakespeare, William. *Complete Works*. Ed. David Bevington. 5th ed. New York: Longman, 2004.

Shelley, Mary. *Journals, 1814–1844*. 2 vols. Ed. Paula R. Feldman and Diana Scott-Kilvert. Oxford: Oxford UP, 1987.

Shelley, Percy Bysshe. *Poetry and Prose*. 2nd ed. Ed. Donald H. Reiman and Neil Fraistat. New York: Norton, 2002.

Simpson, David. "Commentary: Updating the Sublime." *Studies in Romanticism* 26:2 (1987): 245–58.

————. *Wordsworth, Commodification and Social Concern: The Poetics of Modernity*. Cambridge: Cambridge UP, 2009.

————. *Wordsworth's Historical Imagination: The Poetry of Displacement*. London: Methuen, 1987.

Siskin, Clifford. *The Historicity of Romantic Discourse*. New York: Oxford UP, 1988.

Soni, Vivasvan. "Modernity and the Fate of Utopian Representation in Wordsworth's 'Female Vagrant.'" *European Romantic Review* 21 (2010): 363–81.

————. *Mourning Happiness: Narrative and the Politics of Modernity*. Ithaca: Cornell UP, 2010.

Spenser, Edmund. *Poetical Works*. Ed. J. C. Smith and Ernest De Selincourt. London: Oxford UP, 1935.

Spinoza, Benedict de. *A Spinoza Reader: "The Ethics" and Other Works*. Ed. and trans. Edwin Curley. Princeton: Princeton UP, 1994.

Starr, G. Gabrielle. *Lyric Generations: Poetry and the Novel in the Long Eighteenth Century*. Baltimore: Johns Hopkins UP, 2004.

Stelzig, Eugene. "Wordsworth's Bleeding Spots: Traumatic Memories of the Absent Father in *The Prelude*." *European Romantic Review* 15 (2004): 533–45.

Stephen, Leslie. "Wordsworth's Ethics." In *Hours in a Library*. 3 vols. London, 1876. 2:250–84.

Sterne, Laurence. *Tristram Shandy*. Ed. Melvyn New and Joan New. New York: Penguin, 1997.

Stewart, John B. *Opinion and Reform in Hume's Political Philosophy*. Princeton: Princeton UP, 1992.

Terada, Rei. *Looking Away: Phenomenality and Dissatisfaction, Kant to Adorno*. Cambridge: Harvard UP, 2009.

Thomas, Keith. *Man and the Natural World: Changing Attitudes in England, 1500–1800*. London: Allen Lane, 1983.

Thomson, James. *"The Seasons" and "The Castle of Indolence."* Ed. James Sambrook. Oxford: Clarendon, 1987.

Tompkins, J. M. S. *The Popular Novel in England, 1770–1800*. London: Constable, 1932.

Tooke, John Horne. *Winged Words, or the Diversions of Purley*. 2 vols. London, 1786–1805.

Trenchard, John, and Thomas Gordon. *Cato's Letters: or, Essays on Liberty, Civil and Religious, and other Important Subjects*. 2 vols. Ed. Ronald Hamowy. Indianapolis: Liberty Fund, 1995.

Turner, Katherine. "Defoe's *Tour*: The Changing 'Face of Things.'" *British Journal for Eighteenth-Century Studies* 24 (2001): 189–205.

Twining, Thomas. *Aristotle's Treatise of Poetry, Translated . . . With Notes . . . and Two Dissertations, on Poetical, and Musical, Imitation*. London, 1789.

Vallins, David. *Coleridge and the Psychology of Romanticism: Feeling and Thought*. Houndmills: Macmillan, 2000.

Van Sant, Ann Jessie. *Eighteenth-Century Sensibility and the Novel: The Senses in Social Context*. Cambridge: Cambridge UP, 1993.

Virgil. *Eclogues, Georgics, Aeneid 1–6*. Loeb Classical Library. Trans. H. R. Fairclough. Cambridge: Harvard UP, 1935.

Walker, Eric C. *Marriage, Writing, and Romanticism: Wordsworth and Austen after War*. Stanford: Stanford UP, 2009.

Warton, Thomas. *The Pleasures of Melancholy*. In *Eighteenth-Century Poetry: An Annotated Anthology*. Ed. David Fairer and Christine Gerrard. Oxford: Blackwell, 1999. 367–74.

Weele, Michael Vander. "The Contest of Memory in 'Tintern Abbey,'" *Nineteenth-Century Literature* 50:1 (June 1995): 6–26.

Weiskel, Thomas. *The Romantic Sublime: Studies in the Structure and Psychology of Transcendence*. 2nd ed. Baltimore: Johns Hopkins UP, 1986.

[Whipple, Edwin Percy.] Review of Wordsworth's *Complete Poetical Works*. *North American Review* 59:125 (Oct. 1844): 352–84.

Wilberforce, William. *A Practical View of the Prevailing Religious System of Professed Christians in the Higher and Middle Classes of this Country, contrasted with Real Christianity*. 2nd ed. London, 1797.

Wiley, Michael. *Romantic Geography: Wordsworth and Anglo-European Spaces*. New York: St. Martin's, 1998.

Williams, Bernard. *Moral Luck: Philosophical Papers, 1973–1980*. Cambridge: Cambridge UP, 1981.

Wolfson, Susan. *The Questioning Presence: Wordsworth, Keats, and the Interrogative Mode in Romantic Poetry*. Ithaca: Cornell UP, 1986.

———. *Romantic Interactions: Social Being and the Turns of Literary Action*. Baltimore: Johns Hopkins UP, 2010.

———. "Wordsworth's Craft." In Gill, *The Cambridge Companion to Wordsworth* 108–24.

Woof, Robert, ed. *William Wordsworth: The Critical Heritage, 1793–1820*. London: Routledge, 2001.

Wordsworth, Christopher. *Memoirs of William Wordsworth*. 2 vols. Ed. Henry Reed. Boston, 1851.

Wordsworth, Dorothy. *Recollections of a Tour Made in Scotland*. Ed. Carol Kyros Walker. New Haven: Yale UP, 1997.

Wordsworth, Jonathan. *The Music of Humanity: A Critical Study of Wordsworth's "Ruined Cottage."* New York: Harper & Row, 1969.

———. *William Wordsworth: The Borders of Vision*. Oxford: Clarendon, 1982.

Wordsworth, William. *Benjamin the Waggoner*. Ed. Paul F. Betz. Ithaca: Cornell UP, 1981.

———. *The Borderers*. Ed. Robert Osborn. Ithaca: Cornell UP, 1982.

———. *Complete Poetical Works*. Ed. Henry Reed. Philadelphia: James Kay, 1837.

———. *Descriptive Sketches*. Ed. Eric Birdsall with Paul M. Zall. Ithaca: Cornell UP, 1984.

———. *Early Poems and Fragments, 1785–1797*. Ed. Carol Landon and Jared Curtis. Ithaca: Cornell UP, 1997.

———. *An Evening Walk*. Ed. James Averill. Ithaca: Cornell UP, 1984.

———. *The Excursion*. Ed. Sally Bushell, James A. Butler, and Michael C. Jaye. Ithaca: Cornell UP, 2007.

———. *Home at Grasmere*. Ed. Beth Darlington. Ithaca: Cornell UP, 1977.

———. *Last Poems, 1821–1850*. Ed. Jared Curtis et al. Ithaca: Cornell UP, 1999.

———. *The Letters of William and Dorothy Wordsworth*. 2nd ed. 8 vols. Ed. Ernest de Selincourt, rev. Mary Moorman and Alan G. Hill. Oxford: Clarendon, 1967–93.

———. *"Lyrical Ballads," and Other Poems, 1797–1800*. Ed. James Butler and Karen Green. Ithaca: Cornell UP, 1992.

———. *"Lyrical Ballads" and Related Writings*. Ed. William Richey and Daniel Robinson. Boston: Houghton Mifflin / Riverside, 2002.

———. *Peter Bell*. Ed. John E. Jordan. Ithaca: Cornell UP, 1985.

———. *"Poems, in Two Volumes," and Other Poems*. Ed. Jared Curtis. Ithaca: Cornell UP, 1983.

———. *The Prelude: 1799, 1805, 1850*. Ed. Jonathan Wordsworth, M. H. Abrams, and Stephen Gill. New York: Norton, 1979.

———. *Prose Works*. Ed. W. J. B. Owen and J. W. Smyser. 3 vols. Oxford: Clarendon, 1974.

———. *"The Ruined Cottage" and "The Pedlar."* Ed. James Butler. Ithaca: Cornell UP, 1979.

———. *The Salisbury Plain Poems*. Ed. Stephen Gill. Ithaca: Cornell UP, 1975.

———. *Shorter Poems, 1807–1820*. Ed. Carl H. Ketcham. Ithaca: Cornell UP, 1989.

———. *Sonnet Series and Itinerary Poems, 1820–1845*. Ed. G. Jackson. Ithaca: Cornell UP, 2004.

———. *Translations of Chaucer and Virgil*. Ed. Bruce E. Graver. Ithaca: Cornell UP, 1998.

Worthington, Jane. *Wordsworth's Reading of Roman Prose*. New Haven: Yale UP, 1946.

Wu, Duncan. *William Hazlitt: The First Modern Man*. Oxford: Oxford UP, 2008.

———. *Wordsworth: An Inner Life*. Oxford: Blackwell, 2002.

———. *Wordsworth's Reading, 1770–1799*. Cambridge: Cambridge UP, 1993.

———. *Wordsworth's Reading, 1800–1815*. Cambridge: Cambridge UP, 1995.

Young, Edward. *Night Thoughts on Life, Death, and Immortality*. Ed. Stephen Cornford. Cambridge: Cambridge UP, 1989.

Yousef, Nancy. *Isolated Cases: The Anxieties of Autonomy in Enlightenment Philosophy and Romantic Literature*. Ithaca: Cornell UP, 2004.

———. "Wordsworth, Sentimentalism, and the Defiance of Sympathy." *European Romantic Review* 17 (2006): 205–13.

Index